Profitable Garden Center Management

Second Edition

Profitable Garden Center Management

Second Edition

Louis Berninger
University of Wisconsin—Madison

RESTON PUBLISHING COMPANY, INC.
Reston, Virginia

A PRENTICE-HALL COMPANY

Library of Congress Cataloging in Publication Data

Berninger, Louis, 1929-
  Profitable garden center management.

  Includes index.
  1. Garden centers (Retail trade) — Management.
  I. Title.
  SB454.6.B47   1982   381'.4159'068   82-387
  ISBN 0-8359-5633-4   AACR2

Interior production: **Jack Zibulsky**

10 9 8 7 6 5 4 3 2 1

Printed in the United States of America.

Contents

Preface

In attempting to provide a practical guide for garden center managers as well as horticulture students, I have integrated management concerns with the care and selection of quality plant materials and equipment. The resulting book is suitable for a course in retail horticulture or retail garden center management, with each chapter presented as a unit independent of the preceding material. By covering pricing and merchandising strategies, business analysis, personnel, and maintenance practices, emphasis is placed on the practical, real-world concerns of both the present and future garden center manager.

The enthusiasm and spirit of the beautification programs initiated in the 1960's has spurred dramatic growth of the garden center business. Consumers of all ages and from all walks of life have demonstrated great interest in a variety of outdoor and indoor garden projects. The future is indeed bright for those individuals and for organizations dedicated to meeting the needs of gardeners with good service, a large product mix, and quality merchandise.

The interests of home gardeners have spanned the entire field of horticulture. Vegetable gardening has captured the fancy of untold numbers of individuals interested in good exercise and the production of tasty foods for the dining room table. Seed and transplant sales continue to grow each year, and the demand for small plots in urban settings shows no signs of diminishing. University extension personnel in many counties have provided leadership in organizing programs for "city" gardeners often working plots some 30 by 30 feet.

Producers of spring bedding plants continue to find a welcome home for their products each spring. Annual increases of 10 percent have been recorded in the 1970's with gardeners demanding quality plants and new introductions. The All American Program has helped spur sales each spring with some three to five annual flowers and a similar number of vegetables commanding the attention of the gardening public. Hybrid seed geraniums, impatiens, and fibrous rooted begonias have challenged petunias for the leadership in spring sales of bedding material.

Wholesale nursery producers have been booking sales some two years in advance of delivery dates. Street tree planting programs accompanied by growth of home and commercial projects have resulted in shortages of most popular materials.

Turf products including sod, seed, fertilizers, and pesticides continue to move rapidly into the hands of home gardeners. If nothing else, most homeowners want a healthy, luxurious lawn.

The sale of indoor plants lunged forward in the mid-1970s. Overnight, everyone seemed to want hanging baskets, specimen plants, and a wide variety of green plants in small containers. Sales started to level off following a rapid surge that caught everyone off guard.

Sales represent only one facet of the total picture confronting garden center operators. The real challenge is one of holding costs in line and recording a fair return on one's investment. Unfortunately, too many operators have ignored this latter point. They have sailed along calmly assuming that sales automatically bring forth reasonable profits. A sad moment occurs when an individual tries to sell his or her business and is suddenly confronted with the prospect of receiving only pennies for years of hard work.

Garden center operators must focus more and more time on analyzing business records and taking appropriate action to eliminate problem areas. Good business principles and practices must be employed to meet the challenge of competitors and to record reasonable profits.

The profit picture often has been blurred with many individuals combining profits and salaries into one lump figure. This will distort the real situation and make it quite difficult when comparing one operation with others in the same industry. Salaries vary considerably, with some receiving handsome compensation and others working for pennies.

Independent operators have faced a real challenge from large discount operators. The latter often have sold products during the spring season when sales were booming. Operating on much smaller margins, these firms have captured a great deal of attention with attractive prices.

Some independent operators have tried to compete with large operators on the basis of price. Limited buying power often has prevented them from accomplishing their goal. A second approach has focused attention on the sale of services and quality products. The battle has been waged on grounds more familiar to the professional garden center operator.

Consumers have become more and more sophisticated when buying garden products. This trend should benefit those firms featuring quality products and reliable services.

The garden center business does need a continuing supply of well-trained and enthusiastic people. Growth and prosperity will continue to occur providing this industry successfully attracts talented people, focuses attention on the sale of quality products, and offers good services.

Louis Berninger

Acknowledgments

Visits to numerous garden centers and discussions with managers, owners, and store personnel helped considerably in the writing of this book. My thanks to these individuals for sharing their experiences and, in many instances, providing materials for photographs incorporated in most chapters. Special thanks go to Home & Garden Merchandiser and Bedding Plants Incorporated for their permission to reprint numerous items. Colleagues and friends have provided great assistance in gaining better insight into the garden center business. My wife and family have shown a great deal of patience and provided support during all phases of the project. To all of these individuals and organizations, my sincere thanks for your assistance in the preparation of this book.

chapter
one

Introduction

The garden center business has expanded rapidly in the last decade, and with it has come an explosion in the number and types of firms adopting this banner. An examination of the "Yellow Pages" can be most revealing in terms of the products and services offered by firms classifying themselves as garden centers. Some firms advertise in a few areas such as equipment and tools. Other operators "cover the waterfront," handling indoor and outdoor plants, supplies, and equipment rental.

Some groups have been noticeable by their absence from telephone listings and common identification as garden centers. These would include greenhouse and florist businesses that annually merchandise a large volume of bedding plants, including annual and perennial flowers and vegetable transplants. Some of these firms stock supplies of fertilizers, pesticides, and containers. They generally have chosen to be listed under their own headings, keeping themselves distinct from the garden center classification.

Nurseries also have a separate classification, and the operators belong to their own professional organization. They occasionally market bedding plants along with supply items.

Landscape contractors operate on the fringes of the garden center business. They perform a vital service, doing much of the work of landscap-

A modern nursery provides many services for indoor and outdoor gardeners. The center shown here carries extensive lines of trees, shrubs, spring flowers, indoor plants, and garden supply items.

2

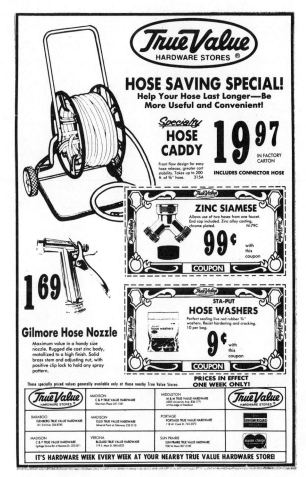

Hardware stores frequently promote nationally advertised garden products at attractive prices.

ing and maintaining grounds around homes and businesses. The products they handle can be found in typical garden centers for those who prefer do-it-yourself projects.

Florists, nursery operators, and landscape contractors might be thought of as specialists in specific facets of the garden center business. They cannot be excluded from a discussion of garden centers, since many of their products and services overlap. A definition of garden centers is further complicated by the fact that many firms have diversified in recent years, the primary goals being simply to expand sales and to operate profitably twelve months out of the year.

Location plays an important role in determining the number of weeks and months out of a year that a garden center operates. Firms located in warmer regions often operate throughout the year, reflecting the long growing season. Many of these firms are able to specialize solely in the sale of garden products. Northern-based operations are restricted to about six months of active business, starting before the last killing frost in spring and ending with the first hard frost in fall. These operators frequently must diversify to generate income during winter months.

The dramatic surge in garden product sales in the 1970s has captured the fancy of many retailers handling product lines totally unassociated with the garden. The list includes supermarkets, hardware stores, discount operators, large retailers, and five-and-ten cent firms. All these operations have found it profitable, in varying degrees, to operate garden centers during the busy portion of each season. They have been criticized by many independent operators for skimming the cream off the top of the bottle. However, large retail chains have become an important segment of the garden center business.

Diversification Program

The garden center business has looked highly inviting to some retailers handling specialized products and looking for product lines to fill in slow periods. This is especially true for operators handling ski and related winter

The successful marriage of a pet and garden center has resulted in a healthy increase in gross sales for this operator. Gardeners support the pet shop throughout the year, and, in turn, pet fanciers return for garden items each spring.

equipment. This business blends in nicely with garden center products for northern firms. Another consolidation has been worked out between pet and garden center businesses. Garden supplies occupy a modest area of space from midsummer through early spring with the emphasis on pets and pet supplies. Floor space is rearranged for the garden season with plants, supplies, and equipment taking over a large percentage of available space. This arrangement has not jeopardized pet supplies sales. Gross sales have increased at a healthy percentage each year with operators servicing two distinct clienteles.

A large number of traditional garden center operators have added indoor plants or related supplies to their total product mix. Avid outdoor gardeners often focus a great deal of attention on decorating the interior of their homes with fresh flowers, plants, and giftware. In similar fashion, indoor gardeners show a great appreciation for developing attractive landscapes for their homes.

Diversification programs also have included hobby and craft products, giftware, permanent flowers, and even roadside markets. The rationale has been to provide gardeners with a wide range of products and, in the process, stimulate increases in gross sales.

Fresh farm produce captures the attention of many suburban and urban gardeners. New customers can be attracted and added sales generated during the roadside market season that often comes during a slow period for many garden center operations.

Large-Scale Retailers

Large retail outlets including supermarkets and discount stores have increased rapidly their share of the garden center business. They have contributed greatly toward expanding sales of garden products and, in the process, captured a large share of total sales. The immediate outlook suggests that they will continue to grow and expand both product lines and services.

A variety of reasons can be offered as to why gardeners like to shop at these giants, including convenience, attractive prices, large volumes on display, regular specials, good parking, convenient location, and extensive advertising.

Convenience. Giant retail organizations have made it easy to buy their merchandise. They were first to offer self-service programs in many parts of the country. Independent operators and especially small business organizations initially resisted "modern" retail practices.

Containers. The self-service approach also required a change in methods for handling bedding plants. A typical flat contains some 70 to 100 young vegetables or flowering plants. Sales personnel had to dig and wrap the desired number of plants for each customer. This time-consuming process just did not fit the mold of a self-service operation.

The creation of a market pack or container holding twelve to fifteen plants

Many bedding plants are now being grown in individual cell packs. The cells vary in size according to the specific needs of each plant.

Digging bedding plants was a common sight at most garden centers prior to the introduction of market packs.

revolutionized the business. No one has to wait in line to select a pack. The supermarket concept finally has been brought to the garden center business.

Check-Out.   Most mass outlets have tried to provide quick check-out service for customers. Gardeners like to browse and take their time while selecting merchandise. They do not like waiting in long lines to pay for merchandise, especially when only one cash register is in operation.

Attractive Prices.   Large retail outlets have had the image of selling products at attractive prices. Gardeners have been attracted to these stores through extensive advertisements appearing in newspapers and through in-store promotional materials. Pricing psychology seems to favor large retail outlets now.

Volume on Display.   Large retailers have been synonymous with massive displays of merchandise. Display techniques also play an important role when projecting the image that one carries a large stock of material. Discount merchandisers are masters of this concept. Massive displays in front of supermarkets and similar stores have captured a great deal of attention. Impulse sales have been triggered with many consumers unable to resist purchasing a geranium or a pack of pansies.

Regular Specials.   Weekly specials have been used effectively to capture the attention of consumers. Many garden products have been used as leader

Massive displays of gardening materials adjacent to large discount stores capture attention and have generated many impulse sales.

Good parking facilities attract many gardeners to large retail stores.

items during spring months, much to the consternation of small operators. This same policy has been applied to the sale of flowering plants at holidays.

Parking and Location.   Consumers know that they can always find a parking space at a supermarket or discount store. Large parking areas have become the trademark of mass outlets. A second feature of these giants has been location. You can easily find supermarkets and department stores. Often, they have been located on major highways.

Extensive Advertising.   The value of advertising has been proved and fully accepted by large-scale operators. An examination of a local newspaper for one week reveals numerous full-page advertisements and supplements sponsored by large retailers. The rapid growth in sales by discounters in the last decade partially attests to the impact of advertising programs.

Full-page advertisements sponsored by large retail operators capture a great deal of attention, especially from new gardeners.

Responsibility of the Independent Operator

An emphasis on bigness should not suggest that the age of the specialist is over. There are still many small, independently operated garden centers that have produced an excellent income for their owners. Some business people have accepted a highly fluctuating sales curve and have put all their energies into making a living in a short span of time. Other operators close their businesses for several months each year and enjoy a life of leisure. This schedule works well for family-operated businesses requiring only part-time help during the busy season. Some successful family-operated firms have remained profitable by avoiding expansion and diversification programs. Such growth programs usually require strong financial resources and managerial talents above and beyond those possessed by most small businesses. Owners should recognize their own assets and limitations before embarking on anything more than a modest expansion program.

The owner-manager bears a great deal of responsibility in operating a profitable garden center. This business, like most businesses, requires that one wear many hats. The small businessperson must be a master of many trades since he or she does not have the luxury of hiring many skilled workers. Some of the most important tasks of a manager include:

1. Buying and recognizing quality
2. Implementing proper practices for maintaining plant materials on the premises
3. Knowledge of pesticides and their use by gardeners
4. Cultural requirements of plants
5. Proper use of soil amendments and fertilizers
6. Buying, selling, and repairing equipment
7. Training personnel
8. Advertising
9. Image building
10. Pricing
11. Merchandising
12. Maintaining and using records

Quality. Buyers must learn to differentiate between poor, average, and good quality merchandise. This applies to perishable as well as nonperishable products. The same assessment also must be made in terms of the reputation of suppliers and their ability to deliver merchandise on time and according to specifications. The product offered should reflect the marketing strategy and image of the firm. The procurement of inexpensive merchandise to cut product costs can affect the reputation of the entire firm.

Maintenance.   Perishable products must be handled with kid gloves to minimize damage and provide consumers with good merchandise. Whether one is handling sod, indoor plants, trees and shrubs, or annuals, personnel must follow a prescribed set of procedures to bring customers the best possible product.

Pesticides.   Gardeners often seem puzzled and reluctant to handle pesticides. These products are dangerous, and there is good reason for many gardeners to have numerous questions. At least one person in the organization, and more with larger firms, should be well trained in the selection and application of pesticides.

Culture of Plants.   New gardeners seem to be arriving on the scene each and every day. They come with a tremendous thirst for information. The operator catering to this massive group of enthusiastic people can rapidly develop a solid image in his or her community. Personnel should be encouraged and assisted in improving their knowledge by reading and attending classes sponsored by technical schools and the local extension service.

Soil Amendments and Fertilizers.   Improper use of soil amendments and overapplication of fertilizers have created many problems for indoor and outdoor gardeners. At least one member of the staff should be trained as a resource person to advise customers regarding proper use of these products.

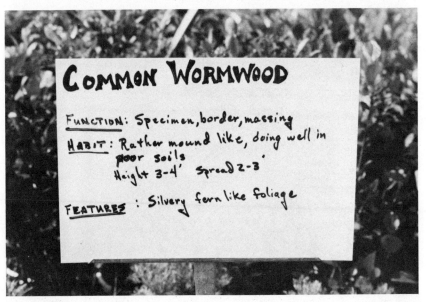

Helpful information placed on attractive posters stimulates sales and helps answer many questions normally raised by gardeners.

Equipment.   The sale, rental, and repair of garden equipment is big business. Many so-called garden centers deal exclusively in this particular area. The inventory of new and repair parts requires a substantial investment in the business. A decision to handle power equipment should be made only after extensive consultation with resource advisers such as bankers. Well-trained people are extremely important in properly handling and servicing garden equipment.

Personnel.   The policies developed regarding personnel often make or break a firm. Mom and Pop operations have not carried the burden of hiring, training, and motivating people. Growth often brings with it the problem of handling people other than members of the family. This can be a shattering experience for some individuals previously accustomed to issuing orders without fear of their being questioned by mom or a son or daughter.

A special effort attracts attention and insures that gardeners will recognize the name of this particular operation.

Advertising.   Word-of-mouth advertising plays a role in attracting customers to a store. Total or near total reliance on this practice can be equal to a game of Russian roulette. You really never know what or when something good is being said about your operation. Aggressive operators recognize that the market is always changing with potential customers arising daily in their community. Advertising dollars must be allocated for steady growth and reasonable profits.

Image Building.   One of the most important, if not crucial, tasks of the owner-manager is to build a solid image of the organization. What do you want consumers to say and think about your firm? The manager bears the responsibility for charting a course and, in the process, developing an identity or image for the firm.

Pricing.   Pricing merchandise is an art and a science. Industry practices often serve as guides to operators in pricing perishable and nonperishable merchandise. The person responsible for pricing must look at all merchandise through the eyes of a consumer. There are times when one can go above or below recommended formulas according to value of the product.

Merchandising.   Aggressive retailers employ a variety of techniques designed to distinguish their operation from other competitors. Newness and product identification are two important merchandising weapons of special value to independent operators. Consumers should be provided choices whenever possible, in terms of both product quality and prices. Unusual products such as geranium trees help firms in their quest for a unique image and identity.

Records.   Some operators see records as a necessary expense item and a worthless endeavor designed solely to satisfy the Internal Revenue Service. Profit-oriented managers recognize that these "useless" records represent valuable resources in charting a course of action for the firm. Operating, income, or profit and loss statements must be analyzed monthly to keep track of rapidly changing conditions. The sale of a business can hinge on the availability of accurate information generated over a number of years.

Conglomerates

The garden center business has attracted the attention of giant organizations that have not previously been associated with this type of product and service. Pillsbury purchased and later sold the European Flower Market. Green Giant opened and then sold a chain of garden centers in the Minneapolis–St. Paul area. The dramatic growth in sales of plants prompted diversification programs and the entrance of these giants into the business.

Success has eluded many, if not most, giants whose track record in other areas was exceptionally good. Poor profit reports coming from these early investors may deter other large business conglomerates from entering the garden center business.

Chains

Local and regional chains have had a significant impact on the garden center business. Franks', probably the largest chain operation, has moved from Michigan to the Chicago and Minneapolis–St. Paul areas. This growth- and profit-oriented firm has steadily increased its penetration in these and other markets.

A number of chains, such as Stein's in Milwaukee, have had a tremendous impact on local markets. Their appetite for merchandise often seems endless in their quest to fulfill needs of consumers. Full-page advertisements in major newspapers have placed the name of Stein's before all area gardeners.

The growth of local and national chains can be expected to continue in the 1980s and 1990s. Their success has been partially based on employment of knowledgeable people and on creation of a marketing strategy aimed at a specific segment of the market.

Management

The quality of management determines growth and profitability of a firm. The unique nature of a product or service may produce growth for a period of time even though management exhibits many deficiencies. Sooner or later, these limitations will come to the front and severely handicap future growth and profits.

Marketing Strategy

There have been many success stories and formulas or marketing strategies fashioned by garden store operators. Each approach has its merits. The tactics used by one individual may not prove acceptable in another situation. The business philosophy of the owner-manager should come through loud and clear in the formation of a marketing strategy for each organization.

Some operators have thrived while at the same time violating many recommended principles and practices. Their success may have been based on finding one or more ways of fulfilling the needs of a significant number of customers. Customer loyalty, however, may be questionable in those instances where operators have directly or indirectly abused shoppers.

Some people like to shop in an environment where sales personnel are always on hand to help make decisions. Other buyers like to browse around without someone looking over their shoulders. You must develop a strategy that meets the needs of the audience targeted for your operation.

Goals

What are your goals in owning or managing a garden center? Will you be satisfied in running an average shop? Can you be content with average? The sign on the wall reminds us that average is either at the top of the lower half or at the bottom of the upper half. An average shop or an average profit has little glamour when viewed from this position. The bankruptcy rate may be high simply because too many business people start off being content with just being average.

Licensing

The sale of nursery stock and perennial flowers normally requires that you obtain a license from your state department of agriculture. The law in many states includes the sale of bare root and potted roses. The local county extension agent can put you in touch with the appropriate agency in your state. A license normally is not required for the sale of bedding and indoor plants. Check with your local extension agent to confirm that a local ordinance has not been enacted in your area.

Pesticide legislation at the national and state levels may have an impact on dealers handling this line of merchandise. Training schools have been sponsored in some states in anticipation of dealers having to take tests to become registered to sell pesticides.

Fertilizers and seed laws regulate the packaging and sale of these two important groups of garden products. Your state department of agriculture normally has jurisdiction over these matters and can brief you on laws relating to the garden center business. Speakers from this agency often have appeared at educational meetings to clarify their role in protecting the interests of dealers and consumers.

SBA

The Small Business Administration was created in 1953 as an independent government agency to encourage, assist, and protect the interests of small business operators. They have made loans to business concerns and victims of catastrophes. A second function has been to improve the management skills of active and potential small business owners through the preparation of well over 300 publications. Contact your local SBA office, often located in the state capital and major cities, for information on their services.

Consumer Loyalty

When all is said and done about how best to run a business, consumer loyalty determines whether a firm runs in the black or red. Every effort must be directed toward making customers feel good when shopping at your place of business.

Ann Landers has taken credit for preparation of "a customer." The statement, with minor variations, also has been credited to Wilson Sporting Goods Company. The author deserves much credit for placing the spotlight on the role of consumers in our expanding industry.

> A customer—the most important person in any business is not dependent on us—we are on him
>
> —is not an interruption of our work—he is the purpose of it
>
> —does us a favor when he calls—we are doing him a favor by serving him
>
> —is part of our business—not an outsider
>
> —is not a cold statistic—he is flesh and blood with feelings and emotions like our own
>
> —is not someone to argue or match wits with
>
> —is a person who brings us his wants—it is our job to fill these wants
>
> —is deserving of the most courteous and attentive treatment we can give
>
> —is the fellow that makes it possible to pay your salary whether you are a truck driver, plant salesman, or manager
>
> —is the life blood of this and every other business.

SUMMARY

The garden center industry is thriving and the future is bright for those engaged in this line of work. It is a rewarding business with the knowledge that our products and services bring great joy and satisfaction to buyers. Firms are growing at a rapid rate and this has placed increased demands on management.

The owner-manager wears many hats. This is true for the small as well as the large operator. A wide variety of products has been offered to consumers as a means of operating profitably throughout the year. Perishable plants require unique knowledge in purchasing, pricing, maintenance, and display practices. The demands are much more intense than when handling most hard goods.

Management plays a vital role for all operators in all successful stores. Many marketing strategies have been devised by aggressive businessmen and women. It becomes increasingly important to target your intended audience, mold an image, and then fire all guns in attracting customers to your store.

Independent operators must identify their strong points and the weaknesses of their major competitors. Marketing strategy will then reflect or capitalize on these strong points. The growing number of firms entering this field and the increasing dominance of large operators make it imperative that small and medium-sized firms accentuate the positive in attracting customers to their place of business.

Two general rules are worthy of being repeated and always remembered by growth-minded people. Price reflects quality, and you generally get in return what you pay for a product or service. Secondly, the customer will always be king or queen. All our efforts and energies must be directed to satisfying gardeners, especially those just coming into the world of plants.

There is room for all parties, large and small, who wish to be a part of the garden center business. No one will receive a share of the pie just because he or she thinks they deserve or have an inherent right to sell garden products. This is a highly competitive world and only those who stay one step ahead of the pack can expect to survive and prosper.

1. Identify three types of retail organizations other than traditional garden centers and discuss why they have been motivated to sell garden products.

2. Why have garden products often been used as leader items by "mass" merchandisers?

3. What prompts store managers to diversify? Give examples and reasons for adding different lines of merchandise.

4. Identify and discuss five attributes of large scale retailers attracting customers.

5. Identify and discuss one of the most important factors enabling "mass" outlets to successfully enter the bedding plant business.

6. What can independent operators do to solidify and enhance their position in the garden center business?

7. To what extent should a firm strive for an "average" postion in an industry?

8. What can one expect from conglomerates in terms of their entering garden center business in future years?

9. Identify five common management deficiencies.

chapter
two

Going
Into
Business

There are a number of reasons for going into business, and even more for not. The profit motive should rank first in your thoughts when assessing any move to start a business. Are you profit oriented? Your business can prosper and enjoy a long lifespan only when profits dominate your plans. Some individuals have been motivated to start garden center businesses largely on the basis of their interest in growing indoor and outdoor plants. It is important to have this motivation, but desires may become so strong that good common sense flies out the window.

Enthusiasm for plants must be balanced with a realistic appraisal of your knowledge and capability to operate a business. Ignorance about a profit and loss statement, and little attempt to correct the deficiency, starts you down the road to bankruptcy. Your willingness to go back to school and learn something about the business world represents an important plus factor in your favor.

Some people have been motivated to buy a business out of fear of job loss. The owner plans to sell and gives an employee first crack at the business. The nature of the current relationship between the parties does not always work in favor of the buyer. The decision to buy out of fear brings dark clouds on the scene. What happens if you do not quite have the money to carry you after the sale? Will all go down the drain including current assets? Do not be forced into a purchase unless it represents a planned action on your part. The risks are exceptionally high when one makes a hasty and ill-timed decision.

Do not start a business unless you are comfortable with the profit motive. Your enthusiasm will blossom providing the firm rests on a solid foundation and is not threatened regularly with extinction.

BANKRUPTCY

Bankruptcy statistics, going-out-of-business sales, and vacant stores have not discouraged enthusiastic and aggressive people from establishing new enterprises. A number of reasons can be cited for high failure rates among new enterprises. Four important reasons are:

1. Your potential
2. Lack of marketing plan
3. Inadequate capital
4. Failure to grow and mature.

The success rate for the first five years of business comes to only one in five. Human failure accounts for virtually all collapses of small business enterprises. A variety of excuses is offered, including cut-throat competition and customers looking for ways to "steal" you blind. When all is said and done, the responsibility for bankruptcy still rests on the shoulders of the proprietor. The successful people are those who have corrected mistakes in a positive manner, and have not blamed other people for all their problems.

Good planning is essential to business success. A young man attended a retail management clinic and asked for assistance in determining the potential market for a pizza and ice cream parlor in his community. He had purchased a franchise the previous year. This question should have been asked and answered prior to establishment of the business. Without a market his investment is worthless.

Many aggressive and ambitious people become trapped through exhaustion of their financial reserves. Fortunately, those seeking bank loans can anticipate rigorous examination of financial resources and plans. This insurance policy is lacking when one puts the finger on family members and friends.

The ability to grow in a business-minded sense is an important element in avoiding bankruptcy. Attending extension and vocationally sponsored business courses can prove most important in expanding knowledge of advertising, personnel, sales programs, and records. Many people become stagnant shortly after opening the doors of a new operation. Further education can turn the tide away from bankruptcy in favor of growth and profits.

YOUR POTENTIAL

The Small Business Administration has prepared a number of management aids for small business persons. Contact your local office to obtain a listing of their resources. They offer several programs that can prove invaluable to those planning to start, those just beginning, or those in business for a number of years.

Your first step should be an analysis of your own potential in managing a business. Do you have the physical and mental stamina to run a business in a highly competitive world? The attraction of operating a business often inhibits an objective analysis of one's managerial potential. Small Marketers Aid No. 71 contains a checklist for those planning to enter business. Truthful answers to the following ten questions can reveal your potential as manager of a new business:

1. Are you a self-starter?

_____ I do things on my own. Nobody has to tell me to get going.

_____ If someone gets me started, I keep going all right.

_____ Easy does it. I don't put myself out until I have to.

2. How do you feel about other people?

_____ I like people. I can get along with just about anybody.

_____ I have plenty of friends—I don't need anyone else.

_____ Most people bug me.

3. Can you lead others?

_____ I can get most people to go along when I start something.

_____ I can give the orders if someone else tells me what we should do.

_____ I let someone else get things moving. Then I go along if I feel like it.

4. Can you take responsibility?

_____ I like to take charge of things and see them through.

_____ I'll take over if I have to, but I'd rather let someone else be responsible.

_____ There's always some eager beaver around wanting to show how smart he is. I say let him.

5. How good an organizer are you?

_____ I like to have a plan before I start. I'm usually the one to get things lined up when the gang wants to do something.

_____ I do all right unless things get too goofed up. Then I cop out.

_____ You get all set and then something comes along and blows the whole bag. So I just take things as they come.

6. How good a worker are you?

_____ I can keep going as long as I need to. I don't mind working hard for something I want.

_____ I'll work hard for a while, but when I've had enough, that's it!

_____ I can't see that hard work gets you anywhere.

7. Can you make decisions?

_____ I can make up my mind in a hurry if I have to. It usually turns out OK, too.

_____ I have to make up my mind fast. I think later I should have decided the other way.

_____ I don't like to be the one who has to decide things. I'd probably blow it.

8. Can people trust what you say?

_____ You bet they can. I don't say things I don't mean.

_____ I try to be on the level most of the time, but sometimes I just say what's easiest.

_____ What's the sweat if the other fellow doesn't know the difference?

9. Can you stick with it?

_____ If I make up my mind to do something, I don't let anything stop me.

_____ I usually finish what I start—if it doesn't get fouled up.

_____ If it doesn't go right away, I turn off. Why beat your brains out?

10. How good is your health?

_____ I never run down!

_____ I have enough energy for most things I want to do.

_____ I run out of juice sooner than most of my friends.[1]

A person with good potential as an entrepreneur will have placed most if not all checks on the first line. You really shouldn't consider embarking on a career as an owner-manager should most checks appear on the third line of each question. A majority of answers in the middle category suggest that you have some potential to operate a business. Realistically, it might be best to look for a partner to insure that things do get done and that the business has a fighting chance.

Analyze the Community

One or more communities may attract your attention as potential prospects for buying an existing business or establishing a new one. The Chamber of Commerce, local newspapers, and city hall are important sources of information regarding a community or segment of a community. Seek out background information to help determine profit potential of a business.

Here are some important considerations:

I. People

   A. Type of employment

      1. Stable—large government employers

      2. Unstable—history of periodic strikes with large percentage of people in this category

   B. Income

      1. Size of disposable income

      2. Growth potential—new employers

   C. Population pattern

      1. Rapidly increasing or stagnant

      2. Large percentage of young or elderly people

   D. Birth, death, and marriage rates

II. Community

   A. Expansion plans—annexation

   B. Services

---

[1]Small Business Administration, "Checklist for Going into Business," Small Marketers Aid No. 71 (Washington, D.C.: the Administration, 1975), pp. 4-5.

      1. Condition of roads

      2. New bypass roads being planned

      3. Schools

   C. New home and business construction

   D. Zoning restrictions limiting expansion or extensive remodeling of present facilities

III. Size of planned market area

   A. Portion of city

   B. Entire city

   C. Size of surrounding market area

For example, a community featuring a large percentage of retired people and declining birth and marriage rates offers little promise for any real economic growth in the next decade. The construction of new homes and business facilities, well-maintained roads and schools, and reasonable services all point in the direction of an economically viable community.

The composition of the community in terms of blue- and white-collar workers also helps determine the feasibility of opening a new business largely featuring nonnecessity items. A high percentage of white-collar workers, especially those employed by government, should assure a high degree of business stability. Disposable income is the name of the game for firms selling flowers, garden supplies, trees, and shrubs. What has been happening to this factor in recent years and what are the projections for the next three to five years?

Remodeling and proposed expansion programs may be hindered by zoning restrictions especially in older sections of a community. Similar restrictions may apply to those locations surrounded by individual dwellings. The vitality of a community also can be reflected in annexation plans and the condition of schools and roads. Poor schools and roads suggest stagnant conditions. Modest or nonexistent annexation programs can lead to the conclusion that a community has entered a rocking-chair period unsuited for aggressive businessmen and women.

Your analysis must focus on the area to be serviced by the proposed business. This might entail only a portion of the entire community. The surrounding market area becomes quite critical when one plans to settle in a rural environment. Information on a county or multicounty basis might be digested to determine the ability of an area to support your planned operation.

Some words of caution regarding plans to service a broad area. This may entail unprofitable deliveries, often part and parcel of the retail florist business. You may have to advertise in several newspapers to reach all potential customers. The loyalty of people some distance removed may be suspect especially in comparison to those residing in the immediate vicinity of the firm. The establishment of a new firm could result in many customers leaving the fold because of convenience and improved service.

Analyze Your Competition

The best way to learn about competitors has been and will continue to be to visit their places of operation. Stop at some local stores and ask people where you can buy a product that you plan to carry. Talk to employees of potential competitors asking questions much like a typical customer. Analyze:

I. Location
    A. Convenient to customers?
    B. New or old part of town?
    C. On major thoroughfares?
II. Advertising
    A. How extensive?
    B. Does it attract attention?
    C. What media are employed—television, radio, newspapers, direct mail?
III. Pricing
    A. Do they focus attention on low, medium, or high prices?
    B. Reasonable in relation to quality?
    C. Emphasis on specials?
IV. Product
    A. Quality of merchandise?
    B. Product mix?
    C. Quantity of merchandise on display?
V. Personnel
    A. Size of staff?
    B. Training?
    C. Courteous and pleasant appearance?
    D. Knowledgeable?
VI. Store appearance
    A. Inside
        1. Traffic patterns?
        2. Lighting?
        3. Displays?

B. Outside
   1. Signs?
   2. Neatness—paint?
   3. Plantings?
VII. Parking facilities
   A. Nonexistent?
   B. Limited?
   C. Reasonable?
   D. Extensive?
VIII. Community services
   A. Contributes to senior citizen organizations?
   B. Holds clinics on plant care and identification?
IX. Business hours
   A. Seven days a week?
   B. Closed on Sunday and evenings?
X. Overall image

This analysis should be conducted for traditional as well as nontraditional outlets like supermarkets and discount stores. One should not be so biased as to ignore large retail outlets. They have been commanding a larger and larger share of the market. Their weaknesses can be capitalized upon by operators of independent firms.

Extensive use of television commercials should suggest the existence of potentially strong competitors in a particular market. Similar clues regarding competition can be gleaned through an analysis of advertisements appearing on radio and in newspapers. These are expensive media, and you may not be able to match these important advertising expenditures.

Pricing practices can reveal much about the business philosophy of potential competitors. Some firms offer highly attractive prices on a regular basis to capture sales. However, prices may not reflect quality, leaving some operators vulnerable to frequent criticism from buyers. Weekly specials often reflect the philosophy and marketing strategy of highly aggressive operators seeking a larger share of the market.

The quality of store personnel plays an extremely important role in capturing consumer loyalty. One or more visits to an operation can reveal a great deal about the staff. A few questions regarding merchandise and guarantees will reflect management's philosophy regarding its staff and customers. The appearance of the store from inside and out often determines customer allegiance and interest in browsing. Poor lighting and crowded displays tend

A unique and attractive advertisement combined with a special sale is bound to attract the attention of new and established gardeners.

to repel all but bargain hunters. Narrow aisles and few signs or prices can discourage even the most persistent buyers. Garden centers require wide aisles, especially those that utilize shopping carts. The exterior appearance frequently contrasts sharply with the products offered for sale. Garden center operators sell beauty. You cannot accomplish this goal when customers must pass through a crop of weeds, antiquated signs and drab structures.

Garden center operators often have been called upon to contribute plants and materials for worthy community projects. You can build excellent goodwill and in the process stimulate sales through an improved appearance of the community.

Consumers often expect garden centers to operate almost 24 hours a day. Every hour and every day is precious to the gardener and the business person

This well-manicured garden center features wide aisles and attractive beds of nursery stock.

As this sign attests, long hours are the norm for customer-oriented operators. Every day is previous to gardeners during the brief planting season.

during the short spring season. Long days are a fact of life and you must be prepared to service buyers.

Good parking facilities are a must for gardeners carrying plants and bulky items. The area should be black topped to avoid problems with mud and holes during the spring season.

Your analysis of competitors can prove to be the most important factor governing success of the proposed business. Do not hurry your study. An extra day or two cannot compare with a business planned to last ten or more years. The biggest temptation might be to view competitors through your own eyes rather than those of typical customers. You may be overly biased in terms of how you like to display merchandise and the overall appearance of the store. Carefully watch customers as they shop and try to determine the extent to which they respond positively to potential competitors.

ANALYZE YOUR ASSETS

What can you contribute to a particular community? Why should people patronize your operation over that of a competitor?

Develop a listing of your assets and your objectives after analyzing the community and your competitors. This step will aid you in molding the image of your new firm. Most of the items to be considered appear on the same list for your analyses of competitors.

1. Product mix
2. Size of inventory
3. Services
   a. guarantees
   b. trained staff
4. Appearance of exterior
5. Appearance of interior
6. Parking
7. Advertising
8. Pricing policy
9. Market area
10. Business hours
11. Community services

It is crucial that you formulate a marketing strategy designed to convince potential buyers that you have something to offer. When all is said and done, the question still remains, "Why should someone come to my store?"

GROWTH AND DEVELOPMENT

Many business operators become stagnant soon after the first day of operation. Some individuals think they know everything about the product or service they offer. Others become so engrossed in day-to-day activities that they find little time to gain control over their business. Growth potential often remains only a potential until management learns to focus attention and resources on

1. Planning and organizing today, tomorrow, and next year.

2. Managing your time and that of your employees.

3. Developing and utilizing meaningful records.

4. Employing, training, and motivating capable people in your organization.

5. Merchandising and advertising products and services.

BUY OR BUILD

The individual planning to enter the business world often faces the dilemma of not knowing whether to buy an existing firm or start a new enterprise. Each situation is unique and must be evaluated on its own merits. Reasons favoring purchase of an established firm include:

1. The firm has a track record — financial records.

2. You can anticipate immediate income.

3. Buying at a bargain price.

4. Acquiring business on a land contract with a small down payment.

5. Assistance from previous owner in learning the ropes and initially managing the business.

6. Acquiring good location.

7. Loyal customers — capitalizing on reputation of former owner.

8. Saving time in setting up business — acquiring equipment and stock.

9. Acquiring experienced workers.

10. Immediate contacts with wide range of suppliers.

11. Mailing list of customers.

12. A "complete" marketing plan from previous owner.

The disadvantages of buying an existing firm may lead one to consider seriously building an entirely new facility and organization. Disadvantages may include:

1. Poor reputation and profit potential of firms in desired market area.
2. Major remodeling costs.
3. Desire to establish in new, growing community.
4. Decline of community; changing traffic patterns.
5. Poor quality staff—low morale, poor productivity.
6. Interference from previous owner.
7. Paying more for business than it is worth—sales and profit goals found to be unrealistic; being misled about previous performance of firm.

High land and building costs may stimulate one to investigate the potential of buying an existing garden center. Limited cash could make it difficult to finance an aggressive advertising program for a new firm. Carefully evaluate financial resources before embarking on construction of your dream.

Newly developing areas of a community offer great potential for a garden center. Homes and light business establishments soon require turf, trees, shrubs, flowers, indoor plants. These areas have much more potential than older, more established sections of a community and areas where existing firms are located on secondary streets.

SUMMARY

A decision to buy or establish a new firm in a community should be based largely on your desire to earn a reasonable return on investment. The hobby approach is suitable only for those with money to burn. Do not buy solely out of fear of job loss when a new owner arrives on the scene.

The prospects of going broke rarely stem the tide of new firms emerging every year. Four out of five businesses normally fail in the first five years of their existence. Careful planning is a must to improve the odds for success in the garden center business, or any other enterprise.

Someone has to take a good hard look at your potential for surviving and prospering in the business world. Critically analyze your personal assets and liabilities before embarking on a business venture. Your answers to the questions devised by the SBA may suggest going into partnership or not venturing forth without acquiring further skills.

Three important areas of consideration in planning to buy or construct a new business are:

1. Community
2. Competitors
3. Your assets

There are occasions when it is most desirable to buy an existing business and other times when one should construct a new facility. Each situation requires careful analysis of the community in question and availability of firms on the market.

1. Identify and discuss three poor reasons for wanting to buy a business.

2. What factors should be analyzed in the planning stage regarding your own potential to operate a business?

3. What three broad factors contribute to the high rate of failure of small business people? Discuss.

4. Identify and discuss five assets your firm can offer a potential buyer.

5. Discuss three ways one must grow in learning to operate a profitable business.

6. Identify and discuss three important areas when analyzing a community for possible establishment of a new business.

7. Identify and discuss seven important areas when analyzing potential competition.

8. Discuss the pros and cons of building a new business or buying an established firm.

chapter
three

Buying
and
Selling
a
Business

Two of the most crucial periods in the life of a business occur when planning to buy or sell an enterprise. The emphasis must be on planning to insure that the best decision can and will be made in each situation. Both occasions can be highly traumatic, given the nature of what will come in the form of a new enterprise and the culmination of years of hard work.

The planning process is similar for both events, with the same questions being asked of seller and buyer. These two concepts are treated in one chapter so that the seller and buyer may gain awareness of both thinking processes occurring simultaneously in buy-sell situations.

A decision to buy should not be made in haste. The sudden desire to be one's own boss should be examined carefully before plunging in. Months and months of planning should precede any decision to buy or build a new enterprise.

Every business ultimately must change hands or close its doors for the last time. The challenge must be faced squarely for a positive transfer of a business to a new owner. Poor or inadequate planning often leads to heartache and financial disaster, especially for survivors of the owner-manager.

Transferring a business to younger members of the family at the right time often represents the most significant challenge facing older persons. Conflicts among family members can be particularly destructive, leading the younger people to find employment with other firms, often in other areas of the country. These problems often can be avoided through good planning.

TIME TO SELL

There is a right time and a poor time to sell a business. Businesses have been sold all too frequently when:

a. the owner dies, leaving a wife or husband with the task of putting everything into order.

b. profits have declined for several years in a row.

c. the physical appearance of the business has been allowed to deteriorate.

An owner should plan to sell a business when the three above factors just described are not working against him or her. This could mean the owner's selling a business while still in his or her middle to late 50s. The transition of a business from father to son can occur during that time frame or even earlier. An aggressive young person in his or her early 30s will probably want to help control the destiny of an organization. Keeping the individual on a string until he or she reaches the 40s can lead to:

34

a. change in employment by the son or daughter.

b. loss of interest in the business.

Neither of these situations will be in the best interest of the parent.

Arthritis of the business may have slowly crept into the picture during the last decade or so. Some owners unknowingly begin to slow down in one or more ways. They

1. Fail to maintain store, nursery, or greenhouse in proper condition
2. Take customers for granted and do little to attract new residents of the community
3. Reject new business concepts
4. Fail to attend meetings or read industry magazines

The warning signs are present, and yet too many individuals fail to recognize them and take appropriate action.

You should take a few hours each year to assess the viability of the organization. Suppose you had to sell it lock, stock, and barrel next month. What is the business worth to you and a prospective buyer?

A smoothly running, highly profitable business can and will capture the attention of potential buyers. You have to capitalize on these assets to lure buyers and acquire a top price for a business.

Age tends to creep up slowly during the 50s and then more rapidly in the 60s. A loss of enthusiasm and energy can spell disaster when the owner finally decides to sell an enterprise. The time to sell is when you still have enthusiasm and the business is generating healthy profits. Sell when you are ahead of the game. Do not wait until the last inning before seeking buyers for your garden center.

PREPARING TO SELL

The selling process should begin several years before one actually intends to put the business on the market, providing time to plan and prepare for the ultimate confrontation with potential buyers. This process is often condensed into too short a period of time. Great pressures are placed on the operator or survivors of the entrepreneur to unload a business. The selling price may reflect lack of planning time and hasty acceptance of the first offer. A minimum of three years will help the operator fully prepare for that day when an offer will be received to buy the business. This period of time may seem too long to some, but it is a must in terms of preparing solid financial records and grooming the physical appearance of a garden center.

POTENTIAL BUYERS

Who might buy your business? A listing of potential buyers would include:

1. Member of the immediate family or another relative
2. Employee
3. Someone in the community
   a. Competitor
   b. Employee of competitor
   c. Someone unassociated with industry
   d. Allied trade
4. Someone from a different area of the state or country
   a. Member of garden center industry
      1) Owner of firm in noncompetitive area
      2) Employee of existing firm
   b. Allied trade
   c. Someone unassociated with industry

Family members are prime candidates for taking over a business. A major barrier is that the older generation owner often does not have confidence in the abilities of a younger person to run the operation. This probably reflects the unusually close working relationship between all parties. Sometimes a parent looks for perfection and cannot quite realize that a younger person has been adequately prepared to assume responsibility for the firm.

Talented employees should also be viewed as good prospects for carrying on the garden center operation. As in the family situation, early planning helps prepare for the ultimate change of ownership. Early planning is also crucial to the buyer's ability to acquire financial resources to buy the business. Negotiations for a buy out can begin a number of years in advance of the target date. This insures that the employee will remain loyal and productive, recognizing his or her future stake in the firm.

Membership in local service clubs can help the owner find potential buyers. A community resident may represent an excellent prospect for purchasing the business. Lack of experience and knowledge of the industry can present obstacles during the buy-sell process. A potential buyer in this situation may have to rely extensively on the owner for briefings before and assistance following consummation of the deal.

Competitors in the market area might be interested in acquiring the business. These individuals should have a sharp eye regarding value of the total business and in particular of inventory and facilities. Previous working relationships with competitors may enhance or hinder negotiations. Key personnel associated with other organizations often are prime candidates to take over ownership of a garden center.

Tradespeople, handling perishable products and hard goods, are good communicators of information. They have contacts with large numbers of people associated with the industry. Their daily contacts include owners and employees of garden centers in both local and distant regions.

Professional agents probably will be employed to contact persons totally unrelated to the industry and living in areas distant from the business in question. A similar situation will develop for transactions involving community people who are new to the industry.

Advertising

Industry trade papers and magazines usually feature classified advertising sections announcing business enterprises for sale. These are an excellent means of disseminating information and contacting prospective buyers. An analysis of advertisements suggests that many sellers want to:

a. minimize expenses in contacting prospective buyers
b. keep all facts secret to prevent competitors from knowing that the business is up for sale

The first advertisement helps establish the image of the organization for sale and current management. A modest-sized ad containing little or no pertinent information may fail to capture the attention of prospective buyers; a successful advertisement presents a reasonably clear picture of a well run operation. A professional writer might well be employed to create the most favorable impression of your business.

Real Estate Companies

Real estate firms experienced in the sale of commercial enterprises should be investigated to help conduct all phases of the transaction. The realtor's previous experience in handling ornamental type businesses is an important factor in selecting the best firm for the job. The commission can be defended on the basis of the realty's assistance in the following areas:

1. Assessment of operation
   a. House cleaning projects
   b. Economic value of business

2. Preparation of appropriate documents — records and promotional materials
3. Contacting prospective buyers
4. Identifying parties truly interested in the operation
5. Advising on negotiations
6. Completing necessary paperwork

A real estate agent may be necessary when a business must be sold on short notice. The owner can try to sell the business himself when there is time for word of the intended sale to filter throughout the industry.

PREPARING THE BUSINESS

A good plan provides adequate time for preparing all facets of the business for inspection by interested buyers. Friends, business acquaintances, advisors, and members of the family can prove extremely valuable in analyzing the assets and liabilities of the existing operation. Both must be examined carefully to insure putting your best foot forward with potential buyers.

Records

A good business operator will want to examine business records going back a minimum of three and preferably five years. The CPA or accountant advising the individual will insist on this information in order to conduct a reasonable evaluation of the operation. This assumes the buyer plans to continue the business as developed by the previous operator.

Your own CPA should be requested to develop appropriate documents to satisfy the needs of his or her counterparts representing other potential buyers. The decision to sell should be made as early as possible, permitting one to construct records reflecting a most profitable business. This process helps one acquire top price for a garden center. Poor records, and especially those showing a series of losses, can work against your best interests.

The potential buyer normally wants to make a reasonable return on his or her investment (ROI). Your financial records are important in projecting future profits. This information, in turn, will help the buyer obtain bank approval for loans to finance purchase of the business.

The desire to minimize taxes may have to take a back seat to showing, on paper, that you have a profitable business. Three years of good records are a must to develop this story.

Small business operators often reject the idea of making financial information available to interested buyers. One such party remarked "its none of anyone's business except the IRS". This philosophy may appear rational from the seller's point of view. Why should one reveal information that may ultimately be passed on to competitors?

A buyer, unless a complete fool or novice, will not proceed with negotiations until all facts are on the table. There is little basis for discussing price in the absence of solid, reliable financial information. The seller's reluctance to expose records should be viewed as a red flag. The warning signals are up and one should proceed with extreme caution.

A fairly common approach by sellers employs the following themes:

1. There is much opportunity to expand the business with someone having a great deal of vim and vitality.
2. The records really don't show how much I'm taking home.

The promise of growth potential often tempts potential buyers. "We should be able to increase sales and profits 20 percent next year." This factor may be capitalized on by the seller hoping to influence the sale price in his or her favor. Fortunately, bankers and other financial lenders have been reluctant to approve loans based on these expectations. There is no guarantee the business will expand and generate substantial new revenues. The prospects for growth should capture your attention. The sale price should reflect your analysis of the business as it exists today.

There is the suggestion, in the second statement, that all income has not been recorded by the previous owner. This practice is against the law. Your CPA will not approve of your continuing to skim off some of the monies to fool the IRS. The present owner may have avoided some taxes in past years, but one must ultimately pay the price when it comes time to sell the business.

You are gambling with your own future when paying a price based on promises. A CPA will have earned his or her salary by cautioning you against falling into the two traps of high expectations and income from under the table.

Physical Assets

"Familiarity breeds contempt." The operator planning to sell a business must avoid the trap of becoming too familiar with the physical assets of an operation, specifically, accepting things as they are and failing to see the building, parking area, and display counters through the eyes of potential customers. One often fails to recognize the gradual decline of a business. Its something like "the feel of an old sweater." The article of clothing feels very comfortable. However, it may have become threadbare and look totally out of place in a business environment.

A good physical inventory can be conducted, preferably with the aid of business friends or some trusted employees. Identify all the attributes of a modern garden center. A listing of some of the more important features would include:

I. Approach
    A. Visibility
        1) Parking entrance
        2) Main facility
        3) Greenhouse
    B. Parking
        1) Safe entrance and exit
        2) Well marked stalls
        3) Adequate number of stalls
        4) Location of primary and secondary areas
    C. Landscaping
        1) Presence of trees, shrubs, flowers, and accessory items
        2) Condition – maintenance of plantings
    D. Signs
        1) Condition – appearance
        2) Size and location
    E. Display beds
    F. Front of main facility
        1) Cluttered and messy or neat and attractive
        2) Sign on building
        3) Landscaping
        4) Window displays
    G. General traffic pattern
        1) From parking to sales areas
        2) Flow from indoor to outdoor areas
        3) Ease of moving carts
        4) Distance from checkout to parking lots
        5) Indoors
    H. Information signs – outdoors and indoors
        1) Prices
        2) Identification of the item in question
        3) Cultural information

I. Outdoor displays of hard goods

   1) Protected from rain

   2) Neat displays

   3) Volume of material on displays

J. Indoor lighting

K. Condition and appearance of display units

L. Interior and exterior directional signs to major departments

   1) Publications

   2) Pesticides

   3) Pottery

   4) Seeds

   5) Soil mixes

   6) Annual and perennial plants

   7) Vegetables

   8) Ground covers

   9) Shrubs and trees

M. Checkout areas

   1) Number of units and location

   2) Speed of operation

   3) Protection against theft

The time spent in conducting a thorough inventory will prove most valuable to all parties involved in a business transaction. A prospective buyer must determine how much money it will take to recondition the business. The cost of this operation, if excessive, may lead to a lowering of the bid price. More importantly, one comes away with a poor or questionable image of the firm. This may have even greater influence on the final decision than the analysis of business records.

The person planning to sell would do well to invest a modest amount of money in upgrading the physical appearance of the business. Good lighting will do much to create a pleasant atmosphere. It does not cost money to maintain neat displays. A few dollars should be invested in appropriate interior directional signs. The outside of the building might need a new coat of paint.

The physical facilities of your operation help tell a story to prospective buyers. Be reasonably critical when evaluating your own enterprise. Take the time to do an accurate inventory of just what the consumer sees when passing by or entering the garden center. The image you create will influence, one way or the other, the decision to buy and how much will be offered for a business.

BUYING A BUSINESS

How much should you pay for an existing business? This is a complex question that fortunately does not face the party planning to construct a new firm. There are several approaches that can be taken to serve as guidelines in arriving at a fair evaluation of a business. The same guidelines can help a party determine how much to invest in a new operation.

Presumably, one has investigated the community and potential competitors. These analyses, combined with your own assets, show a bright green light. What is your next step in evaluating a business?

Assets

One common approach has been to identify and total all assets of the firm. The last balance sheet and tax records can help you assess the combined value of the land, store, home, greenhouse, inventory (including hard goods and plant materials), accounts receivable, and goodwill. The minimum price for a business would be the total of the liquidation values of all assets. What price would the seller receive for land, inventory, and equipment if all were put on the auction block tomorrow or sold on a special sale? The top price might be the cost involved in replacement of all assets. If someone wanted to start an entirely new business, it would require a considerable outlay of funds for procurement of land, supplies, and equipment. A potential buyer might keep this figure in mind when arriving at a proposed purchase price.

A study of the balance sheet must be undertaken with an understanding of the depreciation formula used by the present owner. An accelerated system would lead to undervaluing assets. Will the land appreciate rapidly because of growth prospects in the area? It is conceivable that buildings could be razed and a high rise structure built on the property. This may be on the drawing board for the following decade.

The first four items might be straightforward in placing a realistic value on these assets. The assessed valuation can provide a starting point in placing a dollar value on these items. One must note the extent to which improvement might have to be made to the store, home, and greenhouse. Remodeling programs can consume valuable dollars. Your cash reserves may or may not be adequate for these projects. The real cost of the business should reflect purchase price and those remodeling costs deemed necessary to begin the new operation on a sound footing. What is the condition of the greenhouse and especially the boiler? Will you have to replace it soon at a cost well in excess of $10,000? Is the structure sound and has it been maintained in good condition by its present owner? A run-down structure may represent more of a hazard and liability than an asset.

The value of inventory is often up for debate. Hard goods such as containers and ribbons may be out of date. They could have been purchased by the carload and at a bargain a decade ago. You may want to discount them 50 percent or even ask the owner to dispose of them before the sale. Nursery materials may have become overgrown and unsaleable. The present owner undoubtedly has placed a high value on the materials, assuming someone will take them off his hands tomorrow. Outdoor plantings maintained in poor fashion probably have little value either to the current or future owner. Poor weed control is symptomatic of the problem and should attract your attention. Greenhouse crops may or may not be in good condition. A recent buyer of a greenhouse completely removed and destroyed all plants as the first step in his remodeling program. The listing of assets did not include any dollars for plant materials.

Accounts receivable 60- and 90-days overdue probably have relatively little value. You may create problems trying to collect old bills from potential customers. The current owner should be advised to handle all collections.

The asset approach has been used by firms specifically interested in procuring such facilities as greenhouses or buildings. An entirely new operation may be planned by the new owner. Business records would provide very little if any information regarding the value of the operation. Procurement of assets such as greenhouses has occurred on a number of occasions in recent years. Buyers have been motivated to acquire older facilities in their belief that they could be acquired at a cost much less than that for a new structure.

Buyer and seller must come to an agreement on the current value of land and structures. The former can be arrived at with relative ease from assessment figures and real estate personnel. A fair figure for the structure will be determined on a more subjective basis. What is the price of a new unit? What is the condition of the old unit? How badly does the seller want to sell and the buyer want to buy?

Previous records of a business are believed useless by some buyers and sellers. They reason that an operator was highly successful or an immense failure solely because of business philosophy and ability. The new operator will not follow in the same footsteps. Thus, the only fair way of selling a business should be on the basis of tangible assets. The successful operator would have been rewarded through profits earned in previous years. The poor operator already took his or her lumps in reduced salaries and limited or nonexistent profits. A new buyer simply starts with a clean sheet in the record books.

The asset approach will be advanced by sellers recording few if any profits in recent years. The market value of land, facilities, and inventory becomes a key consideration in arriving at a sale price. Records can be manipulated to some degree to reflect specific desires of the owner at particular points in time. A firm may keep one set of records for tax purposes and an informal set conceivably reflecting more accurately the current status of the business. This has prompted some buyers to ignore records when assessing the value of an operation. Assets such as land and structures can be evaluated by neutral parties.

Profitability of Firm.   A second approach to buying a firm focuses attention on its profitability or track record. The first step requires you to obtain and evaluate the profit and loss or income statements for the last three to five years. How much profit has the firm produced? This figure should be analyzed carefully to insure that it does not reflect unusual income or expense items. The profit figure should be adjusted so that it provides a true picture of the earning capacity of the firm. Profit is the name of the game for someone interested in investing hard-earned dollars.

Some owners refuse at least initially to show their records to a prospective buyer. This is a real danger signal. There is nothing to do but back off and wait or begin looking at other firms. These owners justify their position on the basis that one should have faith in their verbal reports. This line of reasoning has no justification after initial conversations. The owner's position may be justified on the basis that records have been "altered" for tax purposes. The owner must show proof or accept responsibility for preparation of adjusted returns resulting in a lower sales price than might be expected for the business. The ability to manipulate profits to some degree does handicap the accurate valuation of a business. You may wish to employ a qualified accountant or CPA to help analyze the profit position of the firm.

Most sellers will show their books without any hesitation. A three-year analysis should focus on trends and the extent to which profit, owner's compensation, and sales have risen in an acceptable fashion. The trend in an upward direction permits you to extend the lines with a degree of confidence. An up-and-down history often requires that you examine books over a longer period of time. You may wish to average figures for the last three years to offset high and low figures. Your careful analysis will be reflected in the ultimate purchase price. Take time and examine all figures.

"The figures really do not reveal the full potential of this business." So what! Any increase in sales and profits will come from the actions of the new buyer. The potential is only a potential and does not enter into the proposed sales figure. An interested buyer certainly would find it attractive to purchase a business with excellent growth potential. Again, this should not enter into negotiations since one is dealing with a purely hypothetical situation.

An analysis of business records must be undertaken with the knowledge that current owners have been motivated to manage for a forthcoming sale or continued operation. Owners preparing to sell a business often will minimize deductions and expenses to maximize profits. This action will subject the organization to higher taxes in the short run. The goal, however, is to make the business look appetizing to potential buyers.

Those operators planning to continue operation of the business for many years will look for ways of minimizing state and federal taxes. A primary way has been to reduce profits through inclusion of a variety of benefits to management. These might take the form of legitimate business trips, company-owned cars, and similar fringe benefits. The income or profit and loss statement must be analyzed in terms of the presence or absence of such benefits and the influence they have on profits at the bottom line.

Let us assume that profits after taxes and owner compensation come to $30,000 a year. How much are you willing to pay for the business, assuming all other factors appear in proper order? The profit approach suggests that you ask yourself how much one would invest in an enterprise yielding a return of $30,000 a year. This might be in terms of buying stocks, bonds, real estate, or another business. Some individuals think their investment should be returned in five years. This opinion is based on the risk factor and the knowledge that one might receive a safe 10 percent return on some bonds. If so, a purchase price of $150,000 would be in the ball park. This assumes an out-of-pocket investment of the entire figure. Investing $50,000 of your own dollars and acquiring a loan of $100,000 requires minor adjustments in your evaluation scheme. The loan interest will appear in the profit and loss statement, and thus reduce profits by a like amount of dollars. This new dollar amount or profit should be equal to the desired return on your actual investment of $50,000.

You might be willing to use a factor of 6 to 10 based on your own expectations and desires in receiving a return on your investment. You could anticipate that land would dramatically increase in value in 5 to 10 years. This might stimulate one to pay more for the business, accepting a lower return with the promise of ultimately reaping a harvest on sale of the land. This approach is profit oriented. It requires that you have access to reliable records. You must carefully assess trends to insure that the business has not reached a plateau and is in fact sliding down hill. Your desires in terms of return on investment guide the final proposed purchase price.

One danger signal relates to a business based solely on the contributions of one person. The disappearance of this key person could result in a vaporization of profits. A business looks much more attractive when "purchasing" several key employees all capable of helping maintain and improve the profit picture.

Net Book Value and Price-Earnings Ratio

A third and more sophisticated approach focuses attention on establishment of parameters to decide the potential price for an ongoing business. The two parameters are:

1. Net book value (balance sheet)
2. Price-earnings ratio (income or profit and loss statement)[2]

A price-earnings ratio (P/E) of 5 has been recommended by some financial analysts. This means that one expects to receive a full return on an investment in 5 years. You may agree to wait longer and thus increase the P/E ratio to 10 or even higher. This approach was described in the last section of this chapter.

The balance sheet provides information on the net book value of a firm as of a specific date. This figure is arrived at by subtracting current liabilities (those owed to parties outside the company) from total assets. The net book value reflects the amount of money owed by the firm to its shareholders and in retained earnings. This approach recognizes that extensive assets should be considered in determining the value of a business. The extent of liabilities, by the same token, must be considered by the potential buyer.

There are situations when the figure derived from the P/E ratio will be higher than that for the net book value. The reverse situation may be true on other occasions. There is no special significance to which of the two figures appears high or low. You should carefully analyze the relationship between total assets and liabilities. A company heavily in debt means that someone has used dollars from other parties to help run and develop the business. Creditors may show limited patience should a new operator begin to fall behind in payments. You need to have an adequate cash reserve to avoid potential default and ultimate bankruptcy.

A firm with a relatively high net book value provides a measure of security to new operators. They can make some mistakes, as often occurs, and still not have creditors banging at the door. The company has the strength to survive a storm. Here are two case studies to help illustrate the use of this technique. The information has been condensed with attention focused on major categories in the profit and loss statements and balance sheets.

Firm 1 has been working with other people's money. Almost 90 percent of their assets have been procured through loans from creditors. The second firm is in a much stronger position with only one third of its assets based on support from creditors. A strong cash reserve would be highly desirable were one to acquire the first firm.

[2]It is assumed that the figures appearing on these statements have not been modified or adjusted significantly for special purposes.

BALANCE SHEET
DECEMBER 31, 1977

		Firm 1	Firm 2
Assets			
Current		$275,000	$150,000
Fixed		150,000	150,000
	Total	$425,000	$300,000
Liabilities and Shareholders' Equity			
Current liabilities		$355,000	$ 25,000
Long term liabilities		25,000	75,000
Shareholders' equity		10,000	125,000
Retained earnings		35,000	75,000
	Total	$425,000	$300,000
(Net book value		$ 45,000	$200,000)

INCOME STATEMENT
January 1, 1977–December 31, 1977

	Firm 1	Firm 2
Net sales	$1,000,000	$475,000
Cost of goods sold	850,000	350,000
Gross margin	150,000	125,000
Operating expenses	125,000	105,000
Net income before taxes	25,000	20,000
Net income before taxes	25,000	20,000
ratio of 5	125,000	100,000

The present operator of Firm 2 has acquired a sizeable net worth. It reflects a conservatively managed business not unique in the florist, garden center, and nursery fields. The important question is the extent to which this operator can find a buyer to offer something near the net book value of the firm. It has yielded only a 10 percent return on investment (ROI) compared to an almost 56 percent return on equity investment in the first firm.[1]

A shrewd buyer would prefer to focus attention on the low parameter of $100,000. This would offer a 20 percent return on investment (net profit before taxes of $20,000 times a P/E ratio of 5 yields $100,000). The earning power of Firm 1 has been extremely good. It represents the high parameter when bidding on this operation. This figure would command attention especially if you were to have adequate cash reserves for the first year of operation. Poor management, however, would place the firm in serious

[1]ROI for Firm 1, before taxes, of 56 percent based on $25,000/$45,000 and 10 percent for Firm 2 arrived at by $20,000/$200,000. The $25,000 and $20,000 figures represent net income before taxes. The $45,000 and $200,000 figures represent net book values or total investment by owners for the two firms.

jeopardy as creditors have provided most of the money necessary to produce the exceptional income after taxes.

An offer of only $100,000 for the second firm would bring tears to the eyes of the present owner. This is the price to be paid for accepting a low return on investment. Steps should have been taken in earlier years to improve the return on investment.

Profit Approach.   Some sellers and buyers have scorned the profit approach in favor of asset valuation. The performance of current management, so the argument goes, should not enter into negotiations regarding sales price. One simply is selling and the other party buying specific assets. It is true that potential growth and profits cannot be quantified for the benefit of buyer or seller. Past performance has been placed in the same category by those focusing all attention on assets. This is a debatable position.

The profit position of a firm reflects performance and, to a degree, good-will generated by management. A new owner inherits these "assets" at the time of purchase. Should they not enter into the purchase price? Good management as reflected in profits should be rewarded when the business changes hands. Profits are an asset in many respects and rightfully enter into negotiations over the purchase price.

A new and inexperienced operator may suffer losses the first year or so in business. Why should the individual pay a price based on profits realized by past management when one likely will go into the red shortly after change of ownership? There is nothing in the business world that guarantees anyone a profit. One assumes this risk when a decision has been made to buy a business.

The business operator who has recorded profits should be rewarded for his or her efforts at time of sale. By the same token, one who has been a failure will have to pay the price for mismanagement. Selling price should reflect the assets and profitability of a firm. It should not be based on future growth potential. Past records must be carefully analyzed in arriving at a reasonable price.

Price and Value

The final selling price will represent a compromise between the asking and bid figures initially offered by both parties to a transaction. The seller focuses attention on all the positive features seemingly supporting the asking price. A buyer sees the business through different eyes, noting risks and liabilities to be inherited with transfer of ownership. The facility may need a new look, including an upgrading of merchandise. Differences between the two parties must be reconciled to insure completion of the transaction.

The final selling price may well differ from the real value of the business. Both parties, again, will approach the task of identifying value from different prospectives. The seller may focus attention on the monies invested for land, buildings, and inventory. A potential buyer, recognizing these assets, must still focus attention on profit potential of the operation. "Will the business produce profits of a magnitude that can justify the original investment in the business?" The seller, recognizing this approach, may wish to focus attention on future profit potential under the dynamic leadership of a new owner. This action tends to shift the spotlight from current profits and return on investment to future projections. A leading agency will question projections which depart radically from the past performance of the operation.

DETERMINING VALUE OF A BUSINESS

RULE

Firm	Profit[1]	ROI [2]	Years for Payback[3]	Value of Business to Buyer [4]
A	25,000	25%	4	100,000
B	15,000	10%	10	150,000
C	50,000	20%	5	250,000
D	50,000	10%	10	500,000

[1] Before taxes

[2] Return On Investment desired by operator.

[3] A 25% ROI means that profits recorded over a four-year period (25 × 4) will pay back the original investment.

[4] Column 1 × 3.

Value should be viewed in terms of current performance of the operation. How many dollars can you invest given a known or hard profit figure before taxes? Price should be somewhere close to the value figure derived for an organization. An adjustment up or down reflects the nature of the risk, condition of the facility, and some estimate of goodwill.

A factor for goodwill often has been suggested as an addition to that of assets in arriving at a fair value for a business. What is goodwill? Goodwill often has been thought of as the value one receives based on the name and reputation of the previous owner. There is no magic formula in placing a dollar value on the name of the former proprietor. What happens if the owner had a poor reputation and it was sliding every week? You can identify goodwill as that value arising from sales that commence with the first day of operation under new ownership. This is in comparison to sales from a hypothetical and identical unit that just came into existence the same day. You must still decide, however, how much value to place on goodwill. It is quite nebulous and exceedingly difficult to translate into a monetary value. A compromise sales price may include goodwill in terms of utilizing the name of an operation and without applying a specific figure for this item. Goodwill does not appear on typical records such as the profit and loss statement and the balance sheet. Your accountant and tax expert should be consulted regarding identification of goodwill on yearly tax return forms.

Existing Contracts

The individual planning to buy a business must examine, preferably with a lawyer, all contracts signed by the current owner and having a bearing on the new operation. These include:

1. Real estate leases
   a. duration
   b. renewal
   c. improvements
2. Exclusive agent for line of product
3. Employment contracts
   a. key personnel
   b. union members contracts
   c. health and profit sharing programs
4. Insurance policies
5. Assessments or claims against land, buildings, inventory
6. Partnership agreements
7. Corporation documents pertinent to the transaction — authorize sale

Final Contract

A lawyer and accountant (CPA) should be employed by the buyer in finalizing all details of the contract to procure a business enterprise. Presumably, the seller will be represented by professionals to protect his or her interest. The major concerns to be addressed include:

1. A detailed description of what is actually being sold and just as clearly what is being retained by the current owner — clear title
2. Time and place for final signing of the contract
3. The purchase price
4. Method of financing purchase — especially if land contract or similar instrument is being employed to facilitate sale

5. Final adjustments at closing time regarding inventory and operating expenses (rent)

6. The nature and extent of all commitments to be accepted by buyer including disposition of accounts receivable

7. Seller may be required to sign a statement preventing his or her opening a competing business for a given period of time and in a given market area

8. A warranty may be required to protect the buyer against false financial information and undisclosed liabilities to be inherited by the new owner.

The closing date should immediately precede the day scheduled for transfer of the business to a new operator. A time lag may lead to future problems regarding disposition of some assets following signing of contracts and actual takeover of the business.

SUMMARY

The process of buying and selling a business is complicated and often emotional. It is especially emotional for the seller who may have devoted a lifetime to the enterprise. The buyer must carefully investigate all facets of an existing operation before making an offer to buy.

There is a right time to sell a business. A smoothly running, highly profitable operation will capture the attention of buyers. It is much easier to obtain close to the asking price in this situation than it is for a business which has gone downhill in recent years.

An owner needs a minimum of three years to prepare the business for transfer to a new party. Prospective buyers include members of the family, employees, competitors, and persons totally unassociated with the garden center business.

Trade papers have been used effectively by sellers in announcing that a business is for sale. A professional writer may be of value in designing an advertisement that captures the attention of prospective buyers.

Real estate agents can be most helpful in preparing a business for sale. Their expertise in contacting prospective buyers, closing the deal, and placing a value on the business can and will be most helpful to sellers.

Placing a value on a business requires an analysis of both the balance sheet and income or profit and loss statement. The net book value, combined with a P/E ratio of 5, can provide parameters for arriving at a reasonable price. A simple evaluation of assets can prove misleading at times, especially when other people's money has been used to acquire them for the firm.

The asset approach has been used by buyers specifically interested in acquiring land and buildings to be used for purposes other than current operations. This approach also may be used in those instances where a firm has been in the red or producing few profits. Goodwill is hard to define. It is even harder to attach a dollar figure to it.

Avoid the trap of trying to place a value on your business under pressure. A simple and valuable exercise helps develop parameters reflecting the value of a business. Use the balance sheet and income statement each year to analyze the strengths and weaknesses of your firm. Take the initiative in keeping up to date on a realistic evaluation of your business and its potential vaiue to a new owner.

The final step involves the signing of the contract by buyer and seller. A good lawyer should be present to represent each side. This is a critical moment, especially for the buyer, finalizing all details that may well have a bearing on future prosperity of the firm.

Good records are a must for anyone wanting to sell a business at top dollar. A CPA will want to analyze financial information for the last three years. The planning process should provide time for your accountant or CPA to present a clear picture of the operation.

A careful inventory of the operation should be performed by seller and buyer. This includes everything from the time a consumer approaches the operation to when he or she departs from the parking lot. Friends, business acquaintances, and employers can prove helpful in looking at the enterprise through the eyes of a customer. You must avoid the trap of becoming too familiar with the operation.

1. When is it a poor time to sell a business?

2. Identify three conditions of business arthritis.

3. Identify three potential buyers and discuss their attributes.

4. Discuss the role of a real estate agent in finding prospective customers.

5. How does one prepare a business for sale?

6. What approaches can one employ when buying a business and establishing a purchase price?

7. What is the difference between selling price and value?

8. What type of contracts must be investigated and known by potential buyer?

9. Identify five important elements of the final contract.

chapter
four

Financial
Planning

The opportunity to own a business appeals to many individuals. Why work for another person, helping them make a good salary plus profits? The want ads in trade papers and daily newspapers continually provide opportunities for budding entrepreneurs. Running a business, especially when one likes the product or service in question, certainly has a great deal of appeal. The realities become quite evident when one is forced to prepare a financial plan in defense of a proposal to start a new operation. Lofty dreams must be turned into realistic plans unless one has been blessed with a gold mine to support the venture. Your immediate task calls for the development of an indepth financial plan. Lenders of money want adequate assurances that you have thought the proposal through to the nth detail. The process will command your energies and time for many months. Risking your own hard earned dollars should, in itself, provide the incentive for a complete study of the proposed venture. A wealth of details, obviously requiring time and effort, should command the attention of prospective borrowers. Contrast this approach with that of someone's approaching a lender with a napkin bearing a series of miscellaneous numbers. Who has given real thought to the proposal?

You can avoid many of the pitfalls of those who failed in business by careful analysis of your financial resources. You should determine how much money you will need to start the business, prepare it for the first day of operation, and keep it operating until sufficient revenues are on hand to balance expenses. The first item cannot be ignored as you must cover start-up costs prior to opening day. You may have to tap reserves for a number of months to cover operating expenses, often exceeding income. Optimistic projections of sales may exceed the realities. This is especially troublesome to the business offering credit, which then finds cash does not arrive on the scene for some 45 days after the sale. This is a key factor in many first-year bankruptcies. The SBA has prepared a worksheet, their publication S.M.A. No. 71, *Checklist for Going into Business*, to help analyze financial needs.

Some individuals may be tempted to eliminate proposed expenditures for advertising in an attempt to decrease necessary startup costs. They rationalize that this item could be supported once the business is running smoothly. This action could jeopardize the future of the organization. A special effort must be undertaken to acquaint people with the new garden center. If anything, more monies might be funneled into an advertising program than that required for a well-established firm. You should also examine your living standards, and the degree to which you are prepared to sacrifice during the early years of a new organization. Unsuccessful people often have an inability to strike a balance between living standards and reinvesting earnings in the business.

SOURCES OF MONEY

The business entrepreneur can turn to two primary sources of money when financing the acquisition of a firm. *Equity* capital comes directly from the resources of the business person. The individual may have cash on hand or be able to convert assets into cash for the new operation. One normally has to borrow some monies from other parties; this will be referred to as *debt* capital.

Equity Capital

The buyer must determine the extent to which he or she wants to transfer assets from a normally safe investment into one bearing a risk of undetermined magnitude. Lenders of money, on the other hand, will not be willing to risk their hard-earned dollars unless the proposed operator is willing to take comparable risks. The chances of acquiring a loan increase substantially to the degree that one invests his or her own assets in a business.

Debt Capital

The new operator normally will have to borrow money to purchase a business and to establish credit for later transactions. Commercial lending institutions are primary sources of debt capital. High interest rates, especially early in the 1980s, have made it extremely difficult for business people to acquire and afford loans from local banks.

Product oriented businesses require the procurement of a sizeable inventory. In most cases this money must be available well before one generates sales. Family members and friends often function as major source of money to one trying to start a business. Special pressures can be applied indirectly and directly by the borrower on these people. Sometimes this is intentional, and sometimes it occurs accidentally and without any plan by one seeking a loan. The risk factor can magnify unintentionally when one seeks debt capital from noncommercial lenders. A close family or working relationship between the two parties may preclude development of appropriate financial plans and close examination of the borrower's credentials. Lofty dreams and plans may be verbalized without thought of the realities.

The refusal of a loan by a commercial lender should warn all parties, especially the borrower, that he or she is skating on thin ice. Financial plans and projections developed with the aid of a Certified Public Accountant

(CPA) or accountant should be reexamined and revised in light of a loan refusal. Family and friends should not be pressured as one desperately tries to finance a new, and apparently high risk, business.

The current owner or owners of a business may serve as a partial or total lender of funds to a prospective buyer. This source of capital has become increasingly popular from both the buyer's and seller's point of view as interest rates have risen. The seller obviously wants to unload the business. A strong desire to sell, tied in with realities of the financial world, has stimulated many sellers to assume part of the risk.

The sale contract involving debt capital provided by the seller will include provisions for:

1.   down payment
2.   monthly or quarterly payments
   a.   principle
   b.   interest
3.   security on specified assets
   a.   buildings
   b.   land
   c.   equipment
   d.   inventory

One potential drawback of owner financing is that the borrower may be unable to acquire additional capital from commercial lending institutions because a bank cannot lay first claim to the assets should the business go bankrupt. The original owner would have first claim to assets secured in the contract. Owner financing has merit when the borrower can provide enough capital to operate the business for six months or longer.

The seller of a business offering a land contract as the vehicle of exchanging ownership must be prepared to accept risks and the eventuality of reacquiring the business. Age of the owner may necessitate an outright sale in lieu of helping finance the proposed buyer. The financial terms of a land contract (namely, down and periodic payments) must protect the interests of the seller. A scenario, not at all unusual, has the seller bending over backwards to move the business. Terms of the contract favor the buyer to the extent that all risks have been borne by the seller. Whether intentionally or not, the buyer runs the business during the busy season and "escapes" with all the profits. The business is returned to the seller in somewhat poorer shape than it was six months or a year earlier.

SIZE OF LOAN

Your CPA or accountant can help you protect the size of loan that can be requested from a lending institution. The financial statements prepared to support the proposal are the basis for acceptance or rejection of the application. The lender will look at budgeted items for the following:

1. your salary
2. depreciation
3. interest expense

The combination of these three items, coming from the operating statement, will establish the parameters of a proposed loan. Your salary must be considered adequate to maintain a family in reasonable comfort. A banker would find it difficult to accept a statement calling for an annual salary of $12,000 to support a husband, wife, and two children. The opposite extreme would be to project a $50,000 salary for the same family during the first couple of years. A more realistic line of income, given the community and ages of family members, might be around $20,000.

The interest payment category covers all loans secured by the operation to finance a business. A family loan requiring annual interest must be joined with all other loans including those from commercial lenders. The projected gross income for the new enterprise will help determine how much debt can be borne by the operation. Net profit must still look good following payment of reasonable salaries and covering all interest expenses.

A banker often permits one to use depreciation to cover interest payments during startup years, especially for a new operation not anticipating replacement of facilities in the immediate future. One should carefully study an enterprise featuring a greenhouse complex that just might need major overhaul shortly after signing the papers. This would apply to high-cost components such as a boiler. The normal pressures of starting a business are great enough without having to finance major projects.

Working capital is important to the new operator as well as one who has been in business a number of years. It represents the cash available to pay rent, salaries (yours included), utilities, and suppliers each month. The amount of cash available at the beginning of a month will be added to expected cash sales. Collection from accounts receivable will be added to this figure for those firms already in business. Be careful not to overestimate your collections and in the process inflate working capital. A careful estimate of working capital will also help to smooth out the seasonal peaks and valleys that face many garden center operators.

The difference between the categories of cash and expenses represents the cash-flow situation. A new business must have adequate reserves to cover cash deficiencies for the first six months to a year. You cannot expect to receive short-term loans immediately after securing financial support on a longer term basis from financial institutions.

RESPONSIBILITIES OF BORROWER

The person or persons in need of debt capital must develop and provide a wealth of detailed information to and for proposed lenders of money. This particularly applies to commercial banks. The packet of information required by these parties also should be provided to family members and friends. This practice forces one to examine realistically all facets of a business transaction. The proposed borrower should be required to prepare the following:

1. personal and business financial statement
2. supporting information:
    a. general business knowledge
    b. knowledge of particular business — industry
3. marketing plan
4. pro forma statement

Personal Financial Statement

The responsiblity is on your shoulders to prepare and make available to proposed lenders a capsule of your financial history. What makes you a good prospect for a business loan? Major ingredients of a financial statement are similar to those provided when applying for a bank credit card.

1. Identify your own assets
    a. house and property
    b. savings accounts
    c. stock, bonds, and other financial statements
    d. checking account
2. Identify your liabilities
    a. credit card accounts
    b. short and long term loans

3. References
   a. business
   b. personal
   c. credit
   d. banking institutions

What is your track record in building a solid financial image in the community? Consider the following:

1. Have you paid back all loans on schedule?
2. Are your credit card accounts up to date in terms of payments and size of outstanding balance?

The burden is on you to prove that a loan of the magnitude requested is relatively secure. You must help the lender, in every way possible, signal the green light. Much of the information may appear highly personal. Your decision to seek a commercial loan overrides any desire to maintain some element of secrecy regarding past financial dealings.

General Business Knowledge

Every business, whether a garden center, supermarket, candy store, discount house, or amusement park, has one common denominator. Business concepts and practices apply across the board. Product lines and services will vary considerably from one area to another. Financial statement, analysis of business records, and management of personnel, to mention just a few concepts, apply equally well to every retail operation in your community.

Have you sharpened your business management skills before deciding to embark on this venture? Can you demonstrate an awareness of the skills required to operate a business successfully? Your strength in knowing how plants grow will do little to overcome the fears of someone asked to finance a new enterprise.

Good business sense comes from a combination of:

1. practical experience — working for someone else and being given the opportunity to learn varied business skills
2. education — attending short course business programs and conferences; formal classes

Business failures often can be traced back to the entrepreneurs' inability to master management skills particularly appropriate to small enterprises.

These skills should be acquired before embarking on the dream to own a business. The world can and will be cruel to those who come unprepared for the task of managing all facets of a garden center operation.

Knowledge of Industry

A lender recognizes that an element of risk is attached to every loan. Your goal must be to demonstrate in the presentation that risks will be minimized in your particular situation. Your knowledge of the industry and business in question will be crucial in helping the lender support a loan application. This area parallels the previous section on general business knowledge. Hopefully, you can demonstrate both practical knowledge and some formal learning in a classroom type situation. The latter could well take place at industry meetings and short courses sponsored by an extension service or vocational-technical school. Short courses and conferences are held locally, regionally, and nationally to help upgrade people in the garden center business. Industry trade papers carry meeting notices; one trade paper actually has a major role in sponsoring the annual session. These programs help people prepare for changes affecting garden centers throughout the country.

The learning process can be shortened greatly if some in-depth knowledge has been acquired of the business in question. Risks become much more significant when the proposed new owner must learn from scratch. This concern can be reduced by employing one or more knowledgeable people. The former owner of an established business may be "contracted" to work for from six to twelve months following completion of the sales transaction. A person with similar background may be employed to work for an entirely new operation. Good experience represents a real plus for someone wanting to start or buy a business.

Practical experience commands the attention of anyone being asked to lend money. How much do you know about the business? How long have you worked for the existing firm or for someone having a comparable operation? Help the lender gain confidence in your competence to run a profitable business.

Marketing Plan

A detailed marketing plan must be developed to attract the attention of potential lenders. This effort reflects your own intimate knowledge of the business. What do you plan to sell? How do you plan to market your product and services? The marketing plan can be broken down as follows:

1. Identify products and services offered to consumers
    a. product lines
        1) seed-grass, vegetables, flowers
        2) pesticides
        3) equipment
        4) accessory items
        5) woody plant materials
        6) indoor plants
        7) garden flowers — annuals and perennials
        8) fertilizers — indoor and outdoor
        9) gift items
        10) containers
        11) handicraft projects
    b. services
        1) rental of equipment
        2) planting woody materials
        3) delivery of large items
        4) in-store personal service
        5) landscape plans
2. Market area for your proposed operation
    a. geographical area
    b. composition of market area
        1) economic factors
        2) age group
        3) new developments
3. Advertising budget and program
    a. radio
    b. shopper newspapers
    c. direct mail
    d. other
4. Special open houses
5. Month by month breakdown of sales and areas contributing to income
6. Image to be created by management

The attributes of an existing firm you plan to buy should be outlined specifically to blend in with your marketing plan.

1. General appearance of the facility—external and internal
2. Layout—efficiency of operation in terms of customer and employee movement through facility
3. Location
4. Available records—a base for sales projections
5. Image of operation in community
6. Employee morale and loyalty

A description of an entirely new operation should focus on items 1, 2, 3 and 5 from the last section. Paint the most complete picture of how you plan to use monies made available by the lender. A more detailed description of a marketing plan, for a business that is functioning, will be found in Chapter Six.

Pro Forma Statement

An application for a loan presumes that one will have the ability to pay back principal and interest over a stated period of time. A lender wants to know specifically how you plan to fulfill the repayment requirements of the loan contract. Verbal assurances represent more of a red flag than intended by the loan seeker. Realistic financial projections are a must at this stage of the loan presentation. Your CPA or accountant will prove invaluable in helping prepare appropriate documents. The documents in question are essentially those prepared for the business at the close of each fiscal period. What will your operating statement and balance sheet look like in three, six, twelve, and twenty-four months following start of the business? Operating statements can be developed using:

1. projected sales
2. known or anticipated expenses

The top line of this statement contains your best estimate of gross sales for the period in question. An adjustment will be made for returned goods leading to net sales. All expenses are identified as specific dollar figures and as a percentage of net sales. The percentages programmed should be in the ballpark of industry averages. This tells you essentially how much can be spent for interest, wages, products, and all other operating expenses.

The balance sheet also serves as a guide in monitoring the financial stability of a firm. Will you have enough capital to make it through the first year? Or will you need short term loans? This picture will be further clarified by preparing a cash flow report.

THREE-YEAR OPERATING STATEMENT
FORMER OWNER

	1981	1982	1983	
Sales	140,000	152,000	168,000	(Aver. 10%/yr.)
Cost of goods sold				
Gross margin				
Operating expenses[1]				
Profit				

[1] Includes wage to owner

PROJECTED THREE-YEAR OPERATING STATEMENT
NEW OWNER

	1984	1985	1986
Sales			
Costs of goods sold			
Gross margin			
Operating expenses[1]			
Profit			

[1] Includes wage to owner

Sales Projections

Purchasing an existing business can prove extremely helpful in preparing realistic projections for sales during the next three year period. This assumes that the previous owner maintained a good set of records. One should anticipate a minimum increase from the most recent year equal to the rate of inflation. An adjustment up or down would be appropriate reflecting general trend lines for the previous three year period. One might argue that new management will significantly increase sales. The previous sales records may be of little value. You will have to carefully document this degree of optimism. A typical lender has heard this story many times only to find that a more conservative approach would have been appropriate given the realities of the situation.

A young couple, for example, purchased a viable business. They followed all recommendations regarding preparation of financial documents and projections. Sales were expected to increase some 15 to 20 percent the first year. This virtually doubled previous management's record in operating a healthy business. The couple's loan was approved by a local bank. A crucial decision faced the couple just prior to opening day in March. What prices should be charged for their products? They had intended to increase prices from the previous year by at least 10 percent reflecting inflation and prices charged by competitors. All their previous efforts went for naught as special introductory prices were offered for the first planting season. Prices were actually reduced in the hope of attracting more customers. Sales recorded for the first year turned out to be just below those of the former owner. The pressure was on to pay principal and interest on the loan.

Sales projections may have to be revised reflecting local conditions and the actions of competitors. Each change may have a significant bearing on one's ability to fulfill financial obligations.

How does one prepare a sales projection without benefit of past records? This question must be faced squarely early in the game. The answer affects all other financial deliberations. The process can begin with a determination of what one expects in terms of a salary. An owner-manager may determine that an annual salary of $20,000 will support his or her family. To simplify, assume that a working spouse draws a salary and is counted as an employee. Industry statistics may suggest that a salary for management normally runs 10 percent of gross sales. This means that one has to gross $200,000 a year in order to pay management the salary of $20,000. Total gross, using industry average, can be broken down into product lines and in turn by month of the year. Your experience or gut feelings will have to tell you whether or not these projections are in the ballpark.

SALES PROJECTIONS—1985   × ½ COMPANY

Product Line	Year	Jan.	Feb.	Mar.	Apr.
Grass seed	$	$	$	$	$
Fertilizer					
Trees					
Shrubs					
Bedding plants					
Indoor plants					
Potting soils					
Pesticides					
Small garden supplies					
Large equipment					
Gifts					
TOTAL:	$	$	$	$	$

SMALL BUSINESS ADMINISTRATION

The Small Business Administration will provide a great deal of assistance to individuals proposing to buy or start a new business. They have a number of excellent publications designed to help you enter the business world.[1] Staff members in district and regional offices can provide some guidance or direct you to appropriate sources for assistance in developing financial plans.

The Small Business Administration can also provide direct assistance in acquiring business loans. Low interest loans have been made available to qualified people unable to acquire financial support from lending institutions. A waiting period of nine to twelve months has not been uncommon for these direct loans. Special programs have been available to women and members of minority groups.

TIPS ON BORROWING

1. Know exactly how much money you require for the project. Avoid the temptation of underestimating the size of a loan in hopes of generating favorable action by the lender. A banker, for example, should be in a good position to evaluate and determine your needs. You will not impress a professional lender by shooting too low or changing figures from meeting to meeting.

2. Try to talk the language of a banker or professional lender. A "line of credit" normally will be used to finance inventory and accounts payable. You need a term loan, rather than an extension of credit, to finance the purchase of fixed assets.

3. Do not wait until the last minute before applying for a loan. A lender does not look favorably on someone faced with a deadline just around the corner.

4. Come prepared for your first meeting with all appropriate records and plans. This will hasten the process and impress the professional lender.

5. Can you demonstrate a strong measure of optimism for the future? Realistic goals and sales projections exceeding the current rate of inflation will reflect well on your application for a loan.

6. A banker, for example, should be viewed as a real partner. Do not hide information or fail to seek his or her advice. These people want to succeed and their progress reflects your own business success.

[1]See *Buying and Selling a Small Business* and *Starting and Managing A Small Business of Your Own.*

7. Professional lenders are called upon to finance:
   a. new businesses
   b. expansion programs
   c. business survival

It can be relatively easy to finance an expansion program. The firm should have a track record with the lender. A borrower must recognize that few lenders want to allocate monies to a sinking ship. What has brought a business to this critical point? Did the operator fail to work with the banker? One has to prepare well for this type of loan. Financing a new business probably falls in between these two other positions. Nevertheless, one will have to work hard to convince a lender of his or her prospects for success.

SUMMARY

Financial planning separates those operating in dreamland from those with two feet firmly planted on the ground. The realities of the busienss world come into clear focus when one prepares to meet a professional lender. You must be prepared to provide adequate assurances that risks have been minimized in the proposed plan of operation.

Two sources of money have been identified: equity and debt capital. The former comes from your own resources or assets. How much are you prepared to invest in this business? All outside parties, including family members, are potential sources of debt capital. The refusal of a banker to lend money should capture your attention and that of other potential lenders. Your proposal may be too risky or perhaps not enough thought was put into the written financial plan and proposal.

A land contract may prove desirable to both the buyer and seller. The latter must protect all interests to insure that the buyer does not capture short term profits before reneging on the contract.

Your CPA can help you determine the size of loan likely to be granted by a lending agency. Be sure you have adequate working capital to cover the first year of operation.

The borrower must be prepared to provide full information to a potential lender. This includes a personal and business financial statement, supporting information, marketing and sales plan, and pro forma statement. You must be completely open and honest in developing a complete financial plan.

Practical business experience and knowledge of the garden center industry will prove important in building a solid case for your loan. You must demonstrate the ability to operate a business enterprise successfully. The projection for sales during the first year will reveal much about your knowledge of the garden center business.

The pro forma statement consists of your proposed operating statement, balance sheet, and sales targets. This can be developed monthly for the first year and quarterly for the second and third years. Previous records of an existing firm may prove helpful in developing these figures.

The Small Business Administration can provide assistance to persons interested in buying or starting a business. They have numerous publications to help guide the small business person. Direct and indirect assistance has been available in terms of funding loans.

1. Identify and discuss the two main sources of money for financing a new operation.

2. Discuss some of the potential problems of borrowing money from friends and members of your family.

3. Discuss the contents of a land contract and potential problem for current owner.

4. What factors will influence the size of a loan?

5. What are the major components of a personal financial statement?

6. How can you demonstrate general business knowledge and knowledge of the garden center industry?

7. Identify and discuss three components of a marketing plan.

8. How does one formulate sales projections for a garden center business?

9. What is and how does one produce a pro forma statement?

10. Discuss three tips on borrowing money.

chapter
five

Managing
Your
Business

A good set of records is a key ingredient to the success of all organizations. Successful managers have learned to use records effectively in the day-to-day operation of their business. Good records are as important to business success as a roadmap to a driver. Small businessmen and women have a tendency to mix business and personal finances. They see it as "my" money. Their records become so jumbled that potential buyers often have no alternative but to make an offer well below the fair price. A good rule to follow calls for the separation of all business finances from those of the family. Tapping the till to cover costs of a haircut or pair of shoes distorts the true profit picture. This situation ultimately catches up to you.

Some operators start to analyze their business only after red flags start waving in the breeze. The need to borrow money to finance salaries or purchases may awaken some to the danger of their situation. Learn to analyze your business from the very first day of operation. This is the time to know when to spend dollars and when to hold back on purchases.

Two sets of books may be maintained by you or your accountant. One set will be used for income tax records and includes all allowable deductions including the highest depreciation rates on capital assets. For example, a piece of new equipment might be depreciated over a five-year period on your books with 20 percent assigned to each year. A knowledge of certain tax breaks could allow you to depreciate almost 50 percent of the cost of the equipment in the first year. This figure would be used to prepare the balance sheet and profit and loss statements, and to improve your cash flow.

An internal set of records may reflect more accurately the true profit potential of a firm. It accurately reflects all assets and depreciation according to realistic market conditions. An owner planning to sell a business in the foreseeable future should begin to sacrifice, paying higher taxes on a more realistic appraisal of his firm's profits. This could take a couple of years, since interested buyers often require records covering the last three years of business activity.

LEGAL STRUCTURE

The legal structure of a firm must be analyzed carefully and reviewed periodically to determine how well it meets current and future needs. This is especially crucial for those individuals and firms that want to prosper, expand, and continue in business for many decades. Following is a discussion of the various legal structures available.

Proprietorship

The proprietorship is the easiest form of business to bring into this world. It does not require state or federal approval. The goals of the organization can be as flexible as deemed desirable by the operator. All business profits will be taxed as personal income, and the owner is personally liable for all debts and taxes.

Partnership

A partnership can be created by two or more people. It is quite simple to start and terminate this type of business enterprise. Partners will be taxed separately based on their share of the business. A partnership agreement may be in writing or be an oral agreement. The written form provides an insurance policy in case the partnership breaks up under adverse conditions. A limited partnership will appear in written form, specifying the liability and initial investment of each member. It must conform to the laws of the state.

Corporation

Corporations represent the most formal business structure. They have a continuous and separate legal life. The scope of activity is limited by a charter from a particular state. Business profits are taxed separately from the earnings of the owners and operators. The cost of forming a corporation will exceed that for limited and general partnerships. Single proprietors face only the potential costs of a license to carry on a particular business such as selling nursery products.

Aspects of the Various Legal Structures

Risks.   The amount of risk confronting the owner or owners of a firm should play an important role in determining the best legal structure. A single proprietor is liable for all debts to the extent of his or her entire property; liability cannot be limited. Each member of a general partnership, regardless of investment, is responsible for all debts of the firm. Limited partners bear risk only in proportion to the capital they invested in the organization. Corporations have an advantage in that creditor claims are paid only to the extent of company assets. A shareholder will lose only the original investment in the firm. Regardless of structure, creditors still have first shot at business assets in case of bankruptcy before equity capital may be withdrawn.

Continuity.   Single proprietorships have no time limit on them. However, the firm can quickly disappear because of death or old age of the operator. Partnerships are perishable in similar fashion; a partner may die or otherwise withdraw, thus terminating the enterprise. Corporations have the strongest legal structure of all three forms. Stock certificates can be sold, and the business will go on without interruption due to illness, death, or retirement of key people. Stock certificates, representing ownership of the firm, can be sold at a stock exchange or over the counter.

Adaptability of Administration.   One individual guides the destiny of a single proprietorship. This is the case with firms often classified as being in the craft stage. A great deal of responsibility is in the hands of one person. The individual may or may not be competent to handle the reins of a growing business.

A partnership often brings together people who have talent in a variety of areas pertinent to success of a business enterprise. Two individuals may team up to run a garden center. One may have expertise in buying and displaying plant materials. The second may know how to maintain and analyze records and conduct the marketing program. A team approach can provide a great deal of the strength necessary to survive in a highly competitive environment.

Stockholders may or may not participate in the ongoing activities of a corporation. Specialists often have been employed to run the enterprise and to represent the best interest of those investing in the company. Risks tend to be spread out much more in this operation than the other two legal forms.

Attracting Capital.   Additional funds often must be acquired to support a growing business. Single proprietors may raise money by borrowing in much the same fashion as partnerships and corporations. Creditors look much more carefully at the proprietor than they would a corporation since the former must use his or her own resources to guarantee the loan. Partners may be able to borrow money more easily than single proprietors since there are two or more individuals to back up the loan. Corporations may borrow funds by selling securities to the public. This may be in the form of stocks or bonds.

Laws.   A single proprietor can operate in any state without paying taxes other than in the home state. He or she has great freedom to conduct business without restrictions from state governments. The same situation applies to partnerships. Corporations owe their legal life to one state. However, in the normal course of business the multi-state corporation can come into conflict with statutes and court decisions in other states. It is important to have good legal counsel to represent a corporation.

Businessmen and women should evaluate carefully the pros and cons of the legal structure for a prospective as well as ongoing firm. There are distinct advantages to each form of organization. Business growth may necessitate changes to take advantage of tax laws and to protect liability of the concerned parties.

STAGES OF GROWTH

Small business firms representing some 95 percent of all commercial establishments in the country employ less than 20 individuals per enterprise. Many firms in this broad category often have been referred to as "Mom and Pop" operations. An analysis of these firms shows that they fall into one of three categories relating to stages of growth and maturity. A large percentage fall into the initial or craft stage. The promotion stage follows and consists of a smaller number of firms. The administrative and most mature stage contains the fewest number of enterprises.

Retail businesses may remain in the first stage throughout their entire existence or move into the second and possibly third stages. A firm moving into the second stage normally spends little time in this area before graduating into the administrative area. The type of product or cultural background of the owner-manager does not influence movement from one to another stage. The individual running the show and his or her makeup largely determines progress or movement up the ladder.

Craft

Individuals operating businesses in the craft stage often have the following traits in common. They are highly skilled, hard working people with conservative goals. They do not mix much in the community, or take advice from people outside the firm. They follow traditional policies with little creativity to minimize risks. They do not plan on growth, providing fixed roles for people in the organization.

Many independent garden center operators reflect a large number of traits associated with the craft stage. There is nothing wrong with most of these traits, except that they tend to limit growth and stifle development of some employees.

Promotion

Some individuals tire of the craft stage and look for new challenges. The introduction of new capital and aggressive personnel help trigger movement into the promotion stage. A desire to innovate plays an important role in moving a firm from the craft to the promotion arena. The middle stage consists of entrepreneurs who identify specific goals for themselves as well as the organization. A desire to become the biggest garden center in the town or state represents an important goal for all members of the firm. Morale is an important factor in helping management move rapidly through the second stage.

One of the real dangers for a rapidly expanding operation involves the financial support required. Many, if not most, firms focus resources primarily on sales and production. This is where the action takes place and commands the attention of the boss. Cash flow becomes crucial, often sinking the ship before it has time to complete its mission. The financial picture looks like a ship on rough waters with many ups and downs.

The owner occupies the key position in the organization. Everything radiates around him or her. He or she develops policies and controls the destiny of the firm. Staff support largely provides technical services to bolster the boss in the decision-making process. The top person often has modest, if any, fear of failure. He or she can tolerate a great deal of uncertainty in day-to-day operations.

Administrative

The pressures mount on the boss in direct proportion to growth. It soon becomes time for advancement into the third stage and some dramatic changes in management. The final stage often sees employment of skilled managers to replace promotion-minded leaders. This is the time to solidify advances recorded in recent years and to progress in a more businesslike manner. Management focuses attention on risks and limiting or controlling them much more than ever dreamed of in the second stage. The introduction of new concepts often takes a back seat to refinement of known and successful business practices. A great deal of effort is placed on improving quality control programs. The reputation of the firm becomes increasingly important to management.

There appears a tendency to bring people into the organization who think and look like the boss and key personnel. This tends to put the brakes on growth as new ideas and concepts cannot find a home in the mature organization. The change from promotion to administrative stages will occur smoothly providing the key person accepts and recognizes the existence of a new ballgame. It is imperative that the boss spread out responsibilities to a number of people. He or she must use caution in trying to rule everything with a heavy hand. The organization can crumble unless talented people receive a relatively free hand in performing their duties.

This is not to say that movement into the promotion or administrative stages represents the ultimate achievement of a firm. Many individuals have enjoyed prosperity and good health remaining in the craft stage. It is important to recognize your limitations and to establish some specific goals for your business. You are the master of your own fate. Your actions will determine whether the firm remains in the craft arena or moves into the promotion and administrative stages.

USING RECORDS EFFECTIVELY

Financing and production or output records are important keys in the drive for maximum profits. Records have four important uses for your business: as a service tool, diagnostic tool, indicator of progress, and for forward planning.

Service Tool

Business records provide the necessary information for filling out federal and state income tax returns and social security reports. The information collected is essential to providing a basis for tax management decisions.

The rapid growth of many retail organizations in recent years has stimulated use of business structures other than the sole proprietorship. The record system can provide necessary information to divide inputs and outputs fairly among participating owners. It can provide a testing ground for the feasibility of any one business arrangement. You can allocate costs and returns to the business on the basis of the approximate value of contributed assets and reasonable returns to those assets.

Good records are a must when seeking a loan from a financial institution. Lenders want to analyze past and current performance in determining profitability, liquidity, and solvency for the operation. Prospective buyers will and should shy away from firms maintaining incomplete or questionable records. A good set of records helps sellers to put their best foot forward and attract the attention of numerous buyers.

Diagnostic Tool

Your records can guide you in analyzing the strong and weak points of your business. You should capitalize on strong areas and focus attention on correcting weak links. This effort ties in directly with the overall goal of maximizing profits.

Profitability can be viewed or measured from several vantage points:

1. Net income (profit or loss)
2. Percent return for dollar invested (ROI)

3.   Asset turnover

The ratio of current assets to current liabilities provides a measurement of liquidity of the business. It shows how your current assets might be liquidated to pay off current debts. The current ratio should be two to one. Solvency differs from liquidity in that it refers to long-term financial stability of the organization. It is a ratio of total liabilities to total assets. Solvency requires that you have more assets than liabilities, especially since assets may be called for to pay off all liabilities at any point in time.

A measurement of cash flow also aids in helping create a clear picture of the current and future health of the business. It serves as an indicator of cash needs that must be met to insure continued operation of the firm. Some business organizations exhibiting good profitability characteristics at the same time find themselves in a cash flow dilemma. A liquidation of resources might be required to improve the cash flow picture. The nature of the cash flow position must be examined to determine the extent to which it represents a warning signal or a green light.

Indicator of Progress

A good set of records will prove useful from both a business and a financial management standpoint. The owner-manager can chart growth of the organization and compare with industry figures or retailers handling similar products. You can measure growth in terms of sales or profits along with productivity and efficient use of resources. The performance of the firm can be measured against planned growth patterns. Did you reach projected sales and have you maintained a desired gross profit margin? This information can be used in taking necessary and corrective action to put your business back on track.

Forward Planning

Short- and long-term planning must be based on availability of accurate records. The task of planning cannot be fulfilled in the absence of records or when questions arise regarding their reliability. Forward planning has become increasingly important in the highly competitive business world. Growth-oriented operators must plan to keep pace with our volatile economic times and the entry of new firms into the garden center area.

Effective use of records is illustrated in a report on Stauffers of Kissel Hill, Lititz, Pennsylvania, appearing in the *Ninth Proceedings* (1976) of the International Bedding Plant Conference.[1] Each morning a courier visits each store and warehouse, delivering the mail and messages from the executive offices and picking up the previous day's sales information. On Monday evening a report is given to each executive of the sales, customer count, and average sale per customer for each store, along with the average sale per customer of the previous week for each department. This information becomes part of the agenda at the Tuesday morning departmental managers' meeting, as well as the basis for projections of sales for the week. The managers then hold a meeting with all of their employees the following evening. The other weekly report given to each manager contains the "sales per hour of labor" and the "sales per dollar of labor" for their department. Graphs are prepared with this information which compare the present year with the two previous years.

BALANCE SHEET

The balance sheet shows the condition of the firm at a given moment in time. It provides something of a snapshot of the financial picture of a company. This contrasts with the income statement, which covers a fixed period of time, such as a month, quarter, or year. Current assets appear on the left-hand side of the statement. These include cash, inventories, and accounts receivable. With other liquid assets, current assets represent the ability to pay ordinary debts as they become due. Fixed assets include land, buildings, and equipment. They are of a durable nature and depreciate with time. Various depreciation formulas are used by accountants to gain tax benefits.

The right side of the statement includes current and fixed liabilities. Current liabilities include accounts payable, short-term notes, and accrued liabilities such as wages and taxes. Fixed liabilities cover indebtedness of a long-term nature. Those items beyond a one year due date such as mortgages and notes fall into this category.

The net worth section comes just below liabilities on the right side. It represents the difference between all assets and all liabilities. The amount owed by the business to its owners, be they stockholders or proprietors equals the net worth figure. The balance sheet shows how much capital has been invested in the business. It reflects current working capital at the time the statement is prepared. A series of ratios can be prepared from the balance sheet to analyze the health of the business. Following is a sample balance sheet for the XYZ Company.

¹Bedding Plants Incorporated, Okemos, Michigan, page 33.

XYZ COMPANY
BALANCE SHEET
DECEMBER 31, 1975

Assets		
Current assets		
Cash		$80,000
Accounts receivable	$140,000	
Less: Doubtful collections	5,000	135,000
Inventory		150,000
Total current assets		365,000
Fixed assets		
Machinery and equipment		75,000
Automobiles		10,000
Delivery equipment		15,000
Office equipment		8,000
		108,000
Less: Accumulated depreciation		22,000
Total fixed assets		86,000
Total assets		451,000

Liabilities and Shareholders Equity	
Current liabilities	
Notes payable	60,000
Accounts payable	50,000
Accrued expenses	10,000
Income taxes	7,000
Total current liabilities	127,000
Long-term debts	55,000
Shareholders equity (net worth)	
Common stock	200,000
Retained earnings	69,000
Total liabilities and net worth	451,000

PROFIT AND LOSS STATEMENT

The operating statement, otherwise known as the profit and loss statement, represents a simplified vision of the company's operation for a specified period of time. The time period may vary from one month to a quarter or full year of operation. Information at the top of the statement identifies the time period being analyzed. Corrective action can be instituted quite early when monthly reports have been furnished to management. The preparation of yearly reports suggests that this document is not being used effectively in guiding the decision-making process.

The major purpose of the profit and loss statement lies in the determination of net profit. Data included in the report will support and clarify reasons for above average or below normal profit figures. The statement consists of three basic sections:

1. Sales—goods and services
2. Costs incurred in conducting sales and for product
3. Profit or loss

A simplified version of this statement would include the following key categories:

Gross sales	$730,000	
Less: Returns and allowances	5,000	
Net sales	725,000	100%
Less: Cost of goods sold	377,000	52%
Gross margin	348,000	48%
Less: Total expenses	312,000	43%
Net profit (loss)	$ 36,000	5%

Monthly reports can be compared largely on the basis of these main categories. More specific information within each section will be analyzed to help explain variations from the norm.

Sales.   Gross sales represent the total billing to all customers. This will include all services and products provided to customers by the firm. Some returns and allowances can be anticipated because of customer dissatisfaction or malfunction of products. A return involves a refund, exchange, or issuance of a credit slip. An allowance covers a reduction in price to compensate customers for a minor problem with the product or service.

Gross sales	$730,000
Less: Returns and allowances	5,000
Net sales	$725,000

Cost of Goods Sold.   This section includes only those costs associated with products that have left the premises and the costs of servicing customers. It does not include the cost of value of goods still in inventory at the close of the period.

Beginning inventory at cost		$ 80,000
Purchases	$387,000	
Less: Purchase discounts	30,000	
Purchases at net cost	357,000	
Plus: Freight-in	10,000	
Net cost delivered purchases		367,000
Cost goods available for sale		447,000
Less: Ending inventory at cost		70,000
Cost of goods sold		$377,000

A physical count can be made at the beginning and closing inventories. Surprisingly, many small business people have been content to simply estimate these figures. They often undervalue some items simply because they are stored in back rooms and basements. Merchandise purchased at bargain prices may have become outdated. These items should be placed on sale or valued at current market prices. The two inventory categories have a profound impact on cost of goods sold and ultimately the computation of profits. Needless to say, the profit picture can become greatly distorted by conducting sloppy, inaccurate inventories at the beginning and close of each period.

Purchase discounts may occur through early payment of bills. The supplier may also allow discounts on purchase of a stated volume often exceeding normal orders. The cost of freight is also overlooked by many operators. Some formulas for pricing have been based on cost of the item. It is important that all costs associated with acquiring the product, even freight, be accounted for in the operating statement.

Gross Margin.   Gross margin or profit represents the funds available to cover the costs of selling products and services and managing the business. There should be a reasonable profit after covering these expense items.

Expenses.   Expenses incurred by a firm can be broken down into three categories: selling, administrative, and general. A new profit figure is arrived at by subtracting the combined expenses from cost of goods sold. Selling expenses normally account for the largest percent of all expenses incurred by a garden center and related businesses. These include salaries of sales personnel, advertising, and delivery expenses. Administrative expenses include those for the office staff, supplies, interest, and miscellaneous items. General expenses include rent, depreciation, water, electricity, interest, and similar items.

Expenses
  Selling

Sales salaries	$175,000	
Advertising	35,000	
Delivery	7,000	
Total selling		$217,000
Administrative		
Office salaries	41,000	
Supplies	1,000	
Interest	8,000	
Total administrative		50,000
General		
Rent	40,000	
Interest	5,000	
Total general		45,000
Total expenses		312,000

Net Profit. A figure for net profit has meaning only to the extent that all expense items have been accounted for in the operating profit and loss statement. Small businessmen and women often omit their own salaries and those of other family members in determining wages. Net profit then represents salaries plus profit. It is conceivable that this procedure will mask a significant loss. A deficit could appear were salaries shown in the expense category.

Percentages. The figures in the profit and loss statement can be converted to percentages using net sales as 100. It is much easier to compare percentages when net sales vary from period to period. Any deviation from projected levels should be examined carefully to protect the profit position of the organization.

By Departments. Separate statements can be prepared for departments to determine profitability of each segment of the organization. You can allocate operating expenses on the basis of square footage of space utilized by each department. This information is vital when determining how to use scarce resources and pinpointing problem areas in the organization.

Fringe Benefits. The profit position can be distorted when dollars are allocated to cover automobile and meal costs associated with nonbusiness activities of the operators. This fringe benefit should be taken into account when analyzing the true profit position of a firm.

The operating statement represents an important tool to management in guiding the destiny of a firm. Reports should be carefully analyzed over a period of time to determine trends and the extent to which some expense items may be getting out of hand.

FINANCIAL RATIOS

A knowledge of typical financial ratios for the industry helps avoid disaster and proves invaluable in modifying and rebuilding a firm to improve earnings. Ratios are not computed solely to amuse accountants. They represent important tools for aggressive and growth-oriented managers. A financial ratio helps measure business health. An annual review is a must to stay competitive in the complex business world. Ratios play a vital role in conducting this examination. The balance sheet and income or profit and loss statement provide the input data for construction of different ratios. All statistics must apply to the same period of time.

The most common ratio employed by business people is net profit to sales. Neither garden centers or retail florists have been known to produce high profits. A report by Dun and Bradstreet in the mid-1970s showed garden· center operators producing 11 percent. *However, this percentage includes compensation to the owner.* Net sales of $100,00 would have produced only $11,000 to cover both salary and profit categories. These are average percentages and suggest that many operators have been running in the red or have submitted misleading information.

Several other ratios are employed to analyze the health and vigor of a firm. These figures are employed by bankers when reviewing loan applications.

Current Ratio

Current assets can be compared with current liabilities. Ideally, a ratio of two to one or better would appear quite favorable for those seeking financial loans. This ratio states that a firm's current assets are double its current liabilities. Inventory can cloud this figure as its actual market value might be significantly below that shown on your balance sheet. A so-called *acid test* compares only cash and accounts receivable to current liabilities. The desired ratio may shrink to one to one, that is, just enough cash available to pay your current bills. The ratio has most meaning when computed at the close of a normal or moderate period of business activity. Computing the ratio in April or May might prove misleading as this occurs at the highest point of the business year.

Age of Accounts Receivable

Some firms offer credit to customers. The average age of accounts reflects management's control over the business. Thirty days to collect an average account would be considered most acceptable by top managers. This is probably an ideal, as many firms fall into the day category. Accounts receivable at the close of a quarter of business activity should be divided by average daily sales for each working day. This is a much more reliable analysis than using total days for the entire period.

COMPARISON OF TOTAL SALES TO WORKING DAYS IN A QUARTER TO ANALYZE AGE OF ACCOUNTS RECEIVABLE

	Total	Working
Number of days	90	77
Gross sales	$225,000	$225,000
Average sales/day	$2,500	$2,922
Accounts receivable	$100,000	$100,000
Age of accounts—days	40	34¼

Age of accounts receivable should be checked regularly against industry averages. This information also can be employed in charting the progress and health of your own firm. A slowdown in payments can seriously affect your cash position. It would call for increased efforts in collecting delinquent accounts. A steady reduction from 45 to 40 to 35 days would indicate that those in charge of collections have improved the efficiency and effectiveness of their department. Care should be taken, however, as tight credit policies might actually drive some customers away, producing a decline in sales. Collection policies must reflect the desired image of the firm and support overall sales objectives.

Fixed Assets vs. Net Worth

There is the danger that too large a proportion of company resources are invested in fixed assets. Liquid capital is thus absorbed that could be used to finance daily operations. Depreciation charges will go up with increases in fixed assets. Maintenance costs, insurance, and taxes also increase with additions to fixed assets. These increased costs will be reflected in lower profits.

Fixed assets: Net worth ratio	
Fixed assets	$ 86,000
Net worth	269,000

Firms can be compared in an industry only to the extent that they have similar facilities. Fixed assets will vary, for example, among garden centers with and without greenhouses. Most comparisons are made on depreciated assets to avoid problems with different depreciation schedules. Industry figures suggest that fixed assets have ranged all the way from 17 to nearly 70 percent of a garden center's value, with the median around 32 percent. The firm being analyzed does fall exactly at the median for this ratio.

Net Profit vs. Tangible Net Worth

This ratio is arrived at by dividing the net profit figure from your operating statement by the tangible net worth figure from the balance sheet for the same period of time. It will tell you the degree to which your investment has earned a reasonable return based on profits recorded by the firm. Growth-oriented firms should be receiving 10 percent or more for growth. The high degree of risk associated with small business enterprises justifies a higher return than that received by investing dollars in a bank or bonds. The 17 percent return recorded by our firm is reasonably good. It reflects a good management team and a dedicated staff.

Net profit: Net worth ratio	
Net profit	$ 36,000
Net worth	269,000

Current Liabilities vs. Tangible Net Worth

The status of your business can be measured by comparing how much you owe to creditors of your tangible net worth. The latter does not include non-tangible items such as goodwill. It does include surplus and capital stock. Current liabilities are those that must be paid within one year.

Current liabilities: Net worth ratio	
Current liabilities	$127,000
Net worth	269,000

Current liabilities should not amount to more than 50 percent of tangible net worth. A more conservative figure would be in the vicinity of 30 to 35 percent. Some firms have gone way out on a limb, owing as much as 75 percent of their tangible net worth. You can improve the ratio by increasing capital invested in the organization. Earnings can be converted into capital rather than being distributed to owners. Finally, watch your debts and delay purchases as long as possible to maintain the desired ratio. Our example firm shows current liabilities of about 47 percent, slightly under the desired percentages.

Net Sales vs. Working Capital

This turnover ratio measures the extent to which working capital has actually been used productively in the organization. It provides a measurement of strain on available cash. The net sales for the period in question are divided by the difference between current liabilities and current assets or working capital.

Net sales		$725,000
Working capital		
Current assets	$365,000	
Current liabilities	127,000	138,000

Note: $725,000/$138,000 = 5

Sales may actually be so large that they represent a strain and a threat to the very existence of the organization. Net sales of four to six times working capital appear relatively safe and ideal for most business enterprises. Garden centers, according to Dun and Bradstreet, average around five times, with a range between three and eight times.

A slow inventory turnover generally requires much more working capital than a business reporting a high turnover and consequently high sales. Slow payment of bills (accounts receivable), a common occurrence in retail florist enterprises, also requires extensive working capital to finance the business. The only alternative is to borrow and thus add to current debts. Overexpansion has proven to be the downfall of many aggressive operators. Growth must be curtailed to the extent that working capital can support the expanding enterprise. Our firm is right on target with a turnover of five. Management should strive for an above average figure especially when projecting significantly higher sales in the coming year.

Inventory Turnover

The ratio of the value of inventory vs. sales for a given period of time provides a measurement of inventory turnover. This ratio is computed by dividing the average inventory for the period into sales for the same period. This ratio helps management determine if too much money has been tied up in inventory and especially inventory that simply sits on the shelves. A stock turnover in the vicinity of 10 times a year appears to be average for garden and nursery stores based on information from Dun and Bradstreet. This figure also applies to retail florists.

A turnover of something less than nine should suggest that management carefully review buying practices and lines of merchandise. Excess money might be tied up in inventory. Poor turnover may be the result of excess markup. A firm will produce more profits when selling prices attract customer attention. A high markup may frighten customers away leading to fewer sales, low inventory turnover, and lower profits.

COMPUTING INVENTORY TURNOVER

Beginning inventory	$ 80,000	
Ending inventory	70,000	
Total	150,000	
Average	75,000	
Gross sales	750,000	

$$\text{Inventory turnover} = \frac{\text{Gross sales}}{\text{Average inventory}} = \frac{\$750,000}{\$\ 75,000} = 10$$

The size of inventory can have a profound impact on working capital, return on investment, and status of debts. Firm 1 in the following situation turns inventory over 10 times compared to once for Firm 2. The assets required to support Firm 2 are 10 times greater than for Firm 1, with only a fraction of the profit.

COMPARISON OF INVENTORY TURNOVER FOR TWO FIRMS

	Firm 1	*Firm 2*
Sales	$200,000	$200,000
Cost of goods	100,000	100,000
Inventory turnover	10 × yr	1 × yr
Balance sheet asset	10,000	100,000
Debts	low	high

Inventory should be checked periodically to see that it has not grown out of hand. A general rule is to keep inventory within 100 percent of working capital so you will be in a position to meet debts. Inventories exceeding working capital signal that cash and receivables (current assets) will not cover current debts (current liabilities).

Net Sales vs. Tangible Net Worth

A measure of the activity of business capital for a specific period of time can be referred to as turnover of tangible net worth. The figure is arrived at by dividing average tangible net worth into net sales for the same period of time. A median figure for garden centers was a turnover of almost three times. Excessive inventory and slow-moving items can depress this ratio.

Net sales: Net worth ratio	
Net sales	$725,000
Net worth	269,000

Management of our sample firm must focus some attention on this ratio. There is a suggestion of excessive inventory with a ratio of only 2.7.

Leverage

The amount of money owed to others in contrast to the net worth of a firm provides a measure of leverage. This should not exceed a ratio of one to one for most enterprises. Excessive leverage places your future in the hands of creditors. A poor year could lead to bankruptcy or control by outsiders.

REAL PROFITS

An accurate and meaningful accounting system must be employed to arrive at a true profit picture for the organization. It is imperative that the system employed convey a realistic picture of the results of operations. There are four major ways that you can deceive yourself about profits. They are existence, sufficiency, profit mix, and trends.

Existence

Do you have a real profit? Carefully analyze each item in the income (profit and loss) statement and compare it with corresponding information for previous periods. Have any trends been developing or are there any hidden meanings to the figures? The income statement can be prepared on the basis of actual receipts and expenses (cash method). A second approach reflects all transactions that have occurred whether or not monies have been received or paid for products and services. The bottom line will change depending upon the system employed by your bookkeeping firm.

The accrual method, the latter system, reflects more accurately all activities occurring during the period in question. Firms that provide credit and operating under the cash system will not receive a true report for a particular period of time. Garden centers conduct most of their business in late spring. The second quarter would not reflect that portion of the business relating to credit sales. Consumers would make payments in the third quarter which often represents a slower period of the year.

Gross profit is arrived at by subtracting total sales from purchases made during the period, plus beginning inventory minus ending inventory. The bottom line or net profit will be distorted if final inventory is valued at an unrealistic level. This increases gross profit and ultimately improves profits for that period of time. The situation will probably change the following quarter or at the close of the next period, bringing profits below their real level.

Depreciation is an important category that can dramatically influence profits. A simple illustration involves depreciating an item over a five-year period when its useful life is only three years. Profits become inflated, since the item should have been fully depreciated in three years rather than five.

Some expenses such as income taxes, insurance premiums, and rent may not have been prorated accurately over months or quarters. This happens when bills are received once a year. Total operating expenses should include all expenses regardless of whether bills arrive monthly, quarterly, or yearly.

Maintenance and upkeep accounts should be clearly identified in the income statement. Profits for a particular period could be adversely affected when large repair bills are not covered by these special accounts.

A common problem of most small businessmen and women is related to their own salaries. Smaller than average salaries and failure to pay members of the family annually result in inflated profit figures. The prospective buyer of a business should look at the combination of owners' compensation and profit to obtain a true picture of the firm. This figure plus compensation to members of the family will provide a fairly clear picture of the real profit potential along with return on investment.

Sufficiency

Some individuals have lived dangerously by not taking out adequate insurance to cover the building, products, and accidents to customers. The profit picture looks much brighter when dollars have not been invested in insurance policies.

Trade statistics will help determine the degree to which profits have reached a desired level or percentage of gross sales. Dun and Bradstreet, Inc. annually publishes ratios and net profit figures for a host of industries. Salaries must be subtracted from profits when comparing your figures with industry averages. Many business people have lulled themselves into a false sense of security by tying the two together. You are then comparing apples to oranges.

Profit Mix

Does the profit figure reflect the true proportion for all product lines and services? It is suspected, for example, that retail sales subsidize the greenhouse portion of many retail–grower florist operations around the country. Costs should be broken down to determine profitability of each product line. This information helps guide management in changing lines to improve the profit position of products deemed essential to the business.

Trends

Profit trends must be analyzed to determine if the business is on strong ground. A steady, if not increasing, trend line is much more desirable than one bouncing up and down or steadily decreasing.

As manager, you must develop your own checklist of potential trouble spots in the business. Carefully analyze each operating statement to determine strong and weak areas. Corrective action should not be delayed or problem areas ignored in the hope that the next period will improve. Problems do not disappear. It takes a strong hand to operate in the black and to improve the profit position of a firm.

INCREASING PROFITS

There are a number of major ways to improve the profit picture of a firm. Continue to examine all methods to maximize profits. One method relates to the percentage of a particular market captured by a firm. You must maintain and try to increase your market share each year in order to survive competition. A firm focusing solely on one product or segment of the market could find itself in a most vulnerable position. Substitute or new products continue to arrive on the scene often replacing older, well-established lines of merchandise. Consumers may tire of a particular product. A new and aggressive firm could arrive on the scene, capturing a significant share of a limited market.

Gross margin must be watched carefully, especially during periods when costs continue to rise. Your prices must reflect current costs to maintain the desired gross margin and profits.

Operating expenses must undergo rigorous examination at all times. Some business people take telephone costs for granted and accept them as a fact of life. There are times when these costs can escalate and get out of hand. One may find ways of cutting down some items and in the process increase profits. Capital expenses also must be held in check to avoid increasing fixed costs. Some firms like to lease equipment for a year before deciding whether they really need the item.

Pricing policy often determines the existence and extent of profits. Some operators fly by the seat of their pants. Rigid formulas have been adopted by other business people. Prices must be competitive and still produce profit for a firm. The ability to control costs and buy efficiently provides a real advantage to firms essentially charging industry prices for products and services. They will have the greatest gross margin yielding maximum profits.

A final way to increase profits is the ability to make decisions on an objective basis. There must be solid reasons for adding personnel and remodeling a store. All expenditures must be carefully scrutinized to determine their impact on profits.

BREAK-EVEN ANALYSIS

Break-even analysis is a management control device that can and should be employed by both new and established operators. It provides information on the volume of sales that under given conditions will just cover costs, producing no profit or loss. The analysis makes two important assumptions. The first is that you accurately determine fixed costs over a given period of time. These expenses will exist regardless of whether someone buys or does not buy your product and services. They would include rental fees, electricity, water, telephone, and salary for permanent personnel. Variable costs represent the second important assumption. These are costs directly related to the volume of sales. Product costs will increase in approximate proportion to the level of sales. The breakdown of costs into the two categories is important and difficult. Some expenses may seem to fall into both categories at different points in time.

The formula for break-even (BE) is as follows:

$$\text{BE Point} = \frac{\text{Total Fixed Costs}}{1 - \dfrac{\text{Total Variable Costs}}{\text{Corresponding Sales Volume}}}$$

Assume fixed costs of $21,000 and variable costs of $700 for every $1000 of sales.

$$\text{BE} = \frac{21,000}{1 - \dfrac{700}{1000}} = \frac{21,000}{1-.70} = \frac{21,000}{.30} = 70,000$$

A gross of $70,000 will bring the firm to the break-even point. Fixed costs of $21,000 will be added to variable costs of $49,000 for a total of $70,000. Variable costs of $49,000 are derived from the knowledge that $700 of every $1000 of sales (700 × 70) has been identified for this category. An increase in gross sales to $90,000 should yield a profit of $6000, assuming no change in the relationship of fixed or variable costs to sales. Variable costs come to $63,000 (700 × 90) and fixed costs remain at $21,000 for a total of $84,000.

FORECASTING

The manager must consider income-producing assets along with fixed and variable expenses when preparing forecasts for the firm. Both sides of the coin must be evaluated to insure charting an accurate course for a given period of time. A restaurant has a fixed asset in terms of the number of tables and chairs. There is only so much potential for revenue. A forecast can be constructed on the basis of the percentage of utilization of chairs at any moment in time. Secondly, how many times will each chair be used during a meal or day? Increasing turnover of chairs might require:

1. More waiters and waitresses
2. More kitchen staff
3. Increased efficiency from all staff

All these options might be employed when forecasts suggest that customers would patronize the operation in much greater numbers. The situation might be improved through training of all personnel to increase their productivity.

A garden center operator might focus on major product categories. The potential for increasing sales might be substantial for the following:

1. Pesticides

2. Small equipment (e.g., pruning shears)

3. Geraniums

An increase in pesticide sales requires a visible and adequate display area be allocated to this line of merchandise. At least one person on the floor should be knowledgeable about safe and proper use of pesticides. All personnel should be made aware of major problem areas confronting most home gardeners. Questions like, "Have you purchased your herbicide to control the current crop of dandelions?" can help increase sales volume.

Pruning shears or other small tools might be offered on special with each purchase of a shrub, tree, or rose bush. They are a necessary item, and many gardeners simply neglect to purchase them. How many geraniums do you want to sell? Do you have adequate room to display an additional thousand plants? Perhaps you ran out of merchandise last year before the close of the season. The sales increase this year might come in the form of seed geraniums or a new cultivar. The increased number of geraniums can be translated into dollars and cents. To what extent will it contribute to the forecast for increased sales?

Fixed expenses included those items that continue regardless of sales. They include permits, taxes, rent, electricity, insurance, and similar items. Some of these are regulated and some contractual, like pension plans and health programs. A third category are those in the obligated class, including dues to organizations, trade magazine subscriptions, and even salaries to foremen.

All other expenses fall into the manageable category. We can control purchases and part-time help. The latter must be evaluated especially when forecasting a substantial increase in sales. Will you need more people on the floor or can existing staff handle the anticipated volume?

A growing business must prepare for additional accounts receivable and inventory. This will increase the burden on the debt capacity of the firm. Will your current financial position handle new pressures? Will a bank support your expansion plans? Should you slow down your forecast in line with available resources? You will need approximately 30 percent of increased accounts receivable and 50 percent of proposed inventory covered by permanent capital. A bank loan on accounts receivable will be discounted. You must be able to cover a portion of the expansion program. The job of forecasting involves much more than simply pulling figures out of the sky. An expansion program requires close examination of the financial condition of the firm. Will you have sufficient display space and personnel to handle the job? Can you acquire merchandise? A total plan must be conceived to cover all facets of the forecast.

Inventory carried over three months annually takes its toll in reduced profits. A lax system of monitoring inventory, a common occurrence in many small and medium operations, threatens the viability and growth of many operations. There are substantial costs associated with storage of supply items. Money is tied up in inventory that cannot be used to pay other bills or simply earn interest at a bank. A charge should be made for use of the warehouse. The building costs money to construct and to maintain. The product may decline in value when kept on the premises for a year or longer.

Buyers frequently are tempted to acquire supplies in large volume to take advantage of attractive discounts. Early season deliveries often are accompanied by special discounts. The prime thrust of many manufacturers has been to move large volumes of merchandise prior to the normal selling season.

The discounts obtained may be more than balanced by depreciation and storage costs. Carefully evaluate all purchase decisions and maintain a close watch on inventory levels of hard goods.

FINANCIAL PROBLEMS

The erosion of capital often represents a serious problem to small operators. A large part of capital can be invested in assets that often decline in value. Overgrown trees and shrubs may become a liability; they occupy valuable space and have lost most of their potential value because of their growth characteristics. A large inventory of bedding plants in June rapidly shrinks in value. The operator may hasten the decline of plants through improper care.

An independent operator may not establish realistic salaries for him or herself and members of the family. A slow season or a poor year may require that the individual draw on capital to finance high salaries and daily expenses for the family. Some operators live off the depreciation account. This seriously erodes accumulated capital. What will happen when it becomes necessary to replace some assets? Using depreciation monies can be justified only in the short run. The account must be restored as soon as possible. Removal of dollars from the depreciation account becomes exceedingly dangerous when assets must be replaced in the short run or in up to five years. You do not have much time to plow dollars back into the account to insure future earning potential for the organization.

The decline in capital can significantly affect future earnings. Poor, outdated facilities can drive customers away, leading to reduced sales and profits. The firm slides faster and faster downhill with no one capable of counteracting the trend. Capital must be reinvested in the business during good years to offset any funds removed in lean years. This must occupy a top priority position to maintain and enhance the health of a firm.

How much cash does your business need? A rule of thumb calls for cash equal to approximately one fourth of current debts. This ratio helps insure that the firm will remain on strong footing and not be continuously threatened with the need for short-term loans. An adequate cash supply should be maintained, permitting the company to pay its bills on time and to receive all discounts.

An adequate cash supply also provides the means for growth. Some profits may be plowed back into the business to provide cash reserves for expansion programs. A track record of maintaining good cash reserves for "working cash" will help many firms in borrowing on a long-term basis for growth projects.

Working cash will be used in buying raw materials, paying wages, and covering day-to-day expenses. Capital cash covers those costs associated with replacement of assets. You should have a firm understanding of which portion of your cash reserves will be available for each category. Problems with cash supply can be avoided by forecasting future sales. Prepare an operating budget based on anticipated sales. What cash needs will be necessary to reach targeted sales? A cash budget must be formulated to show receipts and expenditures for specific periods of time. This can be prepared on a monthly basis for the next year.

CASH FLOW PLANNING

How much hard, cold cash will you need to operate your business during the month of January? This is one of the truly slow months confronting garden centers operators. Will you have to borrow money on a short-term basis? Did you expect to run in the red? What precautions, if any, were taken to avoid this dilemma? Cash flow planning helps you forecast financial conditions confronting your firm. It is an important tool that has the potential to minimize shock and to avoid any unprofitable actions on the part of management.

Whether starting a new operation or associated with an established firm, it is highly important that you project costs and income over a three- to six-month period. You can prepare your banker for potential loans or a line of credit when forecasts of business activity have been prepared for your firm. A cool reception can be anticipated when emergency loans continue to be requested at various intervals throughout the year.

Cash flow planning is a common problem confronting firms during or just after a heavy selling season. Cash comes in slower than the bills for supplies and operating expenses. There are a few assumptions that apply to the case study of the XYZ firm. First is that exactly one-half of sales occur in the form of cash receipts, and it takes, on the average, 60 days to collect the remaining half. This is the major reason for June cash flow problems. A second assumption is that all accounts payable for goods must be cleared at the end of 30 days. All operating expenses such as staff salaries and electricity will be paid in the month due.

The information relating to a breakdown of sales at the top of the table should be quite clear. Information in the lower portion may appear confusing since information in one column comes from the preceding month or two.

The $750 cash collection figure for March is derived from half the total sales in that same month. The cash figure of $500 comes from receivables dating back to January or one half of total sales of $1000 for that month. We are assuming that it will take 60 days to receive accounts payable. This provides us with $1250 total cash for the month of March. Our expenses include current operating costs of $450, and $720 for cost of goods purchased the preceding month, for a total of $1170. We can wait 30 days to pay these bills. Our cash income exceeds expenses by only $80 for March, but we have a carryover of $340 from February, bringing the total cash going into April to $420. If the projections are accurate, with business activity remaining relatively strong into June, we have a cash emergency that may catch some managers off guard. The difficulty has been caused by slow returns from our accounts receivable. A short-term loan will carry the firm into July when the cash picture should return to a healthier balance, as the accounts receivable become paid up.

XYZ FIRM
CASH FLOW PLANNING STATEMENT

Fiscal Period		Jan.	Feb.	Mar.	Apr.	May	June
Income Statement							
(Accrual Basis)							
Sales	(100%)	1000	1200	1500	4000	6000	3000
Cost goods sold	(60%)	600	720	900	2400	3600	1800
Gross margin	(40%)	400	480	600	1600	2400	1200
Operating expenses	(30%)	300	360	450	1200	1800	900
Net income	(10%)	100	120	150	400	600	300
Cash Flow Projection							
Beginning cash balance		500					
Plus: Source of cash		0					
Collections—50% cash		500	600	750	2000	3000	1500
− 50% 60 day A/R[1]				500	600	750	2000
Cash available		1000	600	1250	2600	3750	3500
Uses of cash							
CGS (30-day A/P)[2]		0	600	720	900	2400	3600
O/E (no day A/P)[3]		300	360	450	1200	1800	900
Total cash needs		300	960	1170	2100	4200	4500
Difference between							
Sources and needs		700	(360)	80	500	(450)	(1000)
Cumulative difference		700	340	420	920	470	(530)

A/R = Accounts Receivable.

CGS (30-day A/P) = Cost Goods Sold, Accounts Payable 30 days.

O/E (no day A/P) = Operating Expenses, Accounts Payable immediately.

DIVERSIFICATION

The drive for stability in year round sales has led many firms into diversification programs. This course of action can prove highly profitable or disastrous. There are many stories of firms that lose their shirts engaging in activities removed from their normal base of operation. A key factor in failure is the complete or near complete absence of qualified people to run the show. Do not take chances with amateurs when the ballgame requires employement of talented and professional people.

A highly successful garden store moved into lawn furniture, ties, candy, and giftware to supplement income during nonproductive months. The size of inventory in several areas brought on a cash flow crisis that almost sank the ship. Incompetent people were employed to run the new departments. Fortunately, management returned to its original formula and discarded attractive but unprofitable lines of merchandise. Diversification programs require employment of skilled people, adequate facilities to display merchandise, product knowledge, and financial resources to support the expanded program. These four elements are crucial to success of all new projects.

EMPLOYEE PRODUCTIVITY

There are several techniques in addition to ratios that can help you analyze the health and vigor of your organization. Statistics available for an entire industry can be used to evaluate performance of your firm. A series of comparisons can be made within the firm over a period of months, quarters, or years.

One method is to compute net or gross sales per employee as a means of measuring staff performance. This information can help determine the extent to which a firm is overstaffed or needs to increase gross sales. Payroll can be computed as a percentage of net sales. This figure normally comes to light in the income statement. It is important when comparing with industry averages to note whether or not compensation to management has been included in this category.

Hiring a new person can be justified partly on potential for additional sales and the changes occurring in net or gross sales per employee. Putting it another way, it can help tell you how much in additional sales must be recorded to justify the hiring of one additional person. A firm reporting net sales per employee of $50,000 will have to increase sales by that same amount to justify one more person. The pressures might be lessened if industry averages run closer to $40,000. This might suggest that the firm delay hiring one or more additional people and would be justified in increasing the size of the staff. The ability of the staff to generate $50,000 without undue strain would have to be taken into consideration by management.
ment.

A rule of thumb in retailing is that an employee generates in the vicinity of $40,000 annually in retail sales. Retail florist shops fall far below that figure with sales approaching $25,000. Garden center sales probably exceed retail florist sales, since relatively little production work occurs in a typical garden center.

SUMMARY

Most small businesses remain in the craft stage from opening day until the firm goes out of existence. Entrepreneurs in this stage are highly skilled, work hard, minimize risks, and often do not aspire to new heights. Some firms graduate into the promotion arena. The operators associated with these firms look for new challenges. Sales start to grow at a rapid rate and cash flow can become a serious problem. A few firms move into the administrative stage. Management focuses more attention on limiting risks and improving quality control programs.

skilled, work hard, minimize risks, and often don't aspire to new heights. Some firms graduate into the promotion arena. The operators associated with these firms look for new challenges. Sales start to grow at a rapid rate and cash flow can become a serious problem. A few firms move into the administrative stage. Management focuses more attention on limiting risks and improving quality control programs.

The single proprietorship can be formed with a great deal of ease. All risks are borne by the individual. The firm often disappears from the scene with the death or retirement of the owner. A partnership can be started with two or more individuals. Limited partnerships specify the extent to which each person benefits from profits and the extent of liability in the case of business losses. The arrangement will be terminated upon death or retirement of one individual. Corporations are chartered by a state and will continue without interruption caused by illness or death of key people. It often is much easier to attract capital with this form of business organization.

Records will be used as a service and diagnostic tool, as indicators of progress, and in forward planning. A primary weakness of small businesses has been the failure to maintain and effectively use records in guiding the destinies of the firm.

The balance sheet provides information on the health of the business at a specific point in time. It shows the amount of liquid assets and fixed assets, like machinery, held by the firm. Current liabilities cover those items owed to others that must be paid within a year. Notes payable and mortgages appear in the long-term debt category. Net worth covers money owed to those starting the business; it consists of common stock and retained earnings.

The income statement or profit and loss statement provides a look at a business for a specified period of time. It contains information on sales, costs of goods sold, and profits. The primary purpose of the statement is to determine profit or loss for a given period of time.

The profit position must be carefully examined to insure that the figures truly represent the performance of a firm. Some owners combine salaries with profit. Expenses such as income taxes and insurance may not be prorated for each month or quarter of a year. The real profit position may be masked by these and other accounting procedures.

Cash flow is the amount of money needed to run the business. Temporary shortages from slow collections or sales can place the firm in an embarrassing position. This problem often arises during periods of rapid growth and only modest capital resources. Unusually large inventories can trigger cash flow problems.

A manager must prepare forecasts for months, quarters, and years. Some advance planning is a must in the highly competitive business world. Business failures have occurred frequently with the only one in five firms surviving five years. Factors contributing to failure include lack of both experience and money, unplanned expansion, poor accounting and inventory procedures, and poor location.

Break-even analysis provides a means of determining feasibility of a new product. You can pinpoint the volume of sales required just to cover all costs. A variety of financial ratios can and should be utilized in assessing strengths and weaknesses of a business. These figures are analyzed by bankers when reviewing loan applications. Your figures will be compared against industry averages. Progressive operators will not be content to reach only industry norms when examining records and ratios. Some industry material provides information for the upper quartile of firms in different categories. You must strive for maximum returns on your investment and this means exceeding the norms for the industry.

1. Discuss the pros and cons of a proprietorship, partnership, and corporation.

2. Identify and discuss the three stages of growth commonly associated with business enterprises. What are the characteristics of individuals in each stage?

3. Identify and discuss the life cycle of a product. How might this information help someone in forecasting sales and advance planning?

4. What benefits can be derived from maintaining and effectively using a good set of records?

5. How does the balance sheet differ from the profit and loss or operating statement? Discuss the primary difference between the two reports.

6. How does one arrive at a figure for costs of goods sold during a year?

7. Discuss three financial ratios and their implications or use to a manager?

8. What does a ratio for inventory turnover tell a manager? How do you compute this ratio?

9. What factors above and beyond product costs and general expenses influence the profit figure at the bottom of the profit and loss statement?

10. Define a break-even point and its use to management. What is the break-even point for a firm projecting (a) fixed costs of $42,000 and (b) variable costs of $1400 per $2000 of sales.

11. Discuss the cash flow concept and its value to management.

chapter
six

Improving
For
Profit

A desire to grow and mature starts one off on the road to success. You must work hard by expanding and broadening your vision every day of the year. Regular attendance at trade meetings, reading industry publications, and periodically attending educational programs helps assure that you will:

1. Continually expand product mix and services
2. Enlarge market area
3. Modernize facilities
4. Try new concepts
5. Build a capable and aggressive staff

The ability to achieve your goals will depend largely on time allocated for planning and preparation. Are you willing to take 20 percent of your time to prepare for the future? Are you willing to avoid the temptation of loading or unloading a truck rather than planning an agenda for tomorrow?

Growth and prosperity will occur when you have established specific goals and then proceed to achieve them. This requires dedication reflected in your willingness, interest, and ability in taking time to plan. Motivation can be assured by reading and attending educational meetings. Success can be achieved only through hard work and a willingness to prepare for the future.

There is a tendency for some operators to opt for an "average" position and in the process ignore planning activities. These people take comfort in reading statistics about the average size of a firm, owner's compensation, and profits associated with the business. Success often has been measured by a firm reaching simply the average. Achieving an average position in no way guarantees that a firm will record a fair return on investment. The salary associated with this position in the industry may be much lower than that deemed necessary to support the family. An average position in the industry simply means that you have reached the top of the bottom half or are at the bottom of the top half. There is little glamour associated with this position. You can rise above average through the process of planning and establishing goals for the firm. This activity helps distinguish those willing to operate in the dust from those leading the pack.

CONTROLLING YOUR BUSINESS

How can you learn to effectively control rather than be controlled by your business? Step one calls for a recognition that the learning process never ceases. You must be prepared to expand your knowledge regarding all facets of the operation. A wide variety of evening and one to three day

University extension and vocational–technical schools offer a variety of programs designed to help individuals improve their managerial talents.

conferences annually are sponsored by the garden center industry and educational organizations. You must broaden your knowledge and expertise to remain competitive in this world. Some individuals have shied away from extension programs because they attract a heterogeneous group of businessmen and women. These sessions provide excellent opportunities for exchanges of meaningful information and experiences that often fail to surface in groups made up solely of people in the garden center business.

Smart business people employ specialists to handle financial records and other facets of their operation. Accountants, bookkeepers, and lawyers represent areas of expertise that can prove invaluable to growth-minded operators.

Working With Former Owners

Inexperienced buyers often turn to former owners for assistance in handling the reins of their new business for varying periods of time. This relationship often makes a great deal of sense for both parties. The retired person or persons slowly winds down while the new folks learn tricks of the trade. A break-in period could best be handled prior to the actual sale. The new owner or owners could work for the old operator for a period of a few months. The salary might be modest, depending upon size of the business, but the experience could be priceless.

The situation is slightly different when the buyer has worked for the previous owner for a period of time. There really is little reason for a break-in period although the retired person often stays on to give the extra boost to his or her protégé. An awkward situation often arises when the new operator wants to try something a little different and strike out in a new direction. How will the former owner react? Can you really tell the "old" boss what to do and correct his or her mistakes? Informal relationships often break down as the new owner wants to be free to operate without someone looking over his shoulder. The retired party does not want to force the issue and soon feels unwelcome. Both parties feel as though they are walking on eggs. A possible answer to this problem is a contract specifying number of hours and wage scale for the former owner. This would protect the interests of the retired person. It might serve as a ball and chain for the new owner, limiting his or her options. Nevertheless, it would help to clarify the situation.

An awkward situation also arises when Mom and Dad retire and turn the business over to their children. Will the "old" folks stick their noses into operation of the business? Dad probably can't resist the temptation of spending a few hours a day at work. A willingness to accept change grows harder and harder as one reaches retirement age. This often adds to tensions between Dad and the younger generation. A clean break often makes the most sense when an operation changes hands. The former owner leaves with a good feeling. The new operator is free to conduct business according to his or her own plans.

Management Process

The manager and those delegated with the task of supervising various departments in an organization have been saddled with a variety of tasks. A manager must be prepared to plan, organize, staff, direct, delegate, coordinate, budget, report, evaluate.

Planning.   Do you take time to plan? Someone in the organization must assume responsibility for establishing goals. A priority system must be established to avoid chaotic conditions involving a host of projects and traveling down several roads at the same time. Too many small businessmen and women find it easy to avoid the planning task by becoming engaged in day-to-day activities. They avoid this responsibility like the plague. You can mask this deficiency only so long before the roof begins to cave in.

Organizing. Resources must be organized to accomplish goals. People, money, facilities, and materials must be blended together in an efficient and effective manner, as discussed in Chapters 3 and 4.

Staffing. A key responsibility lies in the area of acquiring good people and training staff. The performance of the staff reflects on your ability to select good men and women for the organization. Some managers select personnel who can dominate each individual. There appears to be an intense desire to capture all the glory and to look down on other people. The dictator generally forgets that success can only come through contributions of the entire staff. You cannot continue to grow and prosper when the organization has been founded on mediocre people.

A truly good manager seeks the most qualified people to fill important slots in the organization. The entire organization gains stature when one or more members of the staff becomes nationally known and recognized by colleagues around the country. This reflects well on management. The image of one operation started to decline soon after arrival of a new owner. This individual was well qualified in the area of sales. He embarked on several ambitious programs designed to double gross sales within two years. The new owner resisted paying a decent wage for a grower and did not recognize the relationship between quality and image of the firm under the former owner. Quality of crops declined rapidly in the absence of a good grower and almost complete emphasis on retail sales.

A second operator diversified his garden center business, taking on a line of giftware, selected clothing articles, candies, and candles. The expansion program involved employing a manager to handle new lines of merchandise. A poor choice was made. The firm soon found itself operating in the red. Profits from more traditional lines were soon dissipated by the poorly managed new departments. New operators as well as more experienced people run the risk of walking through quicksand by their failure to employ qualified people for key facets of the operation. Ambitious growth programs must be founded on talented people.

Directing. Decisions have to be made each and every day in the life of a business entity. Some people hide in back rooms to avoid this unpleasant task. This type of behavior frustrates the staff and contributes to stagnation of the organization. You cannot hurry the decision-making process. However, once the information is at hand someone must take the lead in arriving at a decision.

Delegating Authority. One of the most difficult tasks confronting the small business manager is that of delegating responsibility to members of the staff. Newly founded organizations generally rely on the enthusiasm, knowledge, and productivity of one key person. The creative individual starting a new firm learns to wear a variety of hats in fulfilling a host of responsibilities including purchasing, pricing, advertising, and stocking shelves. Growth brings on added burdens to management, and part-time and inexperienced help no longer fill the bill. It soon becomes obvious that responsible people must be brought into the organization. However, only if the manager is willing to give up some of his authority can these people do their best. The manager must provide a mechanism for training and upgrading staff, and then create opportunities to allow the use of this knowledge.

Coordinating.   A primary function of management must be to coordinate all parts of the organization. Coordination can be thought of as a series of gears meshing together in smooth fashion. Goals and objectives can only be achieved when the staff works together as a team.

Budgeting.   Fiscal planning, budgeting, and accounting must remain under the watchful eyes of management. Tight controls must be maintained over all financial aspects of the business. Bills must be paid on time and collections maintained.

Reporting.   It is important to communicate decisions to the staff. Do not keep them in the dark about a forthcoming sale or other critical matters affecting their position in the firm. The staff should feel free to communicate with their bosses. A two-way channel of communication assures that everyone knows what is taking place in the organization.

Evaluating.   The performance and progress of people in an organization is important to individuals as well as management. A real effort must be undertaken to periodically measure contributions and growth of all key people. The initiative must be undertaken by management. An owner of a large organization has delegated responsibility to a number of people managing departments and branch stores. Surprisingly, he has never called them in for a heart-to-heart talk on their performance. This may be due in part to his failure to establish goals for each manager over a specific period of time.

Salary has represented the only means by which personnel in many organizations know whether they have made any progress. This is a crude process, since overall profits largely determine individual salaries for the coming year. One person could be highly productive and still receive a nominal raise simply because the firm recorded few profits. A pat on the back brightens the day, but does not substitute for a planned discussion of the progress recorded by a particular individual. Management has the responsiblity of initiating regularly scheduled meetings to review progress of all key staff members.

Each person should receive a thorough, in-depth review of his or her performance, contributions, and progress in the organization.

Managing Time

Time often slips by with management unable to achieve goals for a particular meeting, day, week, or longer. Time must be used wisely to insure the firm prospers and grows. All management personnel are equal to the extent that they have the same number of seconds, minutes, and hours in a day. Some people have learned to use this resource effectively and others find numerous ways to squander precious minutes every working hour.

Good utilization of time begins when individuals put a premium on this resource in much the same manner as money. You have to recognize value before learning to minimize lost minutes and to maximize every hour of every working day. A starting point for most people begins with an examination of how they use their time. Try recording in fifteen minute blocks all your activities for a particular week. You can do this just before lunch for

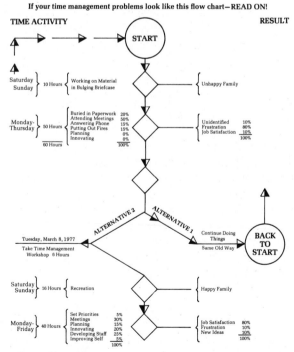

If your time management problems look like this flow chart—READ ON!

TIME ACTIVITY

RESULT

START

Saturday / Sunday — 10 Hours — Working on Material in Bulging Briefcase — Unhappy Family

Monday-Thursday — 50 Hours — Buried in Paperwork 20% / Attending Meetings 50% / Answering Phone 15% / Putting Out Fires 15% / Planning 0% / Innovating 0% — 60 Hours — 100% — Unidentified 10% / Frustration 80% / Job Satisfaction 10% — 100%

ALTERNATIVE 2 — ALTERNATIVE 1

Tuesday, March 8, 1977 — Take Time Management Workshop 6 Hours

Continue Doing Things — Same Old Way — BACK TO START

Saturday / Sunday — 16 Hours — Recreation — Happy Family

Monday-Friday — 40 Hours — Set Priorities 5% / Meetings 30% / Planning 15% / Innovating 20% / Developing Staff 25% / Improving Self 5% — 100% — Job Satisfaction 80% / Frustration 10% / New Ideas 10% — 100%

Department of Business and Management • MANAGEMENT INSTITUTE • University of Wisconsin-Extension

Wise use of time plays an important role in bringing success to one's organization.

the morning period and again before calling it a day. A second approach records time in terms of four major areas. They are:

1. Repair time — correcting mistakes, yours or someone else's
2. Lost time — talk about the football game; unaccounted for time
3. Constructive time — positive discussions to achieve stated goals; learning, planning
4. Maintenance time — keeping things in running order

TIME ANALYSIS

Time	Repair	Day_____ Lost	Construction	Date_____ Maintenance	Comments
8:30					
8:45					
9:00					
9:15					
9:30					
Total					
Week Ending: (Date)_____ _____					
(Date)_____ _____					
(Date)_____ _____					
(Date)_____ _____					
Total—Month _____					

A reasonable breakdown of time into the four categories would include 15 percent each for repairs and lost time, 30 percent for construction, and 40 percent for maintenance. Poor utilizers of time will find that they spend over 50 percent in just the repair and lost time categories. We never seem to have enough time to do things right but we always have time to correct our mistakes.

Time does not have to go down the drain. We can learn to use this resource wisely and in the process live a more productive and enjoyable life. Physical and mental health and a state of alertness are important keys in squeezing out more productive minutes every day.

CREATING A PLAN

The accelerating pace of change has placed the spotlight on individuals capable of good planning. Garden center operators must continually battle change from social, political, economic, and technological arenas. A successful garden center operator will plan for change and remain flexible and open to new and better ideas and methods.

Planning is an organized method for making decisions and solving problems. It maps out what we want to accomplish in the future by stating goals and the means to achieve them. Scarce resources like personnel and money will be used wisely and efficiently by those willing to sit down regularly and engage in the planning process. The planning process also helps to overcome communication problems that plague most small as well as large enterprises. It represents a giant step toward breaking down barriers that often arise when people fail to communicate or are pulling in different directions.

Planning is a skill that must be learned in much the same fashion as pricing merchandise and evaluating the quality of perishable products. The more you practice, the easier it becomes to plan and the more effective you become in planning.

Planning represents a formal method for effective utilization of all resources in an organization, the primary objective being to maximize a return on investment. It is not busy work designed to keep members of the staff out of trouble or laboring ten hours a day. Rather, it is a serious and well-conceived effort to propel a firm forward and to improve its competitive position. The complexities of running a profitable business demand a formal management process.

Stumbling Blocks

Good planning often eludes many small business operators. A primary reason involves failure of top management to make a serious commitment to planning. Some operators think they have all the answers and others are just too busy to spend time at the drawing board. Some plans go down the drain because relatively few if any, line management people have been brought into the overall process. Key employees must be brought in as members of the team. Their support and enthusiasm often determines overall success of the plan.

A schedule must be developed for each phase of the operation. A timetable serves to guide all members of the staff. There is a tendency to feel that management is not serious when no one takes responsibility for specifying dates for achievement of different phases of the program. Common problems that sidetrack or delay planning include:

1. Dealing with minor problems and needs of people
2. Lack of accurate information
3. Dealing with unknown factors
4. Inability to handle unexpected situations and interferences
5. Budgeting necessary time
6. Opening yourself to potential criticism and analysis from others

Stages

Planning can be broken down into three basic areas. First is the creation of a specific plan. This is followed by the action or "do" stage. Finally, the job can be stamped completed only after the plan has been evaluated to ascertain that the goals have been achieved.

A plan should be built on a number of known facts or conditions. Changes may occur in the marketplace during the do stage that warrant a return to the drawing board. These decisions can be made through an ongoing evaluation process that begins soon after the action stage. New conditions should trigger a modification of the original plan. The three stages should form a continuous process. In reality, it can be likened to a circle. There must be some flexibility in all plans. The job of evaluating progress at various points in the program insures that the plan will not lead down a dead end road.

Retail florists often have been criticized for not looking ahead while planning a variety of activities crucial to the success of their operations. This applies specifically to the area of purchasing and submitting early orders for holiday plants. Good planning has contributed greatly to success of many aggressive retailers. They have taken the time to look ahead and forecast product needs for a holiday. This activity insures that they will acquire adequate merchandise and have a fighting chance of meeting sales targets.

Written plans distinguish the serious planner from one who tends to operate in a dream world. You must be willing to expose your thoughts, dreams, and desires to colleagues. Some people do not wish to expose themselves to ridicule and thus resist putting ideas down on paper. A plan becomes operational and has a chance for success only when it appears in black and white.

What are you trying to accomplish over a given period of time? This information is crucial in later attempts to measure accountability and performance of each member of the team involved in the plan. Guideposts help chart a course for the firm; you need to know when the plan has gone off track.

Specific plans must be formulated to achieve stated objectives. How are you going to realize an increase in sales of $25,000 next year? What specific steps will you take to improve the profit picture? Dreams must be converted into something much more tangible. The act of preparing plans in black and white starts the process down the road to success.

One approach to planning involves asking a series of questions about each problem or opportunity confronting a firm.

1. *Why* are you concerned about a specific situation? Can you justify allocation of resources to correct or take advantage of a particular situation?

2. *What* are the specific facts surrounding the question at hand? This is the time to identify all obstacles and to shed as much light as possible on the topic or project.

3. *Who* in the organization is well qualified for this task? Someone must be delegated responsibility for the project.

4. *How* do you propose to achieve your stated goals? This will involve a blueprint containing information on methods, procedures, and systems. Staff time and facilities also must be worked into the program.

5. *When* is the best time to tackle the project? Are you prepared to start today or will some time be necessary to marshal all resources needed for the plan?

6. *Where* is the final question. Some plans provide options regarding location. Careful consideration must be given toward conducting the project in the most desirable area.

Planning a Marketing Program

Marketing programs often tend to dominate attention of management. Here are some steps that can be employed in planning a marketing program.

Organize. This step clearly defines the roles of the persons in charge of marketing programs. Who has responsibility? A line of command should be formulated to insure that all individuals and departments know and understand their relations to the plan and the top person in marketing. This action represents the foundation of the structure.

Evaluate. What are the strengths and weaknesses of your own organization? You must approach this question with a critical eye. This is not the time to downplay weak links or exaggerate the contributions of key individuals. You should take a hard look at the inventory, product mix, caliber of store clerks, location, and appearance of facilities. How does your facility compare with that of competitors?

All marketing plans must take into consideration industry trends and general economic conditions. A gradual decline in green plant sales might suggest that you avoid allocating scarce resources for a special sale. It is important to determine where your major products are on the growth curve.

Place your bet on those that are still picking up steam and climbing higher each year.

General economic conditions will affect your marketing strategy. There is a danger of becoming overly pessimistic as well as going in the opposite direction. Valentine's Day in 1976 looked to many like a disaster because of the economic slump. Flower sales were exceptional with consumers looking to brighten the dull, gloomy atmosphere prevailing at that point in time.

A major strike in a community will have a profound impact on sale of luxury items. You may have to pull in your horns during the layoff period. Higher prices and shortages of gas, surprisingly, have helped spur sales of plant materials. Many homeowners apparently have decided to stay home and spend their vacations gardening and grooming their lawns.

Take time periodically to inventory your marketing resources. Focus attention on your products and services. Each product line and special service should be analyzed in terms of price, special features, packaging, and unusual technological advances. Innovative annual and perennial cultivars and nursery stock are important advantages for a firm in competition with someone working with older selections.

The market position of your firm should command a great deal of attention from all key personnel in the organization. What is your image? How do consumers see you in comparison to competitors? Strong firms can capture a great deal of attention with promotional programs in contrast to those struggling to find some daylight.

Guideposts. Someone in the organization must take responsibility for preparing written guideposts. This information remains worthless as long as it is confined to someone's head rather than appearing in black and white. General objectives regarding products, markets, and the overall mission of the firm need to be clarified before you embark on growth strategies. Specific policies regarding pricing, quantity, and advertising can be brought into focus after identifying objectives for the firm. The next step involves establishment of specific targets including growth rate and proposed share of the market. Retail florists associated with a "wire" organization such as FTDA receive monthly reports regarding share of outgoing and incoming business in their market.

Growth Strategy. Step four focuses attention on selection of growth strategies. This is the time to discuss alternatives for growth such as expansion of nursery stock sales or diversification programs. Write down the merits of each option that appeals to the staff. The growth strategy selected should relate to and be consistent with identified objectives. Will you maintain quality and will the proposed growth area coincide with the mission of the organization? Your growth program might concentrate on internal development. You can improve old products and services. Unprofitable lines could be dropped to provide room for new merchandise.

It is conceivable that you might expand through the process of acquisition of other companies in the same or different communities. You must carefully assess potential contributions of the staff of newly purchased firms before automatically keeping them on the payroll. Your growth strategy might also involve expansion in other market areas. The local market might be saturated and maximum profits could be attained through establishment of a new outlet in a neighboring city.

Plan of Action.   The operational plan begins with a set of assumptions. Internal and external conditions may change, calling for some modifications or perhaps abandonment of the entire plan.

Your plan begins to take form with the preparation of market forecasts for a particular product or service. What type of business can be expected within the next year? Surveys may be available to help guide each forecast. Each new program will require support from various segments of the firm. Will they be adequate or will additional manpower be required to meet objectives? How much will it cost to implement a new program? What volume will be required to reach the break-even point? Financial concerns cannot be ignored even though all signals appear green.

Implement.   The time has arrived to implement plans and to activate controls. One final review should be undertaken to determine feasibility of the project. Be sure that everyone is ready to coordinate activities and fully support the mission. The project must be accepted by all key people in the organization.

A key task involves assigning responsibility of major jobs to specific departments and individuals. It is crucial that everyone know what to expect and what is expected in the performance of their jobs. Timetables will help guide and motivate staff in carrying out assignments. The schedule should be reasonable and provide some flexibility for changing developments in the market place. Periodic reports should be issued, briefing all parties on the status of the project. This is the time to shine a bright light on progress and unexpected hurdles.

A financial budget must be prepared for each main task in the marketing program. Do not force individuals to take dollars from other programs and in the process sabotage important segments of the business. Performance standards can be constructed to help individuals measure individual progress toward achieving specific goals. Those individuals pulling their weight should receive full credit while those asleep on the job must be identified, with the hope of stimulating them to improve their performance.

Review.   Marketing plans must be reviewed periodically and at the conclusion of the program. Some modifications may be called for as reports filter in from members of the team. These reports should be compared to performance standards and expected progress at various points throughout the project.

Corrective action should be initiated when necessary to insure that the program does not become sidetracked.

A final or annual review brings together all relevant information concerning the project. The plan may be revised and the program continued for another period of time. The review session is crucial to successful conclusion of the current program. Each person can see a beginning and an end. Staff members can chart their own progress and performance. The stage is now set for tackling other marketing projects.

SUMMARY

Your chances for success can be greatly improved by attending seminars and short courses offered by vocational-technical schools and the extension service at most universities. A wide range of programs have been developed to help small business operators improve their skills.

Good personnel are an important ingredient, especially in firms that survive the first couple of years and start to expand. One individual encounters an increasing number of problems in trying to cope with all facets of managing the operation.

Great care should be exercised in working with former owners of the business. They can help new people over the transitional period. The relationship begins to deteriorate after longer periods of time when new concepts are explored and implemented by the new owners.

Managing time represents one of the real keys to success for managers of all types of enterprises. You can record your time in 15 minute blocks on the basis of that designated for repairs, lost, constructive, and maintenance time.

One of the most important functions of management lies in the area of planning. The manager must personally become involved in developing plans for the organization. The manager has the task of describing what should be accomplished by the firm over a given period of time. The means by which one expects to reach objectives should be put down on paper. Involvement of key subordinates represents an important factor assuring success of the plan.

The planning process tries to arrange for the orderly and efficient utilization of scarce resources in an organization. Increased competition and higher costs for input factors have necessitated more and more planning activities in all firms, regardless of size.

The manager must not be content to engage in primarily the initial stages of the planning process. It is critical that time be allocated for the evaluation phase. Staff progress and performance can be measured through continual review of the extent to which goals have been achieved by the firm.

Planning begins when someone sits down to ask: why, what, who, how, when, and where. The process goes on every day and every week in organizations moving to higher levels. Failing to take time to plan ultimately dooms a firm to repeating past mistakes and failing to take proper advantage of new opportunities for growth and profits.

1. Identify and discuss three ways for a manger to remain current and to effectively control the destiny of a firm.

2. Discuss the pros and cons of employing former owners for a period of time following purchase of a business.

3. Identify and discuss five tasks of management designed to insure growth of an organization.

4. What are the four major areas involving utilization of time during a working day? What percentage of a working day should fall into each category?

5. Describe the roles of energy and alertness in improving effective utilization of time each working day.

6. Identify and discuss three stumbling blocks that delay the planning process.

7. What are the six questions asked in one basic approach to planning? Discuss each item.

8. Identify and discuss five steps in planning a marketing program.

9. Many firms flounder and fail to keep pace with inflation and competition. Discuss three reasons leading to this dilemma.

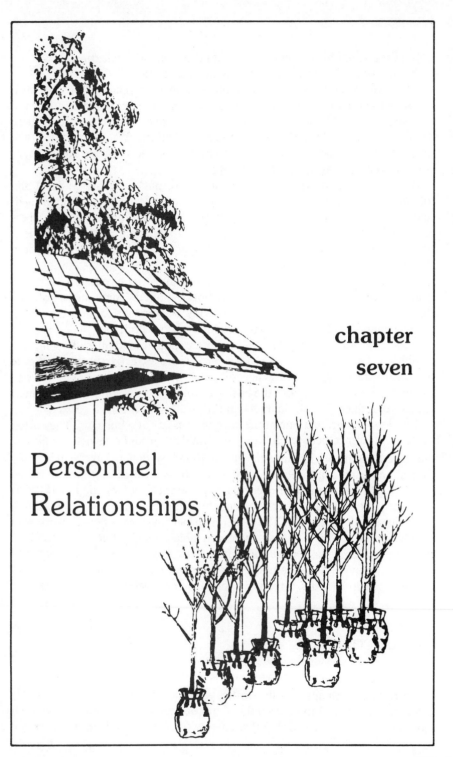

chapter
seven

Personnel Relationships

"The shop really hums when the boss takes an extended vacation."

"You just can't find good, dependable people today."

The two observations represent the extremes of relationships between employer and employees. They may be said in moments of frustration and at times in jest. The frequency in which they have occurred suggests there have been deep feelings underlying the two positions. Why should this type of conflict exist and what can and should be done to improve the relationship between management and employees?

The problem may arise in a firm from lack of understanding and training of employers in proper personnel management. A large number of firms in the garden center industry start out as "Mom and Pop" operations. Members of the family provide virtually all of the labor force required by the firm. Pop often dominated the environment, issuing orders with little or no concern for their impact on "employees."

As the firm prospers and other individuals must be hired on a part- and full-time basis, dictatorial policies may not be altered. There just is not time to go to night classes or special one-day conferences designed to help management develop realistic and productive work policies.

Low wage rates and poor fringe benefit policies often lead to morale problems. Good employees soon leave for more attractive positions. Some bosses frustrate employees by suggesting that they and only they know everything there is to know about the business. Little or no credit goes to talented employees, since this would undercut the position of the head person.

Employees represent one of the most vital assets of a business. They often are the difference between a highly profitable year and one yielding little if any return on the original investment. Thousands of dollars have been invested in training each employee for his or her job. A firm cannot remain in the black with a perennial turnover of key personnel. One of the key tasks of management is development of an enlightened personnel policy and training program for all employees. The owner-manager must learn how to work with and handle people. "You can't find dependable people" often is an admission that the manager has failed and failed miserably in one of his or her key tasks. Employees are a valuable resource and management must learn to motivate them to work effectively for their own welfare as well as that of the firm.

FAMILY CONFLICTS

The flower, nursery, and garden center business has a history of sons frequently finding themselves in conflict with their fathers. While supposedly grooming their sons to succeed them, all too many fathers have driven their sons out of the business or left them highly frustrated. Dad was the boss and made all the decisions until the day he passed away. Junior turned 50 and still had about as much authority as the high school student employed to mix soil on a weekend.

The employment of relatives and especially members of the family requires a high degree of skill on the part of the owner. A careful analysis must be made of the potential of each individual in much the same fashion as for a nonmember of the family. Sons and daughters must be clearly appraised of their future role in the business. This might begin with their being given a target date relating to ownership of a part of the business. A new corporation might be formed immediately, renting space and equipment from the old firm. This procedure could reduce the amount of money required by the young person to buy into the business.

Family conflicts often arise when death of the primary owner occurs before all legal matters have been handled in a satisfactory manner. The problems become compounded when one or more of the inheritors have not participated in the business. How will the estate be handled and will one person deeply involved in the business lose his "investment" of time and hard work?

SMALL DICTATOR

Some individuals occupying the top seat have truly enjoyed the position of a dictator. They have taken a rather narrow view of how one prospers, grows, and achieves success. The magic formula rests somewhere between their own ears. Employees, no matter who they are and whatever their background, are not allowed to offer their full talents to the growth of the business. This philosophy and environment breeds contempt on both sides of the fence. Management and employees soon engage in a tug of war rather than pulling together to reach a common goal.

A firm may prosper even though employment practices mirror those of the Dark Ages. What might have been accomplished were all systems go and employees and employer wearing happy faces? A recent study conducted by the Wichita State University Center for Human Appraisal[1] reported that an authoritarian boss causes his workers to fail and a permissive boss causes himself to fail. The six-year study found permissive bosses produced rebellious workers, giving power away and losing control of the job. The authoritarian assigns obligations but does not give his workers the power to do the job right. He tends to program them for failure. This action permits him to take more power and justifies the abuse heaped upon the staff.

What is the ideal situation? It is one in which the boss listens to workers'

[1] Arthur B. Sweney, *Response to Power Measure Handbook* (Wichita, Kansas: Test Systems Inc., 1972).

complaints and acts on them without being permissive. The boss must be cooperative and critical depending upon the individual situation.

THEORY X AND THEORY Y

Two views of men and women on the job were described by Douglas M. McGregor[2] of the Massachusetts Institute of Technology several decades ago. Employers' attitudes toward employees largely determine the nature of their performance. An enlightened view of man can bring about a desired performance in contrast to the unenlightened downgrading of personnel.

Theory X, the unenlightened view, sees employees as by nature indolent and performing with a minimum of effort. They prefer to be led like animals and shed all forms of responsibility. Employees resist change and are self-centered and indifferent to organizational needs. Finally, they are gullible and greatly influenced by demagogues. All these attitudes can be found in the real world. Why? Failure to satisfy basic needs such as self-preservation, safety, belonging, esteem, and self-fulfillment contribute to the type of behavior associated with Theory X. The authoritarian boss, stomping on employees every day, breeds resistance, laziness, lack of responsibility, and indolence. The final straw often has been ever increasing demands for economic benefits.

An enlightened view of the employee creates an environment where people work hand in hand with common goals for the benefit of the organization. Theory Y assumes that man inherently has the capacity to assume responsibility and to work effectively within the framework of an organization. Management has the task of helping people recognize their abilities and develop desired traits for themselves. The authoritarian boss in contrast inevitably leads people to a more passive role and an increasing degree of resistance to organizational needs.

An enlightened manager sees his or her role as creating the right environment and arranging organizational conditions so that employees can achieve their maximum potential. The manager must help direct people along a freeway created to achieve stated objectives of the organization. Many employees can be motivated by creating an environment that breeds enthusiasm and spirit from within the individual. This individual has the capacity to contribute to organizational objectives and to provide leadership in achieving stated goals.

Management by objectives is a philosophy of business life that seeks employee participation rather than employee control by the boss. It recognizes that employees are important assets and should be so recognized by management. Personnel represent one of the most important, if not the most

Douglas M. McGregor, *The Human Side of Enterprise* (New York: McGraw-Hill, 1960).

important, assets of a business. The balance sheet does not identify this asset beçause of our inability to place some specific value on the contributions of the staff toward success of the operation. Some day, our accountants may find the mechanism to credit personnel properly as a viable and specific asset to the company.

WORK ETHIC

I was brought up in a household where Dad worked six-and-a-half days a week to help a struggling business gain a foothold in the wholesale florist market on 28th Street in New York City. You just could not survive unless the front door was open from six in the morning until late afternoon with the exception of Sunday afternoon. Employees formed a union back in the late thirties or early forties. One of the first demands was to reduce work to only six days a week. This demand was thought bound to destroy the wholesale market. What a surprise to find that buyers adjusted and business prospered with the shorter work week. Labor soon asked to work only five-and-a-half days a week. Well, the florist business could not survive if wholesalers closed on Saturday afternoon. Surprise! The new market hours worked and even management could relax on Saturday afternoons and Sunday.

Why did not management provide leadership in developing realistic work schedules? They were probably so busy worrying about day-to-day details that it was not possible to see the big picture. Here are some examples of management that suggest they prefer the responsibilities of an employee to those of employer.

1. On the job at five in the morning to personally load a truck.
2. Taking the wheel of a truck in preference to employment of a good driver.
3. Preferring to spend time in the nursery, greenhouse, or garden center handling a hose and stacking displays rather than in the office shuffling papers.
4. Maintaining a crew six days a week just because it has always been done that way rather than figuring out how the work could be accomplished in five days.

Some owners still worship a distorted picture of the work ethic. They tend to measure success and performance by the number of hours worked rather than by the bottom line or profits.

1. Retail florists traditionally have worked exceptionally long hours prior to major holidays. The owner often speaks with pride when relating the fact that his or her staff worked almost 24 hours straight to handle all orders.

   The enlightened manager has found himself in something of a quandary to explain the fact that his staff worked only a normal day. They handled more business than a year ago because of better organization. Should one be proud of this accomplishment or does it go against the work ethic?

2. The manager of a garden center and his assistant put in twelve-hour days six and seven days a week from April through the end of May. This is considered normal for a garden center. The owner compounds the problem by continually harping on everyone regarding little matters such as a hose out of position. The work ethic seemingly requires perfection as well as long hours. Is this the mark of success?

   Working exceptionally long hours over an extended period of time requires that management carefully evaluate the effect of the work load on employees. A tired body does not function well and employees soon lose enthusiasm and sight of organizational goals. Why cannot one initiate two shifts, each headed by the manager and assistant manager? There is no need for both to be on hand every day and every hour. The pressures are so great during this period that the owner should demand a realistic work schedule.

3. The typical greenhouse functions seven days a week. Plants require water, and facilities must be vented. A six-day work week has been commonly accepted by many owners. This schedule helped thin out the weak from the strong. Only a dedicated plant lover would work long, hard hours in a hot greenhouse.

   One young man observed that the crew traditionally employed on Saturday produced little revenue for the firm. They worked in halfhearted fashion and wasted many hours. He recommended that most of the work could be performed Monday through Friday with only maintenance activities conducted on Saturday. The proposal was rejected by management.

The work ethic should not require blind adherence to preconceived concepts. It is not an outmoded concept in our society. Rather, some have lost sight of the real objectives. The number of hours worked each week does not represent the goal. Productivity and profits arising from work output should be used as the criterion in determining performance and viability of the work ethic.

EMPLOYEE TURNOVER

Why do employees disappear from the scene and often go to work for a competitor? Some turnover should be expected as a natural phenomenon in our society. There are people who float from job to job and just cannot stand to stay put even though you pay good wages and provide benefits and job security.

Management is not generally concerned about the loss of incompetent people or those who really will not produce a day's work for a day's pay. It might be productive, however, to review hiring policies to help weed these people out before they join your staff. It does cost money to train someone and the investment cannot be recouped in just a few months.

Here is a checklist of the factors that often contribute to the loss of personnel. How do you rate?

1. Reluctance to challenge and give responsibility to capable people
2. Continually finding flaws in performance of staff
3. Inability to recognize contributions of employees
4. Poor or nonexisting fringe benefits
5. Lack of job security
6. Low wages
7. Inadequate program for reviewing progress of employee
8. No reward for exceptionally long work hours
9. Reluctance or refusal to discuss records and performance of firm
10. Refusal to accept responsibility for mistakes

Responsibility and Challenge

Capable people thrive on being challenged and given increasing amounts of responsibility in a firm. Boredom leads to frustration and desire for a new job. For example, a college-trained person was sought for a job as a floral designer by a firm. The primary, if not sole responsibility of this individual was limited to the design room. Most college-trained people with an ounce of ambition would tire of this position in a few months.

The problem may be largely one of management's inability or failure to clarify the nature of the vacant or new position. What are the exact responsibilities of the position advertised in a trade paper? Do you need someone with sales experience? Do you want to hire a person capable of moving quickly into a management position? Do you want someone just to water plants? What do you need? You can save much time, energy, dollars, and needless frustration by matching the qualifications of a productive employee with those responsibilities identified for the vacant position. This is not the time to try to fit a round object into a square opening. A cardinal sin involves placement of a person in a postion of responsibility when that individual is not qualified or interested in the job.

It is the responsibility of management to provide opportunities for continued growth of its employees. This will vary from individual to individual. It must be consistent with capabilities and ambition of each member of the staff. Some good people quit after being on the scene several or many years. They have progressed up the ladder and suddenly reached the top rung. There is nowhere to go and little excitement to the job. They find themselves beginning to stagnate and are looking for greener pastures.

Finding Flaws

Some employers continually look for mistakes and errors in the performance of employees. This negative philosophy discourages even the most competent and enthusiastic person. The problem is compounded when employees have been putting in exceptionally long hours. Criticism, especially petty gripes, cannot easily be tolerated during or immediately following periods of heavy work loads.

The performance of employees often reflects the degree to which management has prepared them for a particular job. The mistakes that keep popping up should be a warning signal to management to spend more time in reviewing assignments and job responsibilities of each staff member. This should be done in a positive manner, during a slack period when few pressures have been placed on the staff.

Criticism of employees should be handled tactfully at all times. Above all, direct or implied criticism should never be made in front of a mixed group consisting of a few members of your own staff. There is the suggestion that unflattering comments are being made about all members of the shop and not just a few. Management must learn when it is proper and how best to correct a staff member to assure improved performance in the future.

Commendations

How often does management pat someone on the back? Most employees want to do a good job and exhibit pride in their performance. The atmosphere becomes increasingly cold and unfriendly should the manager ignore the performance of the staff. It is crucial that employees be rewarded to insure that their performance does not deteriorate. The best time to give credit to an employee is at the time or shortly after they have handled a task in top fashion. Waiting a week or longer to say "thank you" for "a fine job" has as much impact as a five cent an hour raise.

Fringe Benefits

What happens when a staff member becomes ill? Do they lose a day of pay or do you provide several sick days a year? Surprisingly, a number of firms still provide few, if any, fringe benefits for their employees. Aggressive operators have carefully considered and implemented fringe benefits including partial medical coverage, holidays, sick days, and pension and profit plans. This route must be considered by those employers seriously interested in minimizing turnover of personnel. The programs contribute toward a feeling that management really has an interest in the staff.

Job Security

Management may schedule the number of full-time staff on the basis of workers needed for slow or average periods of the year. Part-time personnel are then employed to handle extra work during rush days and weeks.

The manager of one firm hired people to work full- and part-time with all on an hourly wage. The work load lightened during one period and the manager simply sent everyone home from the job. The full-time staff found themselves working 30 hours instead of 40 hours a week. State and federal laws do not provide protection to nonunionized staff in terms of number of hours worked each week. The policy can only be termed highly unethical.

Accepting Responsibility

As a manager, do you readily accept responsibility for mistakes and seek help in correcting problems? Growers often have been prone to hide mistakes. This philosophy also has prevented them from seeking professional help in diagnosing the problem and trying to avoid it in the future. Mistakes in the production of bedding plants, fresh flowers, potted plants, and nursery crops will continue to occur unless corrected. Honesty and openness will always mark the progressive operator.

Wages

Wages do not always represent the most crucial factor influencing employee satisfaction with a particular job. Other factors such as job security, participation in the decision-making process, and knowledge that the owner appreciates contributions of employees all determine rate of turnover within a firm. Salaries often command more attention than they should simply because management does a poor job in showing an interest in employees. The frustrations soon become channeled in the direction of dissatisfaction with wages.

A good wage reflects experience, length of time with a firm, responsibilities of employees, and contributions to profits. Salaries must be competitive with other firms in the community and industry levels. A good manager recognizes that employee wages must be analyzed in terms of their relationship to total costs and profits. High wage rates often stimulate exceptional productivity and in the process push profits to record levels.

Rewards

One aggressive operator rewarded all personnel immediately after a major holiday with a substantial bonus. This was done as a reward to employees for their efforts in far exceeding sales quota for the holiday. Employees were made aware of their contributions almost before they had time to recuperate from the long work days.

Progress Reports

How often do managers sit down with employees to review their progress with a firm? Many managers simply do not have the time for this important task. Often, their inability to discuss performances reflects their failure to outline the responsibilities of a job. Employees operate in a cloud and management becomes frustrated at their inability to accept responsibilities for certain daily tasks.

The initial job of management must be to write down the responsibilities for each employee. This can and often has been done in consultation with each employee. Management by objectives is a philosophy and program whereby employees and employer develop goals.

The second most important task in employee relations relates to periodic and regularly scheduled review sessions. The original goals established by management with each employee then served as benchmarks in the review process. Employees like to know how they are progressing in a firm. Do not keep them guessing. The wise employer schedules regular meetings and carefully reviews the progress of each employee.

Records and Performance

How much information regarding performance of a firm should be related to employees? Some operators keep everything a big secret. Other managers like to discuss targets and performance. Key employees should not be kept in the dark. Their performance will be adversely affected when management hides the monthly profit and loss or income statement. A wise manager knows that employees can be motivated by being able to share information relating to sales and costs. A growing number of firms regularly share information with virtually the entire staff. They believe that people can and will be motivated by management's willingness to discuss information formerly stamped secret or classified.

LOOKING FOR A JOB

Another way of analyzing your managerial capacity would be to view the firm through the eyes of a prospective employee. What should an ambitious young man or woman look for when applying for a job? Major concerns will include wages, growth potential of firm, periodic review of progress, and discussion regarding objectives and methods of reaching goals. These and other important questions are raised below.

1. Does the firm have short- and long-range goals? The extent to which management has identified short- and long-term goals and is willing to share them with its personnel reflects a modern and aggressive organization. This does not necessarily suggest that detailed plans be revealed to all parties, especially those starting at minimum wage levels. One can and should anticipate more information the farther up on the ladder one considers entering a business. The complete absence of any goals should suggest poor chances for advancement. Growth becomes more a matter of chance than ability.

2. Has the boss taken a vacation in the last decade? The older generation prided itself on opening the shop every working day. Vacations were something of an extravagance that only the foolish could afford. A good manager must be able to delegate responsibility to key employees. Failure to do so often stymies growth of the firm and personal development of its employees. Regular vacations insure that the burdens of management will be shared with the best members of the staff.

3. What about past employment practices? One young college man was enticed to work for a particular grower with promises of an attractive salary and personal advancement in the firm. His dreams were shattered within a year when he was asked to leave the firm. He was the fourth college graduate in a row to be treated in this fashion. No one could measure up to the owner's standards. The pattern appeared quite suspicious, and one wonders if it all was not designed to boost the ego of the owner.

4. Does the firm have a training program? Some bosses believe in throwing people right into deep water to see how well they can swim. This practice works well when the individual has had some previous experience. A conscientious employer will set up a training program designed to acquaint a new employee with all aspects of the job. The program can be quite brief for someone learning to drive a truck or water greenhouse crops. It should be much more extensive for those groomed for major responsibilities in the organization.

    A large, modern bedding plant operation often features a well-coordinated production line for the transplant operation. It takes experience and a certain flair in supervising people with a myriad of responsibilities. The production line consists of transplanters, someone feeding seed flats to transplanters, flat fillers, and those removing flats from the end of the production line. The best supervisor for the transplant operation is often one who has actually worked at different jobs on the line. This experience provides the confidence and knowledge of how best to coordinate all facets of the operation. A manager plays with fire should he or she plunk someone down into this job with little or no training in transplanting seedlings.

5. How often will management review your progress? A definite policy of one, three, six, or twelve month review sessions assures you that someone is watching your progress with the firm. One can become lost in the shuffle

and virtually forgotten by management. A periodic review on a predetermined basis assures a new employee that he or she will have a fair chance with the operation.

6. Will management spell out your specific duties? Progress can be measured only through benchmarks. Are the responsibilities of the job clearly understood? Will it be possible to measure growth and development at the end of stated periods of time? A clear job description works to the advantage of employer and employee.

7. Does the firm subscribe to industry trade papers? Key employers and those interested in growth should be encouraged to read trade papers and to keep abreast of new developments in the industry. It has been said that one who does not read soon finds himself or herself employed by one who does.

8. Does the manager-owner attend trade meetings and in turn pass on information to employees? The manager too busy to attend trade meetings soon runs the risk of operating in the dust of those regularly attending local and national meetings. It is a good policy for management to take time to review the highlights of a meeting. Skip the cocktail party details and focus on the meat of the sessions. All parties returning from trade meetings should disseminate information regarding ways of improving the business.

9. Will management send you to trade meetings? A good manager will provide expenses for key personnel to attend selected industry meetings. Growers, for example, should regularly attend short courses sponsored by universities and trade associations. The dollars spent will be returned manyfold by information transmitted at these educational sessions. Some employers may be afraid of losing key employees who attend industry sessions. There is little danger providing management has recognized and worked hard in helping fulfill the basic needs of its people.

10. Will you participate in a profit sharing program? More and more firms have instituted profit sharing programs to encourage and stimulate greater loyalty of the staff. This incentive has great appeal and helps stabilize the work force. The provisions often require that an employee work so many years before being able to withdraw funds upon termination of employment.

11. How clean is the operation? A greenhouse or nursery with a high crop of weeds suggests sloppy management. The appearance of facilities often provides a real clue as to overall talents of the employer.

12. Seeking professional help and recognizing mistakes improves the image of the employer in the eyes of employees. There may be a tendency and temptation to shift blame to employees when one avoids professional help.

13. How does management handle sales personnel from suppliers? The owner too busy to meet with sales personnel may reveal an inner desire to remain blind to new developments in the industry. Most sales people have a wealth of information to share about new concepts, products, and developments in the trade. Progressive operators find time for a chat and an opportunity to keep pace with our world of change.

14. Does the manager-owner take time to plan? The boss who prides himself or herself on working ten hours a day in the garden center, design room, or greenhouse reflects a real dislike for the role of manager. The successful operation must have someone guiding the steering wheel. It is not a task that can be taken lightly or regarded as a part-time activity.

15. Does management have the philosophy of starting you out at the bottom of the barrel with respect to wages? Can you really justify starting a graduate of a two- or four-year program at minimum wages? This attitude tends to suggest that the owner likes to look down, way down, on his staff. The wage offer itself can go a long way in reflecting management's attitude toward:

   a. Nature, responsibility, and importance of job

   b. Employees as an integral part of the organization

   c. Growth potential of its staff

The wage offer also can reveal management philosophy of its own role in achieving success. A large gap between employer and employee salaries may suggest the existence of a dictator who feels he has been blessed with all the wisdom allocated to a particular firm.

A minimum wage or something in that vicinity often attracts only those capable of providing a minimum effort for the firm. One ends up with a large number of unenthusiastic bodies who tend to foul up the works. A minimum wage can be offered to untrained people with the understanding that rates will go up in reasonable fashion and according to performance of the individual. Each employee has an incentive to reach for the clouds.

What should a graduate of a two- or four-year institution expect from a florist, nursery, or garden center operator? The wage must reflect living conditions. One will have higher expenses in Chicago than in Utah. A salary of $15,000 is not out of line for a university graduate with some experience, slated for a position of responsibility in a firm. The salary is not nearly as important as what the individual can produce for the firm. As an employer, you must be interested in receiving maximum productivity from all employees. Your key people must receive an adequate, if not generous, wage.

The nature of the job must be reflected in the wage scale. An individual employed to conduct the total pest control operation for a large production facility carries a heavy burden. This is not the time to play Russian roulette by offering something suitable for an office worker with minimum responsibilities.

There are many reports of individuals leaving a firm because management was unwilling to pay a fair salary. The replacement, however, often has been brought in at a much higher salary than the former employee. This suggests that management was out of touch with reality. Management now has to contend with someone new and possibly inexperienced.

There are few, if any, bargains in employing people at low wages. Employee turnover, sloppy work, and disinterested personnel are the products of an unenlightened wage scale.

16. How family centered is the operation? The family-run operation often appears the rule rather than the exception in the florist, nursery, and garden center business. An outline of the chain of command including names of persons filling key jobs can be highly revealing to prospective employees as well as management. Inbreeding represents a distinct and major threat to firms staffed largely or exclusively by members of a clan. The tendency has been to move members of the immediate family into new and vacant positions. Outsiders often have been relegated to minor positions with few opportunities for personal growth.

Organizational growth requires and thrives on the introduction of new ideas from a variety of people with different experiences and backgrounds. It is a healthy situation when management recognizes the need for new blood. Good people often depart from a firm after gaining some valuable experience. Their departure frustrates management. The loss of valuable assets can be minimized through realization that nonfamily members be provided with opportunities for growth.

A family operation can run the risk of shared responsibility and confusion regarding assignments of key personnel. Failure to identify and clarify roles hinders growth of the firm. The entire staff must comprehend lines of responsibility and roles of their immediate supervisors.

17. Potential colleagues should be met to gain a better feel of an organization. They can reveal much about management. Their enthusiasm will reflect an enlightened staff policy.

GUIDELINES FOR HIRING

What should you look for in hiring a graduate of a two- or four-year institution? A diploma provides only an indication of what to expect from a graduate of a horticulture program. Look a little deeper in assessing the real qualifications of someone seeking employment with your firm.

The grade point average reflects the performance of the individual in the classroom. It is an indicator of future potential with your firm. This information represents only one part of the total picture, and should not dominate or color one's image of a candidate. Here are some other guidelines for consideration:

1. Participation in a horticulture club. To what extent has the individual learned to work with other people? The acceptance of responsibility in carrying out various programs signals a candidate with some excellent potential.

2. Recommendation of instructors. Some students never or rarely confer with their instructors out of the classroom. This individual may be risky, especially when groomed for an important role.

3. Practical experience. The person with only book knowledge often will require an extensive training period. The nature of the job can determine the extent

to which this is an asset or liability. Practical experience in a number of firms should prove highly important and be reflected in the salary offer.

4. Limited employment area. Young persons desirous of living within a short distance of home may have limited potential for finding opportunities with a growing and ambitious firm. Their framework may be limited in scope along with ambition and desire for personal growth. It is especially important that a spouse be willing to move to a new location. This part of the team often determines the extent of motivation and desire of the employee to remain a part of the firm. The wife or husband of a person groomed for an important position should be interviewed along with the spouse.

5. Unsure of future goals. Some graduates have not matured to the point where they can realistically identify potential jobs that have some appeal. This type of person can be very risky and could require extensive patience before arriving at a point of being classified as a real asset to the firm.

6. Regular hours. The person desirous of working a regular 40-hour week probably does not belong in horticulture unless at a low level in an organization. The nature of the business requires a commitment to an unusual and flexible work schedule revolving around holidays, planting seasons, and Mother Nature.

7. Flexibility. A growing number of graduates arrive on the scene with an extensive background in production and identification of crops. Your opening job calls for someone having this background, but also willing to manage a shop. Does the individual welcome the challenge to broaden his or her scope of knowledge and ability? Flexibility is an important trait for someone interested in personal growth.

SUMMARY

"You just can't find and keep good dependable people today." This does represent a major concern of management. The opinion has been heard on many occasions and for many decades. It will still echo throughout meeting rooms until management looks realistically at its own policies. You can find productive people and retain their loyalty providing you:

1. Carefully develop clear job descriptions and employ only qualified persons
2. Begin with a realistic salary and provide advancements reflecting productivity and responsibility
3. Establish a sound training program
4. Review progress at stated intervals
5. Provide praise when appropriate and at time of contribution by employee to advancement of firm

6. Minimize petty gripes, especially during periods of unusual pressures arising from long working hours

7. Provide opportunities for growth

Good people are not hard to find and keep. Management has the means to solve this problem and in the process build a strong, loyal, ambitious, happy, and productive organization.

1. What approach might be taken to avoid family conflicts in a business?

2. Compare theory X with theory Y. Which concept helps develop the fullest potential of an individual?

3. Does the work ethic still apply to current conditions? Discuss.

4. How can a manager reduce employee turnover? Discuss seven ways that can be employed by management to achieve this objective.

5. What should one consider when interviewing for a job? Identify and discuss eight areas important to a potential candidate.

6. What should an employer consider in evaluating a potential candidate? Identify and discuss four important areas.

chapter
eight

Your
Image

Every business develops an image. The image may be good, bad or neutral. Everyone may agree on your image, or your business could have different images to different people. In any case, you acquire an image from your first day of operation. Your image can be consciously formulated as part of a concrete plan of action, or it may come about in a unknown fashion. You have the choice of consciously trying to mold an image ("We Care") or permitting the shifting breezes to control your destiny.

An image cannot be developed or changed overnight. Once established, it may take hard work and a long period of time to mold a new image. The desired image for your firm might look as follows:

1. Handles only better than average quality products
2. Realistic prices
3. Always stands behind a product or service
4. Above average service
5. Pleasant personnel
6. A nice, cheery place to shop

Many factors must be considered after you decide on a general image for your firm. The first task should be to identify clearly the type and scope of image desired for your firm.[1] Then, set about building that image and reviewing practices regularly to keep the operation on the right track. Here are some further important considerations.

AGE

A firm that has been in business 25, 50, 75, or 100 years often focuses attention on its length of service to a community. It can be very comforting to do business with experienced people in contrast to "newcomers" who opened for business just a decade ago.

The red flag might be raised as firms add stripes to the sleeve of a jacket. Has management kept pace with the changing world? Are they still doing business the way they did back in the "good old days"? Some highly respected firms have forgotten that new people continue to move into their communities each year. The older generation retains strong loyalty to an oldtimer. The newer generation often demands something a little different and tends to be less impressed with age.

[1]This also applies to that person seeking employment and trying to decide which firms offer the most potential. Your image of a good firm in a specific field should correspond closely with that of the prospective employer.

Established firms give a comforting sense of stability. Successful marketers must remember to keep abreast of the ever-changing needs and wants of their customers.

A resident of a relatively large city was surprised to find that a shop in the downtown area was really operated by a florist. The gloomy, dull appearance and few flowers in the window suggested a funeral home. What an image!

How can you get out of the rut of doing things the way they were done a decade ago? How can you keep the train on the right track maintaining the desired image of the firm? Try employing some younger people periodically to bring new blood into the organization.

Age can be used effectively as a potent marketing weapon. It represents an important component of overall image in the community. Take precautions to see that it does not work against the desired image through neglect and the general attitude of taking life easy.

PERSONNEL AND PERSONNEL PRACTICES

A firm decides to enter a new field and in the process employs people at the minimum wage level. Pinching pennies may result in a dramatic change in image of the entire operation in just a matter of months. Assume that a business firm expands from that of landscape-nursery to selling green plants.

Neither management nor existing personnel have had any experience with procurement, display, and care of this new product line. They compound their problems by employing someone at minimum wage and without experience. The errors committed by an inexperienced buyer and sales personnel will show through to most customers in a matter of weeks.

Turn the situation around and consider the merits of a typical retail florist expanding the operation to sell trees and shrubs in the spring. An inexperienced person has been employed to water the plants and "occasionally" answer questions. Can you attract a qualified person when you are offering only a minimum wage? Or the manager buys stock unsuitable for the area. A business run in this manner can be expected to disappear from the scene in one or two years. Two ridiculous situations? Yes. But, they have occurred and keep occurring every year.

Employing persons at the lowest rung on the ladder is nothing short of an extreme case of inept management. Your personnel on the firing line can make or break the organization and its image. People in the greenhouse business have been fond of saying that the man on the end of the hose represents the key to success of the whole growing venture. Both statements have much meaning.

"Just a moment and Otto will answer your question." How many Otto's have truly built an image for a greenhouse, garden center, or nursery? Untold numbers of unsung heroes have helped firms provide the service required by many operators for their customers. Those individuals with the green thumb have been and continue to be worth their weight in gold. Employers who pay minimum wages to valuable personnel may lose part of their image when the facts become known to customers. A well-paid crew demonstrates their allegiance to management every day of the year.

Telephone Manners.   "Hello!" Have you ever had this response when calling a business firm? I tried shocking the woman by responding with: "I'm sorry, I thought this was the XYZ Nursery." It never worked, because she had handled the phone this way for many years. Where was the manager and why didn't he provide just a little training in the proper way to handle a telephone? You could rationalize that this approach blended in with the desired image of the firm, but why not have the person begin the conversation with a cheery "hello" and then identify the organization?

How about the voice at the other end of the telephone line that sounded like you just made her day by calling the firm? Or the individual who responded with a dull, tired voice and said, "Jim isn't in and I don't know when he will return." A receptionist at one particular firm was really clued in when she stated that Bill was in a meeting and asked if Ted could be of help.

Dress.   What is the appropriate dress for someone working in a nursery or greenhouse and coming into contact with customers? A tie, shirt, and sports jacket are surely out of place in this environment. You can expect a clean, shaven face and a fresh set of work clothes every day. Sloppy dress and whiskers tend to suggest a poorly run operation and questionable merchandise.

Greeting.   What kind of a greeting can customers expect when they enter your place of business? A standard and unfortunate opening goes something like, "Can we do something for you today?" Obviously, the person entered the store to make a purchase or inquire about a product or service. Try formulating a more cheery and appropriate greeting such as:

1. It's nice to see you again (assuming an old customer).
2. The weather has been just beautiful.
3. We are happy to see you and to take care of your needs.

STORE HOURS

A visit to a small garden center around 9:00 A.M. during the middle of May proved unfruitful since the operator had not arrived on the scene. The individual later stated that they were open until 8:00 P.M. and just couldn't see arriving for business until 10:00 A.M.

Store hours must be based, whenever possible, on the needs of your customers. Retail stores extend their business hours during the Christmas season. Garden center operators must do the same each spring.

EXTERIOR OF STORE

Greenhouse, nursery, and garden center operators depend on consumer appreciation of beauty to provide a livelihood for themselves and their employees. The products they produce and sell have been designed to beautify both the exterior and interior of our homes. The beautification programs of the late 1960s and 1970s spurred sales of plant materials. More and more consumers recognize the role of plants in improving our environment and our lives.

Step across the street from a greenhouse, nursery, or garden center. Look at the establishment through the eyes of a customer. Does the sight in front of you blend with the desired image of someone selling beauty? Does the operator tell you that he or she really has been convinced that plants add beauty to our lives and the community?

The typical greenhouse operator seemingly does not have time in the spring or summer to plant geraniums and bedding plants. Rather, one is likely to see a nice crop of weeds, discarded containers, and dried up plants that couldn't find a home. This dismal picture certainly does not apply to all greenhouses. Relatively few, however, plant spring flowering bulbs in the

Aggressive garden center operators use their own materials to attract attention. Hanging baskets and plant materials displayed in attractive fashion will stimulate impulse sales from travelers passing this outlet.

fall to insure some color in early spring. A few dollars invested in employing high school students in October and May could insure a tremendous display of color all summer.

A rapidly growing garden center operator in a Midwest state plants well over ten thousand spring flowering bulbs each fall. His sale of bulbs has increased each year although they never will support the cost of the planting. Why does this operator invest time and money in a project of this nature? The publicity and traffic each spring have helped increase his overall business at a rate much higher than that normally dreamed of by most individuals. He sells beauty. His actions speak with much more authority than words appearing in a newspaper advertisement.

A combination nursery–garden center operator has constructed a large demonstration area to help customers visualize the impact of plant materials, stone, and other landscape materials. Virtually every item for sale has been incorporated into the display garden. What better way to convey the message that plants are a necessity in our lives?

A small garden center chain features large outdoor displays of peat moss and related products in full view of passing motorists. The tremendous volume gives the impression that this firm stocks a great deal of merchandise. Surely, one must be able to find a good supply of almost every conceivable item for the gardener.

An attractive outdoor planter was ablaze with color throughout the entire summer months. This demonstrated in most effective fashion what gardeners could expect from plant materials purchased from this garden center.

Here are some examples of the exterior of retail outlets that enhance the image or occasionally run counter to the desired image of management.

1. Three hobby horse style planters filled with cascading petunias recently appeared in front of a large garden center associated with a seed firm. Customers were greeted with additional displays on a large patio where tomatoes and impatiens were growing in a vertical wire meshed structure. The total display painted an excellent picture of a quality organization.

2. An exceptionally large garden center looks shabby and cluttered from the outside. It reflects crowded haphazard conditions inside the operation. Bargain village is the theme and image created by management of this highly profitable firm. There are no frills and customers must rely on their own ingenuity when shopping for merchandise.

3. The front of a small operation looked like a typical junk yard. Weeds, old flats, and torn plastic greeted customers in late spring. Wilted plants and haphazard displays seemed to go hand in hand with bargain basement prices. Buyers had to be willing to take some chances in procuring merchandise from this operation.

4. A new redwood lath structure was attached to a modern garden center. The unit was designed to display hanging baskets, fruit trees, and some nursery stock. It blends in well with the existing structure and looks warm and inviting. Customers view this as a good firm and expect to pay prices consistent with the quality of merchandise and appearance of the organization.

This attractive redwood display unit helped to place the spotlight on high-quality hanging baskets and market packs.

5.   A roadside market lined the driveway to its retail store with pumpkins in early fall. Farm wagons were loaded with all types of multicolored squash and gourds. Customers were attracted to this colorful operation and to management which demonstrated some life and vitality in decorating the premises with farm produce.

6.   A number of retail florists have remodeled gasoline stations and historic buildings. This action has captured the attention and fancy of many people. It has demonstrated a concern for the environment and preservation of old structures. This has to be considered a real plus in terms of building a desirable image in a community.

7.   A roadside market has captured the flavor of an old-fashioned general store. Cracker barrels, smoked meats, and individually sold bedding plants all provide the desired flavor and atmosphere for this charming store. The exterior of the operation looks much like something seen in a 1930s movie.

8.   The front window of a retail flower shop looks exceptionally "busy". It has been designed to appeal to shoppers and impulse sales. All merchandise must be priced, and the quality of the plants and giftware must reflect the desired image of the firm.

The window must be changed periodically to avoid the feeling that the shop owners are tired, lazy, and worn out.

9. Many garden centers and similar types of businesses have expanded rapidly in recent years. New additions have been added onto existing structures in order to better service customers. Store additions must be carefully planned and often handled by a qualified architect to maintain the desired image of a firm. A large retail organization in an eastern state decided to construct a small plastic greenhouse adjacent to a modern structure. The addition was designed to display plants in proper fashion and provide more room in the store for gift merchandise. To what extent would a temporary, plastic structure easily visible from the highway conflict with the modern design of the building? Perhaps additional dollars should have been invested in a glass structure that blended in much better with the large glass windows of the modern building.

The materials sold by greenhouses, garden centers, and nurseries are the best advertising and promotional weapons available to management. Use your own products to beautify your place of business.

Checklist

A checklist of items should be employed in evaluating how the front of your operation looks to a potential customer.

1. *Signs.* Has a nearby billboard been repainted in the last couple of years? What is the condition of the sign right in front of the establishment?

2. *Parking.* Have you provided reasonable and adequate parking for customers? Is it safe to park in the assigned area? If one has to park down the road, have you made it easy to walk back to the front door?

3. *Paint.* When did you last paint the front of the establishment?

4. *Clutter.* Have you taken care of weeds, containers, and old plants that often accumulate in front of the operation?

5. *Atmosphere.* Does your place of business radiate a special glow that says "Welcome, we are pleased you came to see our merchandise"?

INTERIOR OF STORE

What type of world awaits the potential customers as they enter the front door of your establishment? It should be difficult to terminate the visit without just one more look at those beautiful geraniums. Consider the following factors as they help develop your image:

1. *Safety.* Can you move throughout the store and greenhouse without running into obstacles? Wires often protrude from greenhouse benches catching a piece of clothing.

Narrow aisles and uneven surfaces make shopping a real hazard and deter gardeners from patronizing this type of greenhouse.

2. *Price tags.* Have you taken the time to price merchandise or do prices remain a mystery to customers and clerks?

3. *Cleanliness.* How often do clerks dust the shelves and merchandise?

4. *Paint.* When was the last time you painted the interior of the shop?

5. *Lighting.* Do you need the aid of a flashlight to find the price tag? The interior should be well lit, bright, and gay.

6. *Displays.* When was the last time you rearranged display counters? A "new" look attracts attention.

7. *Traffic flow.* Can you move easily throughout the store and greenhouse? A store cluttered with merchandise and limited aisle space does not encourage browsing.

How long does it take customers to pass through check-out lines? A major food store lost a substantial amount of business because management cut corners and had only a few check-out lines open at any one time. A nearby competitor capitalized on this error and rapidly attracted shoppers who didn't want the inconvenience of waiting in line fifteen minutes or longer.

Have you really tried to make it easy for your customers to shop? Enter your store and walk through all areas just like a potential customer. Did you enjoy the experience? Try taking some notes of changes to be implemented to improve the atmosphere and image desired for your operation.

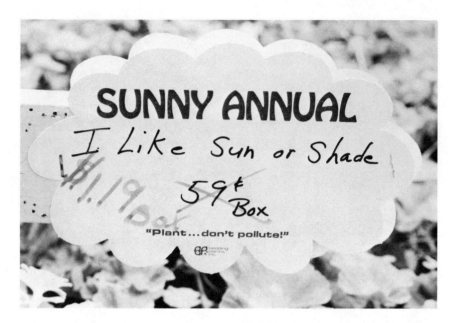

BEDDING PLANTS INCORPORATED has developed special signs for use in promoting bedding plants. Using an old sign to save a few pennies and especially quoting a new, higher price casts a negative impact on one's image.

OTHER IMAGE BUILDERS

Product Mix and Volume

The largest selection of pottery always can be found at one particular garden center in a community of 100,000 people. Everyone knows that they have the best selection available in a wide range of prices. What can people say about your store? Are you known for having just a little of everything or do you concentrate on a few specialties plus the normal inventory of regular items?

A typical gardener might develop a shopping list including an impatiens hanging basket, white geraniums, wax begonias, petunias, and marigolds. What might be the reaction of this customer to learn that you handle only the more popular red and pink geraniums? Your selection might be limited in midseason to only some petunia and geranium baskets. Will your customer return next year or find another supplier with a better product mix? As a specialist, you should strive for an excellent product mix to firm up your reputation and image.

Holes were drilled in an attractive barrel to permit planting of vine type plant material. This is an excellent item for a patio and will capture the attention of discriminating gardeners.

This display has been manhandled and has no appeal even to gardeners looking for special sales.

Quality

Mass outlets often bear the burden of handling poor and questionable merchandise. Poor handling techniques on the premises may have led to a rapid decline in quality of plants. An independent retail florist, garden center, or nursery operator must strive to accent the positive, in terms of quality, to differentiate their operation from firms focusing on price and volume. Quality is further discussed in Chapter 12.

Information Service

Can a customer expect to receive assistance from your clerks regarding planting tips and maintenance of plant materials? This valuable service can make or break the desired image of a firm. The ability to answer most questions stamps the operation as a real "pro" in gardening. You are the specialist in town.

A major garden center in the Minneapolis–St. Paul area has constructed a special education building to service the needs of its customers. The facility was planned to provide meeting space right in the midst of garden supplies and plant materials. A number of lecture–demonstrations have been planned, especially in spring, summer, and fall, to help gardeners. Top speakers from the firm and area have been employed to educate novice as well as experienced gardeners. The building also houses a large collection of books, magazines, pamphlets, and mimeographed material. Some items have been made available at no charge and others at a fee depending upon the source of material. Personnel at this establishment are never too busy to answer questions. The customer is *king* and it's the job of clerks and management to do their best in servicing needs of customers.

Guarantee

"We guarantee all products until they leave our premises." You can smile and perhaps applaud the courage of the creator of this statement. It does tell you bluntly what can be expected from this firm. Contrast this policy with that of another operator who guarantees everything including bedding plants throughout the growing season. Which image would you prefer?

Management

One manager has made an effort to train personnel to answer questions from customers. The staff is well groomed and courteous. The owner-manager does spend a great deal of time on the sales floor. Unfortunately, he has not listened to his own sermons. Customers report his offensive and condescending comments. We should expect more from the owner than the sales staff. Perhaps some owners should invest some time and money in a Dale Carnegie course!

Advertising

The type and frequency of advertising tells an important story about a firm. Some retail florists have focused attention on advertisements promoting funeral flowers. This part of the business still represents an important segment of gross sales for many organizations. What does it say to the person interested in wedding flowers or a gift for someone in the hospital? Each person will respond differently with some accepting and some receiving very negative vibrations.

Extensive advertising on television might support the image that the shop has been expensive, the rationale being that it does take money to support an extensive program on television. Carefully consider the allocation of dollars for advertising. The style and approach should support the planned image of your firm.

Location

A great deal has been written about location and its impact on sales. The move to a new location often has been credited with an upsurge in sales. A move into an expensive complex, however, will have an immediate impact on your image. By the same token, remaining in an older, rundown section of the city suggests that management has lost contact with its customers. Carefully choose a location suitable to your desired image and then sales will blossom. Location is discussed in depth in Chapter 7.

Specials and Discounts

What happens when you run out of a product placed on a special sale for a weekend? A smooth way to handle this situation is to provide interested customers with a raincheck. This permits them to return in a stated period of time and to purchase the product at the sale price. It demonstrates that your firm is interested in the welfare of its customers.

Some firms seemingly hide specials under a bushel basket and in the back forty. It becomes a chore to find the merchandise. One soon has the feeling that management really didn't want to sell the product at the advertised price. A good operator will make it easy to find specials. Appropriate signs can be used to identify merchandise advertised for sale. Store personnel should be instructed as to location and prices of all specials.

In the long run, how productive is it for the customer to receive a discount in lieu of a guarantee on nursery stock? The "good" deal often turns sour for both parties when the tree dies and the home gardener realizes that he or she forfeited the guarantee. Will the gardener return to the same nursery or garden center for future purchases? Why program for disaster in offering a discount in lieu of a guarantee?

Pricing

Your pricing policy and the line of merchandise carried rank as the most important factors in the overall image of your firm. Consumers can quickly identify your firm as being high priced or offering reasonable prices. Even though handling some expensive lines, it's important to convey the feeling of reasonableness. Pricing practices should reflect and enhance the desired image of the firm. You can't be all things to all people. Choose your merchandise carefully and price according to the image constructed for your firm.

Merchandise

The type or quality of product offered for sale has a profound impact on image of the business as seen through the eyes of a consumer. Hazy and double images often greet customers when product quality fails to reflect an image created through advertising programs, store personnel, store appearance, and personality of the manager.

A large garden center has tended to create an increasingly hazy image through procurement of questionable merchandise. Here are some examples:

1. Potted chrysanthemums have been acquired for a number of holidays, at inexpensive prices, from sources in a far distant state. The product normally goes into supermarket channels. Quality varies a great deal and rarely compares with locally produced merchandise.

2. Poinsettias have been bought in volume from a major producer normally servicing mass outlets. This product has represented the bulk of poinsettias stocked by the store. Prices have been set near the normal florist price, and far exceed those of nearby mass outlets handling the exact same product.

3. Inexpensive and often poor quality carnations have been purchased for use in traditional retail work.

Poor or questionable quality merchandise frustrates store personnel and counters the productive efforts of other departments in the organization. Morale of personnel can be adversely affected as they work with inferior merchandise and are then questioned about their productivity.

A second operator also has turned to inexpensive sources for virtually his entire poinsettia and bedding plant crops. This move was made to compete directly with a mass outlet selling low-priced merchandise. In fact, both outlets have been acquiring merchandise from suppliers in the same general area. The new marketing strategy has had a profound influence on the image and customer loyalty of this old and well-established firm. Gardeners have recognized the change in quality and have started patronizing other independent firms in the area.

SUMMARY

After all is said and done, some firms appear highly successful while at the same time building a poor image of their operation and staff. Does this mean that the importance of image is overdramatized? Some people can fall into a mudhole and come up smelling like a rose. This often occurs in the business world. A reasonable explanation is that they have done some things right and in exceptional fashion. The good points seemingly have outweighed their errors. The absence of strong competitors also can result in excellent sales and profits.

How long a firm can continue to ignore its image and prosper often remains debatable. A new, aggressive operator may suddenly arrive on the scene and capture the lion's share of business.

The development of a strong positive image requires hard work and continuous monitoring throughout the year. All facets of your operation including facilities, products, and personnel play vital roles in helping mold an image for every organization.

Some operators fall into the trap of failing to recognize that one's image flows from internal as well as external factors. Personnel and personnel practices affect performance of the entire staff. A discontented staff will take its toll in terms of service to consumers. The way one handles a telephone and dresses have important bearing on image.

Many garden center operators seemingly have forgotten that they are selling beauty. The exterior of many stores looks shabby, and too many fail to plant flowers, trees and shrubs.

Shopping should be an exciting adventure for gardeners. One must focus attention on traffic flow, checkout procedures, volume of merchandise on sale, and extent of product mix. Your strategy must be based on filling all the needs of indoor and outdoor gardeners in trying to mold the desired image.

You have a choice of consciously trying to mold your image or unconsciously allowing things to develop in haphazard fashion. Creating a good image requires a great deal of hard work. It is a never-ending task. The rewards in terms of profits and a well-respected operation more than compensate for your efforts and those of your employees.

1. Why is "image" important to management? Can it be altered overnight? Why?

2. Identify and discuss seven factors other than age that help build an image for a firm.

3. Discuss the pros and cons of age in building a solid image in a community.

4. What type of dress would you recommend for garden store employees?

5. Why should management periodically view the operation through the eyes of a customer? What should one look at and analyze?

6. What impact does product mix and volume have on potential customers?

7. How can one destroy an image or blur it in the eyes of a customer?

8. Should management let nature take its course or deliberately try to mold an image for a firm? Why?

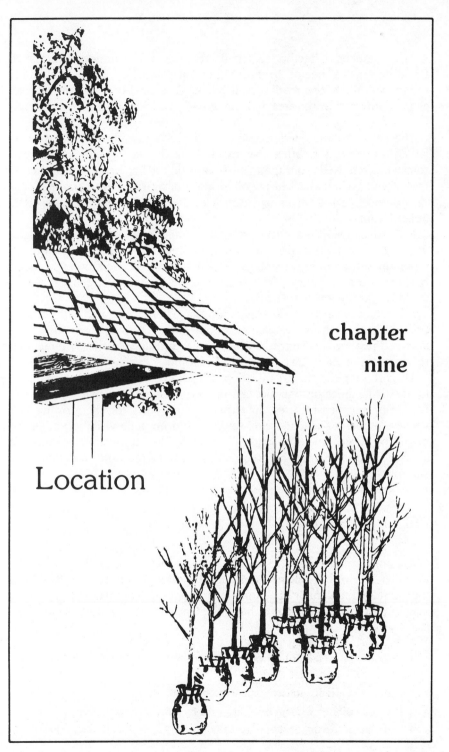

chapter
nine

Location

A large number of factors contribute to success of a business enterprise. Location ranks as one of the most important considerations when planning to buy or build a new retail establishment. The final decision must reflect growth potential of the area and changing traffic patterns in the community.

The nature of the operation, including products and services for sales, largely determines whether one requires maximum visibility or an area somewhat removed from the main stream of traffic. Rental or land costs fees often have a major bearing on location of a firm. The operator should view these costs as a percentage of projected net sales rather than as specific dollar figures.

Fast food operations and developers of shopping malls allocate many dollars for site analyses prior to the construction of facilities. These dollars represent only a minor percentage of total dollars expended for a new facility. This insurance policy, while expensive, helps avoid costly mistakes that could jeopardize a new enterprise.

A number of garden center operations have been associated with production facilities such as a greenhouse and nursery. Some firms also have operated retail flower shops. A few organizations have vertically integrated to the extent of featuring a wholesale division.

The full scope of the organization will help determine whether or not to locate all facilities on one piece of property. One alternative would be to choose an inexpensive area, in terms of land costs for the growing and wholesale operations. The retail outlet, requiring high visibility, might be placed on more expensive land. These and other considerations must be analyzed by the operator before finally selecting a location for the business enterprise.

RETAIL OPERATION

What constitutes a good location? Just as "beauty is in the eye of the beholder," so will the elements of good location vary to some extent from individual to individual. The ultimate test might well be that customers find and do patronize your place of business. One can identify a dream location as follows:

1. Situated on a major highway or one used by large numbers of local and area shoppers in contrast to truckers and business vehicles.

2. Ease of entrance and exit onto a major highway.

3. Good visibility without being crowded by other business enterprises.

4. Adjacent to a major shopping mall or facility attracting traffic every day.

5. Good parking.

Often the operator must face the reality of being situated on a back road miles from potential customers. This liability, or what appears as one at first glance, can be turned into a major asset. You must accept the challenge of finding ways to attract buyers to your remote location. Here are some case stories to illustrate:

1. A rapidly growing garden center has been located in a rural setting some 17 miles from a major metropolitan center. Potential customers must spend 45 minutes to an hour traveling to and from the operation which also features a nursery and landscape service. Why travel this distance? The operator features:

a. A tremendous spring bulb show enabling customers to see every cultivar in bloom before placing an order

b. An excellent seleciton of quality merchandise

c. Well-trained and courteous employees

d. Specially developed literature to aid in planting and care of garden items

e. Attractive displays of plant materials

Many gardeners look forward each spring, summer, and fall to a pleasant drive and relief from the hustle and bustle of city life. A potential handicap has been turned into a real asset by this aggressive merchandiser.

A well-designed bed of spring flowering bulbs helps stimulate advance sales of tulips, hyacinths, and daffodils and encourages gardeners to plant a wide variety of flowers each spring.

2. A roadside marketer has capitalized on the public's desire to get closer to nature. This firm is located about 25 miles from a major metropolitan area. The traffic jam on weekends throughout the spring, summer, and fall has been almost unbelievable. They feature:

    a. A pick-it-yourself operation for strawberries, tomatoes, and several other crops. If you can't pick, then buy their freshly harvested corn and tomatoes.

    b. An old-fashioned store where you can buy "homemade" jams and jellies and crackers from a barrel. Their specialty foods, including cheeses and hams, capture attention even though produced in faraway places.

    c. Good quality merchandise.

    d. A special on tomato plants at 5¢ a plant. They have had to ration plants to customers.

3. A florist in a moderate sized community of 13,000 formerly operated a small retail store in the downtown area and a greenhouse on the outskirts of town. Travel distance was five minutes between the two facilities. Should he close the retail store in favor of the greenhouse location? The downtown store was almost a hole in the wall. Yes, they had foot traffic, but the small display area limited sales. A move was made including remodeling of facilities at the greenhouse. Business has boomed at the new location.

What prompted people to come to the greenhouse? The natural environment of the greenhouse always has attracted attention. People like to see plants growing under glass. An improved selling and display area helped turn the trick.

Location has been turned from a potential liability in some instances to a real asset. A nice pleasant drive now appeals to many people who annually look forward to that trip for fresh strawberries, selecting their own tree, and viewing the tulips.

Visibility

Good visibility is an important asset for most retail enterprises. This frequently has been interpreted as visibility from a main highway or interchange. Land is extremely valuable in these areas and not everyone can find space at an interchange.

A prominent and appropriate sign will attract attention of potential customers. National retail outlets commonly have adopted a special shape, colors, or message that easily identifies the organization.

The presence of a greenhouse, preferably up front, serves as a landmark and captures the attention of passing motorists. There is something unique and almost magical about a greenhouse that entices people to stop and browse.

A parking lot, preferably to one side, provides an open area helping set off a garden center. Contrast this with a string of business establishments packed together into a small area.

Operators of existing facilities should take time to cruise the area approaching their stores from all directions. How would you rank visibility coming from the east and west? What can you do to improve visibility and increase customer traffic?

Location Next to Competitor

Good locations in a community already may be occupied by existing garden centers. Should this prevent you from situating in the same area? A small, independent operator awoke one day to find that a giant, multiple shop operation was under construction across the street. Should this small operator look for another location? The dramatic growth of shopping centers around the country helps testify to the economic feasibility of locating near one's competitors. Shoppers and business operators have accepted an environment where numerous firms compete under one roof. Customers are attracted to areas featuring several stores handling a particular commodity. One can shop at Sears, Wards, J.C. Penney, and a host of smaller sized operations all at a single location.

The same philosophy can be employed when considering the location of a garden center close, if not adjacent to, a major competitor. Two stores may attract more customers than the combined total of both stores in different locations. The direct challenge from a nearby competitor forces one to improve merchandising and business talents.

A new operator evaluated the potential for locating an operation in the same area as two well established firms. Knowledge of the area and the two businesses revealed:

a.   The immediate community was still growing at a most desirable rate.

b.   Operator 1 had a nasty disposition repelling some customers, poor quality plants, haphazard displays, and a limited product mix.

c.   Operator 2 charged high prices for ordinary products and services.

The individual's proposal was to capitalize on the weaknesses of the two established operators. Ultimate success also would reflect one's ability to develop and implement a positive strategy featuring strengths of the individual in question.

Free-standing Operations

A number of garden centers currently occupy valuable land and have been surrounded by housing developments. They were probably considered to be in the country several decades ago. Should these operators move to new locations or absorb heavy taxes while retaining their prime locations?

One garden center operation is associated with a small nursery and land-scape service. The business has been completely surrounded by private dwellings for more than a decade. The business partners have shown no interest in moving because of the many unique features associated with the operation. It represents one of few locations in the city where buyers actually can see plants in the field. There is no question that trees and shrubs can tolerate local conditions. While space is at a premium, they can still display material in an attractive fashion.

The construction of bypass highways or beltlines around major cities has stimulated relocation of many businesses. New car dealers have sprung up along these highways and generally feature many acres for storage and

An attractive, large, and well-landscaped sign welcomes gardeners to this retail operation located on a main highway just outside of a thriving community.

displays. A number of garden center operators have followed the pack and occasionally led other businessmen in seeking greener pastures and open space. The new highways carry a great deal of traffic. Other business enterprises have brought people to the area and away from older sections of the community.

New shopping centers have sprung up along major highways leading to and from our cities and along bypass routes. A location adjacent to a shopping center can prove highly beneficial in terms of car traffic. The shopping center attracts thousands of people. An adjacent garden center will benefit for the simple reason that customers must pass near the store. Attractive signs and a good display of merchandise can bring many customers to the garden center while traveling to or from the shopping center.

High speed highways tend to limit sales of firms on frontage roads unless drivers have good visibility and are made aware of the proper exit. A strong advertising program and a good image easily can overcome this potential barrier. Customers will become discouraged, however, when finding it difficult to exit at the proper ramp and locate the frontage road.

Which side of the road represents the best location for a garden center? The answer depends to a large extent on the frequency of special sales and the nature of merchandise for sale. The homeward-bound side has captured attention of those merchants offering specials designed to attract consumers returning from work or shopping in the downtown area. This location will prove beneficial during the week to a garden center featuring fresh flower and potted plant specials. Most garden center sales occur on weekends during spring and fall. This means that customers were probably making a deliberate effort to visit the store. One might question the advantages of locating on a particular side for those operators featuring trees and shrubs along with bedding plants. The nature of the product and services may contribute more to attracting shoppers than store location on a particular side of the highway.

Shopping Centers

Large numbers of customers passing in front of a store every day have lured some business people to shopping centers. Retail florists and some garden center operators have tried to capitalize on this modern retail phenomenon. The track record of a shopping center should be investigated early in your deliberations. Here are some considerations regarding new and older shopping centers:

New Operation. You have the advantage of getting in on the ground floor and selecting a prime location. However, you must pay relatively high fees for installing facilities and decorating your shop. Sales may be slow for the

This unique kiosk stands right in the traffic pattern for most shoppers patronizing this mall. All four sides are open to the public and stimulate many impulse sales.

first year or two, requiring extra cash to support the operation. Newness should attract customers, especially from older shopping centers in the trading area.

Moderately New. There will be a limited selection of locations in the mall. However, the center has a track record and has probably passed break-even point for most operations. You can acquire a facility with modest expenditure to remodel, and may be in position to bargain over rental rates. You will face potential competition from a new center in same market area.

Mature. What is the image and condition of mall? The expected life span of a mall runs some 15 years. A major remodeling program must be undertaken to insure that the mall remains competitive with newer facilities. Enclosing an older mall reportedly resulted in a doubling of sales for occupants within the first year. You should be in a position to bargain over rental rates, especially when other shopping centers have been constructed in the same trading area. Space selection will be limited and you will face potential competition.

Three types of shopping centers have sprung up around the country. Large regional complexes feature two or more major chains such as Wards and Sears. They attract customers from a wide shopping area and involve a large complex of diversified retail businesses. Neighborhood centers often have revolved around a supermarket and a drugstore. A number of moderately small retail outlets occupy space, including pizza, bakery, ice cream, beauty parlor, and dry-cleaning establishments. Medium-sized shopping malls can be referred to as community centers. They feature one large retail outlet along with a host of supporting stores offering a multitude of services and products.

A garden center in a shopping mall faces the problem of finding adequate and reasonable space to display merchandise. Rental fees are quite high and often preclude the sale of bulky, moderately priced merchandise. On the surface, you might be inclined to feel that the typical image of an independent garden center would not necessarily blend with that of a large shopping center. Customers associate many garden products with outdoor displays and greenhouses. The environment of most shopping centers would appear overly formal and not conducive to large soil piles and bulky plants displayed on the floor.

The Sears organization, as one example, has constructed garden centers as unattached units alongside one of the entrances to the operation. A wire fence has been used to enclose the facility. Cars can drive up to the area to pick up plants and supplies. This operation, on the periphery of the shopping center, preserves and enhances the image of the garden center, and takes advantage of heavy traffic associated with malls.

A garden center may be the prime occupant of a smaller neighborhood shopping center. The complex may have been financed by the garden center. Reasonable space also may be much more available than that at major shopping centers.

Some malls feature free-standing stores also known as kiosks. They probably enjoy much more traffic than most stores of similar size in the mall. Shoppers must pass by all sides and often are tempted to buy well-displayed merchandise. Impulse sales of plants, flowers, and containers represent an important segment of total sales. Stolen merchandise may be greater due to clerks being unable to observe all sides of the display. Available space may be limited in size and restrict one's ability to display merchandise.

Urban Districts

Apartment and condominium dwellers slowly but surely are being recognized as strong prospects for the purchase of some products and services offered by garden center operators. They work with a different set of parameters than those of the typical homeowner or renter. Grass seed and lawn products will take a back seat to patio planters, window boxes, and hanging baskets. These dwellers grow horticultural plants on an intensive basis.

Some garden center firms in an urban environment cater to apartment dwellers and those with extremely limited space for gardens. Their product line reflects the specialized needs of a local clientele which often travels on foot to their place of business. Parking facilities are virtually nonexistent with the exception of metered stalls on the street.

A unique operation has been established on the roof of an older building in mid-Manhattan, New York. It features a wide variety of containers, fertilizers, soil mixes, and plants for indoor locations and small outdoor patios. The construction of a greenhouse has attracted a considerable amount of attention from city dwellers. Downtown locations, especially in the older sections, often have limited parking facilities. Foot traffic from local area tenants probably accounts for most sales. Mini-sized materials are the order of the day rather than the exception.

Each operator must define the location and needs of a targeted audience. The urban audience, often without benefit of automobiles, likes to shop at local specialty garden centers. Business success in this environment requires careful analysis in identifying products lines and services for the urban gardener.

RENTAL FEES

One should treat rental fees as a normal expense in the same fashion as labor, advertising, and electricity. Our example (operating statement) on page 81 shows rent to be just over 5 percent of net sales. Rental fees as low as 4 percent and as high as 6 percent would be considered in the acceptable category. This expense item will not appear in statements where the operator owns the building and land. Some business people, partly for tax purposes, have set up two corporations. One owns the land and buildings and rents these assets to the second firm. The rental fee becomes a legitimate business expense. A good real estate firm can help determine a range of rental fees for the property and buildings in question. This practice minimizes the potential for locating a business on property that is much too valuable for a garden center.

How can you compare rents from competing locations, assuming that you are planning to establish a new firm or open a branch operation? Rental fees should be viewed as a percentage of anticipated gross sales. Will the competing locations produce the same gross? If so, the lower rental fee, at first glance, looks like the best decision for management. But the location with a higher fee could have substantial merit if it were capable of producing significantly higher sales than the other location. The pro forma statement, showing the rental fee as a percentage of net sales, will help clarify the situation.

Some operators contemplating opening a store in a shopping center have found it difficult to accept all facets of the rental contract. They must bear the expense of installing equipment and decorating or remodeling, plus the initial rental fee. Typical contracts also call for a small percentage of gross in addition to the base fee, when sales exceed a certain volume of business. Paying the extra fee ultimately reflects great success in managing the business. After all, you are more interested in gross than in minimizing rental fees. A prime location will command top price. A poor location in the back 40 looks tempting and can be rented for a very nominal fee. Which location ultimately will help achieve your sales targets?

ALLIED OPERATIONS

Many garden centers are part of larger operations featuring a nursery, flower shop, greenhouse, hardware store, or farm market. The development of a full-fledged garden operation might represent the last of several growth moves by management. One has relatively little choice in the selection of location unless deciding to physically separate each major component of the organization, given an existing operation. This is comparable to developing one or more branch stores tied into the main firm.

WHOLESALE PRODUCERS

A growing number of firms, both wholesale nurserymen and florists, have found it economically feasible to open retail operations. Location of the main plant largely dictates whether or not the new facility should be located on the premises or at a separate location.

The advantages of having all operations on the same premises include:

a. The image of a firm producing and selling its own merchandise
b. The large volume of product and product mix available and on display
c. Minimizing transportation problems arising from servicing a remote retail outlet
d. Ease of managing the new facility on existing premises

Assuming that there will be adequate space for establishment of a retail facility, the advantages cited must be weighed against several potential disadvantages which include:

a. Nearness of facility to potential customers
b. Additional advertising and promotional expenses required to attract buyers to a distant location

Greenhouse and nursery wholesale operators often located themselves on the perimeters of metropolitan areas. They wanted to be relatively close to markets. Slowly but surely over the years, these sites became surrounded by homes and shopping centers. The land became too valuable for a strictly wholesale operation. Some operators have sold the land and moved further into the country, seeking cheaper land. A different approach called for establishment of a retail outlet situated on a small parcel of land. One or two greenhouses or a small planting of nursery stock would be retained to enhance the image of the retail operation. The wholesale facility would be moved to a new site.

The process has been reversed in a few situations. A highly successful and rapidly growing garden center moves a large volume of products each year. This growing appetite for merchandise has led some operators to integrate vertically by establishing production facilities. The initial venture may be on the premises and adjacent to the retail outlet. This move enhances the image of the firm as a producer of plants sold through its own store. Success in this venture soon leads to further expansion programs involving location of the primary wholesale facility at a more remote location. Management must consider the following when locating a wholesale facility designed to support partly or totally a retail outlet:

1. Soil and Climate.   Nursery location has been influenced by soil and climatic conditions to a much greater extent than by distance to metropolitan centers. Some firms ship hundreds and thousands of miles. Several major azalea producers are located in Mobile, Alabama. Very large nursery producers have located in Iowa, Oklahoma, and Texas, shipping throughout most of the country. The decision to locate in remote areas often has been based on availability of good and inexpensive land. Most important has been that of a desirable climate and soil, permitting digging of plants at market time. A long growing season has attracted many firms to south and southwest areas of the country.

High light intensity is another factor in the production of greenhouse and nursery crops. Clean air and soil free from pollutants have become increasingly important to these specialty growers. You must carefully survey the area to determine the presence of industrial plants potentially contaminating the environment. Locating a firm near paper plants would appear extremely foolish. Prevailing winds could bring air pollutants and decrease available sunlight during winter months, causing a decline in crop quality.

2. Labor.   Qualified labor from the surrounding area is a must for any wholesale operation. A pool or labor interested in part time work, composed of women and high school students, often can be found in rural areas. One major rural bedding plant operator employs a crew of high school students from 4 P.M. to 7 P.M. to transplant seedlings and pot young plants.

3. Highway.   The wholesale greenhouse operator normally sells merchandise all 52 weeks of the year. This is especially true when foliage plants have played an important role in the production program. An operator marketing flowering plants for holiday and nonholiday periods also must consider a location adjacent to one or more major highways. Fast and economical delivery service is important to producers and especially those located in highly competitive markets.

A primary question relating to the market or markets targeted for the new operation is "Will you ship to one major metropolitan area or several centers in a radius of 100 or more miles?" One Milwaukee, Wisconsin greenhouse producer sells primarily to retail accounts in the immediate metropolitan area. A location just off the freeway system has minimized lost time due to travel on congested streets.

A producer shipping to several markets should have access to the freeway system and major highways. The primary population centers normally are located along the interstate highway system. You might try to select a location near the center of the area to be serviced yet adjacent to a major highway.

The demand for nursery products is highest at the beginning of the planting season. It tapers off rather rapidly during the remaining growing months. Good highways are important to minimize transportation problems during foul weather in early spring.

The nature of the nursery business has been much different than that of greenhouse operators with respect to frequency of deliveries. On the surface, a prime location in terms of transportation would not appear nearly as essential as for producers of flowering plants. The current locations of many large wholesale nurseries would suggest that factors other than roads played a major role in site selection. A nursery location with relatively easy access to main roads will facilitate transportation of stock to buyers. Higher land costs associated with close proximity to major roads could discourage location of a nursery along the interstate system.

SIGNS

Small or large signs may be employed to capture attention of potential customers. These outdoor signs may be located on the premises, approaching the business establishment, or in high traffic areas remote from the actual location of a firm. Billboards may point out that a particular firm is just down the road. This prepares a motorist for an appropriate turn into a parking lot.

The intent of signs and billboards is obvious to everyone. There is the continuous desire to acquaint new and old residents of a community with the fact that a particular business offers a range of products and services. One cannot rely on word-of-mouth information's being transmitted, for example, to new families arriving in a community.

Signs play a role in strengthening or reinforcing the image of a firm. A poorly designed and maintained sign does not reflect well on a firm. Customers begin to question whether products and services of an organization are in the same state of disarray and repair.

A prime mistake involves the length of the message placed on the sign. Readability should be of major concern to the operator. Keep the message simple and sweet. Use large letter and focus attention on good color contrasts with the background.

Signs on the premises often provide opportunities to include a message that can be changed periodically. One pet store operator features a new slogan each week with a play on words, for one of the pets for sale. Passing motorists look forward to each new message. Keep the message up to date. Feature information such as timely garden tips—"Time to control dandelions."

Portable signs with flashing lights are commonly seen on the highway. The modest expense for the unit must be balanced against the image created by this "loud" sign. It may or may not reinforce the type of image one wants to project to potential customers.

Directional Signs

A number of directional signs may be employed by operators in more rural locations and off the main stream of traffic. Good directions help establish the right buying mood for buyers. Customers can be turned off should they have difficulty finding the most direct route to your place of business. No one enjoys consuming extra gas and spending time trying to find the location of a business establishment.

The process of locating directional signs begins when you place yourself in the position of a prospective buyer. How do you find this garden center traveling from the east, south, west, and north? With the aid of a good map covering your location and immediate market area, pinpoint the roads and intersections that will be traveled by most customers. Take to your car and actually travel the roads from different locations to your business establishment. Identify problem areas requiring directional signs or landmarks that can be referred to in advertisements. Permission must be obtained from landowners and the highway department to locate signs along the way.

Good directional signs are:

1. Freshly painted and repaired each year
2. Located at crucial points — before changes in direction
3. Visible, easily read, and of appropriate size
4. Uniform in color, size, and lettering style
5. Sturdy — appropriately constructed to reflect desired image of your operation

READABILITY OF OUTDOOR SIGNS

Height of letter	Maximum distance for easy visibility	Approx. time visible at 35 mph
1 in.	25 ft	½ sec
2 in.	50 ft	1 sec
3 in.	80 ft	1½ sec
4 in.	100 ft	2 sec
5 in.	140 ft	2¾ sec
6 in.	170 ft	$3^1/_3$ sec

SOURCE: James Milmoe, *Roadside Marketing* (Newark Del.: University of Delaware, Food Business Institute, 1965), pp. 46–50.

Warning signs are a must for drivers having to enter a blind entrance. They need time to slow down for a turn into the parking lot. Other motorists should be cautioned to watch for slow moving vehicles entering and departing from your establishment. The removal of trees and shrubs on both sides of your entrance way increases visibility for drivers, greatly reducing hazards associated with a blind entrance.

PARKING AREA

Gasoline prices have not dampened the enthusiasm of gardeners in traveling many miles to their favorite garden center. Operators continually tell of loyal customers coming from faraway locations each year for plants and cultural information. Good parking facilities continue to rank as an important element in attracting customers regardless of business location.

An existing business can rely on past records and observations in determining the number of parking spaces required for customers. A good rule of thumb calls for 15 spaces for every 100 cars expected on an average day. The real key is determining what constitutes an average day for your enterprise.

The large volume of traffic associated with each new planting season can and often does create serious problems for potential customers and the operator. Northern operators conduct much of their business during a span of some four to six weeks. The flow of traffic tapers off following the spring rush each year. How much space can one really allocate and justify for a parking lot?

Smaller operators often plan, gauging from the size of parking lots, for only a few cars at any one time of the day. Customers find themselves parking illegally on busy highways. Traffic congestion irritates customers caught in a small parking lot or on a narrow driveway. Bent fenders occur all too often in these tense situations.

A temporary lot will be required to handle the overflow common during the main planting season. This can be located in back of the premises or to one side. A good gravel base, reasonably well maintained, should prove acceptable to your customers.

The typical parking lot found at many medium-sized shopping centers features lots of blacktop and few trees and shrubs. Providing space for a maximum number of cars seems to have ranked first for many designers.

Spacious parking and easy access are major factors when choosing a location for a garden center.

This philosophy should contrast markedly with that of the garden center operator selling beauty in the form of trees, shrubs, and flowers. The operator has a golden opportunity to expose customers to a wide range of products, in an almost natural setting, immediately upon arriving at the parking lot. A variety of accessory items, such as mulches, decorative stones, fences, and railings, can be employed to landscape a well conceived parking lot.

Local ordinances should be checked prior to planning and construction of parking facilities. Some communities have laws covering size of stalls, surfacing, exits and entrances, and landscaping. A typical stall requires 400 square feet of space. The increase in numbers of small vehicles has prompted some operators to program appropriate stalls for these cars. The stalls should be well marked, and appropriate signs should guide drivers.

The size of the parking area will be related to available space, angle of parking, and number of spaces required. The angle of parking will help determine width of the lot. Larger numbers of compact cars may call for separate parking of these vehicles and modification of suggested guidelines.

ANGLE PARKING SPACE REQUIREMENTS

No. of Rows	Width Lot Required		
	90°	60°	45°
1	43'	39'	32'10"
2	62'	60'	49'5"
3	105'	99'	79'
4	124'	120'	98'10"

Two-way traffic can be utilized when parking cars at a 90° angle. This design increases accident potential compared to one-way driving associated with 60° and 45° angle stalls. Generally, more cars can be placed per linear foot with 90° parking than with either of the other two systems.

The shopping experience should be safe and enjoyable. Do not force people to park in unsafe areas. Plan the flow of traffic to insure that customers can safely enter and exit from your premises. Customers should remember your product and services at a later time—not the hazards of finding a parking spot.

SUPPORTING A GARDEN CENTER

The purchaser of an existing business may look at the question of location differently from one planning to establish an entirely new firm. The track record of an ongoing firm can provide much information regarding potential for continued growth and prosperity. Presumably, one identified a particular business because of these factors and desirable characteristics of the community. Nevertheless, one cannot ignore the element of competition. Several new firms may have emerged in recent years with the potential of capturing a large share of the pie.

The potential buyers or planner of a new operation may benefit from one guideline pertaining to the number of residents normally required to support a garden center. A 1967 statistic provided by the Bureau of Census, U.S. Department of Commerce, much out of date, indicates that the average garden center serviced 65,000 people at that time. This figure applied to a fullfledged garden center in contrast to the host of part-time operators such as hardware and discount stores currently providing some of the products associated with garden centers. The figure can prove of some value even today in initially assessing ability of a community and section of a larger metropolitan area to support a new operation.

PERMANENCE

Garden center operators often point with pride, as they well might, to the fact that their business has occupied a specific location for a long number of years. Customers readily identify with a firm occupying the same location for a long time. Many operators are in a position to continue maintaining their historic location for years to come. Others must look forward to a change within the foreseeable future.

Land prices have risen steadily and especially in those areas being developed rapidly. Agricultural land just outside the city of Denver and near to the north-south interstate highway was selling for $4.00 a square foot in the early 1980s. Small businessmen often cannot afford the taxes placed on a retail operation situated on high priced land. A steady increase in land values often forces one to seek greener pastures for the firm.

A rapidly expanding business requires that one have adequate room for sales areas and parking. Should one retain the old site or move to a new location? The shrewd business operator must plan ahead a minimum of five years. New locations must be continually scouted just in case it becomes necessary to move. The rapidly changing world makes it imperative that one keep an open mind about business location.

SUMMARY

How important is location? There is no question that a poor decision can haunt you for many years and lead to bankruptcy. There appears to be, on the other hand, wide latitude in terms of what constitutes a good choice.

Wholesale producers of plant materials must consider soil and the environment. The absence of air and soil pollutants looms more and more important each year. Access to major highways and markets is exceptionally important to the producer shipping supplies throughout the year.

Retailers must select a location permitting them to display merchandise in proper fashion. The product and services you offer can prove so enticing that buyers will travel extra miles to your location. Focus attention on developing the best image and problems of location often fade into the background.

A prime location should be carefully considered in a shopping mall. Low rental fees should warn you of minimum foot traffic and limited sales potential. You must select a good location to capitalize on traffic generated by the mall.

Many garden center operators have benefited from locations adjacent to shopping centers and other large retailers. High traffic drawn to neighboring areas has helped increase sales with consumers stopping in while going to and from their intended shopping expedition.

Location becomes valuable only to the extent that it is capitalized upon by the retailer. An aggressive, profit-oriented retailer wisely uses all resources, including location, in building a strong, viable business. A good location features high traffic, easy access, return to major highways, good visibility, and adequate parking facilities.

Steadily increasing costs of land and rental fees make it likely that some garden center operators will have to move in the 1980s. A location in the vicinity of one or more competitors often makes good business sense. Consumers like to travel to areas featuring several firms handling similar or related products.

Specialized stores in urban areas will find a clientele largely residing in apartments and condominiums. These gardeners have special needs as they intensely "farm" terraces and window gardens.

Rental fees must be viewed as a percentage of net sales. This provides one the opportunity to compare competing locations with each other and industry averages.

Good directional signs are important to operators located off the main highways. Signs should be legible and uniform in size, color, and lettering. Do not try to include too much information on a sign or billboard.

Customers expect reasonable parking facilities including easy and safe access to and from the garden center. The lot should be well landscaped and preferably to one side of the main building.

1. What factors have an important bearing on location of wholesale florist and nursery producers? Discuss.

2. Discuss the role of location as an important factor in helping achieve success for a retail firm.

3. To what extent should rental fees guide a decision to locate or not locate in a particular building or shopping center?

4. Discuss the pros and cons of locating in new, moderately new, and mature shopping centers.

5. What problems might confront an operator of a garden center desirous of opening a store in a shopping center?

6. What type of clientele would be most attracted to a downtown location? Discuss the needs of these gardeners.

7. What advantages and concerns can be identified for firms located on bypass routes and major highways?

8. What are the advantages and disadvantages of location near a major competitor?

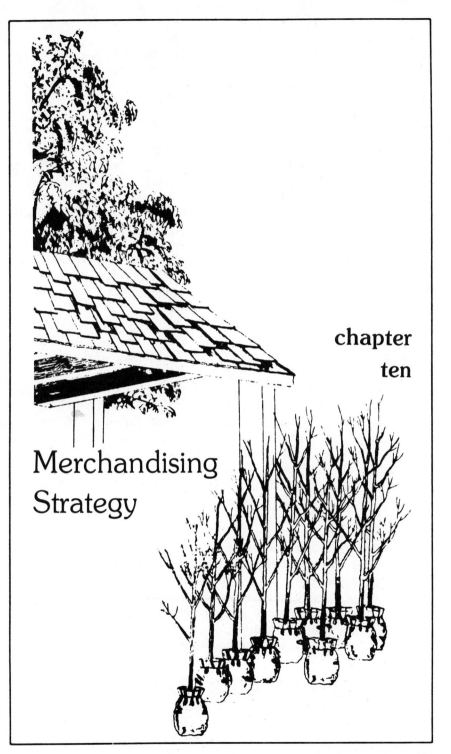

chapter
ten

Merchandising
Strategy

Merchandising strategy must occupy a major percentage of planning time from management in the garden center business as well as all other retail endeavors. It is the key ingredient in building a profitable organization capable of surviving in the highly competitive business world.

Why should someone shop at your store? This is an important question that must be asked and answered every week of the year. What do you offer that warrants consumers patronizing your firm? The market is always changing, with new competitors entering the arena each year. Their tactics may require changes in your merchandising strategy. Also, as new residents move into your community, you may find their needs and wants differ from those of your steady, old time customers. The entrance and success of mass merchants into the garden center business has had a profound impact on independent operators. Consumers do not automatically turn to traditional garden center operators for plants and supplies. Convenient shopping and attractive prices found at discount operations have captured the attention of many consumers. These factors will have great impact on your merchandising strategy.

A good merchandising strategy often will begin with an analysis of your strong points. What can you offer to consumers that makes you different from other competitors? To what degree can and will your product and services truly benefit gardeners patronizing your operation? A similar effort must be made in pinpointing the weaknesses of your operation. Does product quality, for example, truly reflect the desired image of the organization?

The same process should be employed in analyzing the strengths and weaknesses of your competitors. How do your products stand up against those of other independent operators? Can buyers recognize the differences in product quality between your operation and mass outlets?

Your strategy should capitalize on the strengths of your staff. Talented people should be used to develop sales concepts designed to attract customers and stimulate impulse sales.

Price represents a major concern of many operators confronted with a mass outlet just across the street. Merchandising strategy, in this situation, often involves price and only price in the struggle to capture attention and allegiance of gardeners.

A number of studies have been conducted over the years to determine why consumers shop at a particular location. What really seems important to shoppers? Surprisingly, price often ranks rather low. Surveys have shown that quality, variety of selection, convenience, and store atmosphere all rank above price in influencing shopping patterns of many buyers. Garden center operators can and should take advantage of these considerations when formulating merchandising strategy for their firms.

BUSINESS PHILOSOPHY

How many flats of bedding plants or poinsettias will you order for the coming season? Garden center operators like many business people seem to fall into one of three categories when ordering merchandise. A small group of operators rely extensively on sales from the previous year to guide current decisions. In fact, suppliers often remind them of the exact order and find that purchases remain relatively stable from year to year. This group continually looks at business trends with a suspicious eye. They tend to be highly conservative and anticipate a depression each spring or just before each major holiday. Their philosophy seems to be one of minimizing unsold merchandise and losses rather than on maximizing profits. The second group probably includes the largest number of operators. They tend to play it down the center of the road. Sales from the previous year and recent retail trends influence the purchasing practices for plants and supply items. These operators often have been prone to increase purchases just a moderate amount over the previous year. They recognize that growth must be recorded to stay even with inflation. Nevertheless, a cautious approach can be anticipated from this group.

A small number of business people maintain a highly optimistic view toward the state of business. Their actions often confuse competitors and keep them off balance each holiday and spring. How can they buy heavily and advertise so extensively when the rest of us anticipate only fair business? The secret of success really amounts to a good dose of common sense, an awareness of the business climate, and a positive attitude toward the garden center business. These ingredients, especially the latter, often elude the operator bordering on bankruptcy or remaining on the fringes of success.

The florist industry traditionally has relied on holiday business for a large percentage of its gross sales. A majority of retailers cut back purchases in February of 1976 anticipating poor Valentine's Day sales. A few aggressive retailers recognized that consumers had spent money during December and undoubtedly would buy flowers for Valentine's Day. They stocked up on merchandise and recorded excellent sales. Most retailers were bewildered by the rush of business in February and some took their phones off the hook. They couldn't handle business without any merchandise. Surprisingly, many operators remained highly conservative preparing for Easter and Mother's Day in the same year. The strong response of consumers in February could have signaled better than average sales later in the spring.

One of the major wire services associated with the floral industry prepares forecasts for each major holiday. Too many business operators have remained skeptical of this information and have relied on their own conservative analysis of business trends. They have not benefited from optimistic projections often advanced by this organization.

A positive approach often goes hand in hand with a course designed to achieve maximum growth for a firm. Purchase decisions have been made with one eye on a realistic appraisal of the business environment. The second eye focuses attention on sales necessary to achieve stated growth for a month, holiday, or period of time. How many flats of bedding plants, geraniums, or poinsettias will you have to sell in order to reach your sales objectives? Your merchandising strategy must be built on a positive philosophy. Every facet of the operation, whether you are a grower, a wholesaler, or a retailer, will reflect the attitudes and enthusiasm of the top position in the organization.

BUSINESS HOURS

Store hours should reflect consumer shopping patterns, action by competitors, and the hours of neighboring shops in small and large shopping centers. Extended hours are the name of the game during spring planting season in the same fashion that other retailers cater to business in December for the Christmas season. Community standards may have a bearing on stores doing business on Sunday. The so-called "blue laws" in many areas have been repealed and Sunday store hours have become quite common. Some small communities frown on stores remaining open on Sunday and most if not all retailers abide by the standards.

Store hours must reflect those of competitors and nearby shops. Retailers occupying sites in a shopping center must often abide by business hours established by the local association. Nearby competitors featuring long hours may, in turn, trigger comparable practices by other firms. This can be carried to the extreme with food chains operating 24 hours a day.

The independent operator must develop a policy that largely reflects the needs of his or her customers. Store hours based largely on the needs of the proprietor and staff can adversely affect the image of the firm. A large operator in Toronto, Canada reports that over half his sales occur on weekends, especially Sunday. The extent to which these sales could be made upon other days of the week in the event of Sunday closing is highly questionable. Consumers might shop at competitors or delay long enough to miss the best time for planting.

PRODUCT CYCLE

Products also go through various growth stages from introduction to decline and ultimate disappearance from the scene. Sales can be expected to remain low during the introductory period. A good product or service begins to gain momentum and sales rise in dramatic fashion during the growth period or second stage.

The nature of the product and extent to which it is a fad largely determines the point at which it enters the maturity period. Once there, it could stay for an extended period of time or rapidly move out of the picture. A product in the sales decline stage has little appeal to most operators. It may yield some profits to the few individuals who remain in the picture to service a specified group of consumers. Some of our older tomato cultivars would fall into this category.

Hanging baskets and green plants seemingly were given a new life in the early and mid-1970s. They had been relegated to the third and possibly fourth stages when consumers suddenly saw them as "new" and interesting products. A new generation of buyers helped propel both groupings of merchandise back through the introductory stage and into the growth period in a matter of one or two years. Sales rose at a phenomenal rate for several years. Both product groupings moved into the mature stage in or around 1977. Terrariums and sand gardens enjoyed great popularity in the same period. The latter especially moved rapidly from the introductory to the declining stage in just a few short years.

Seed geraniums occupied the introductory stage for something approaching a decade. They just didn't take off in most parts of the country until 1976. The introduction of several cultivars spurred new interest and sales suddenly blossomed. Industry projections heard at national meetings of bedding plant growers suggest that seed geraniums will command almost 50 percent of the market in the 1980's. This crop can be expected to occupy the mature stage for many years to come.

BUYING COOPERATIVES

One of the prime tasks of an independent garden center operator is to distinguish his or her firm from all other competitors. This is especially important when faced with strong competition from mass outlets. A prime strategy involves acquiring unique merchandise that appears far different from that offered by competitors. There often comes a time, however, when some form of cooperation must be considered to survive threats of extinction from large mass outlets.

Independent operators in some areas have joined together formally and informally in buying supply items and advertising on a cooperative basis. This action has been prompted by the nature and extent of competition arising from large scale retail organizations in the garden center business. One such organization consists of eight firms. Brand names have been established for products such as grass seed and fertilizers. They have effectively countered attractive prices offered by discount firms using their own name brands.

Supply items such as pesticides have been purchased in large quantities assuring individual members of prime discounts. This action has enabled members to compete more effectively with discounters in the same market. Plant materials also have been purchased on an individual basis. Members have maintained their independent identity through procurement of perishable material.

A key factor in the success of this cooperative has been the agreement to support an advertising program. Large advertisements have appeared in local newspapers throughout the spring season. These announcements have compared favorably in size to those sponsored by large scale competitors. Members of this organization fortunately service distinct areas in the metropolitan market. The normal concerns of competition or competitive spirit among members have been more than countered by their newfound ability to compete effectively with the giants.

ADDING VALUE

There are occasions when an operator can enhance the appeal of a product by adding some value in terms of a related product or service. The final price provides added profit in addition to covering new costs. One retail operator has decorated green plants with a variety of moderately large and colorful insects. A large, gaily colored lady beetle focuses consumer attention on a particular display of green plants. These products can be acquired at many supply houses servicing retail florists.

Retailers handling fresh flowers should provide a package of a preservative to enhance the life of the product. Small packages have been available for use by consumers.

An inexpensive brochure on care of green plants can be provided at no cost with purchases exceeding a specific dollar value. A wire service associated with the florist industry has produced a special publication on green and flowering plants for its members. This product can be sold or given free to consumers. Green plants could be shifted to decorative plastic or clay containers. This practice might be adopted for selected items and especially those found in a variety of competing outlets.

A small package of house plant fertilizer can be offered at a reduced price with each purchase of a foliage plant. The added sale essentially occurs without a comparable increase in operating costs. Similar programs can be devised when merchandising nursery products and other plant materials. Flowering plants can be decorated with colorful foil. This practice normally has been associated with retail florists in contrast to the bare product sold by many discount outlets. The added touch supplied by aggressive merchandisers has played an important role in stimulating sales and profits.

Look for ways of making your products and services just a little different from those offered by competitors. A small package of floral preservative can prove to be the difference in a firm's effort to build weekly sales of fresh flowers.

OFFERING CHOICES

A technique employed by some enterprising operators has involved sale of a small volume of material at prices competitive with those offered by large discounters. This merchandise may be acquired from a special source or from material selected from regular supplies. The special group of plants can be located on a display table nearby quality merchandise.

The story has been told by a well respected florist of his frustrations to counter sidewalk peddlers who arrived each Memorial Day to sell peonies. This flower was used extensively in decorating graves. The peddlers purchased poor quality flowers and priced them well below the retail florist. One year the retailer finally took some drastic action. He bruised and battered a couple dozen flowers. They were placed in a bucket of water outside the shop and advertised at a price below that of the sidewalk peddlers. A sign "proudly" proclaimed the attractive price. Customers came into his shop and quickly compared the "special" to quality blooms. They made a quick decision to buy his normal line of merchandise. You should be careful when handling products that differ greatly from the normal image of the firm. The competitive spirit must be kept in bounds so that it doesn't undermine the foundation of the organization.

CLOSE-OUT SPECIALS

Memorial Day was often regarded by many operators as the close of the spring planting season. This applied primarily to bedding plants. Special sales were advertised in early June and annually attracted attention of many gardeners. It really wasn't too late to plant flowers and tomatoes in many northern areas. The early sale often worked against the best interests of the operators. Customers delayed purchasing plants with the knowledge that a two for one sale was just around the corner. These sales started disappearing from the scene in the 1960s. Shrewd operators recognized that they actually were not accomplishing the intended goal. A new day arrived when some operators programmed for a profitable market in June with material at normal prices. Some gardeners lost an early crop, others just had the opportunity to plant around a new home and still others had been busy with spring cleaning chores.

Memorial Day sales do capture attention. This operator on the outskirts of a major metropolitan area has effectively used a map along with the special sale to attract attention.

Greenhouse operators in the north have come to recognize that they can produce June plants at much less the cost than an early May crop. Warmer temperatures and increased light intensity help hasten the development of the crop.

Close-out specials have been an important tool for those operators needing space for other activities and crops. The value of extending a normal season must be weighed against utilization of space for other, more profitable enterprises. Perishable products must be moved before they have declined to the point of being candidates for the compost pile. Store personnel should continually monitor plants and adjust prices to reflect condition and shelf life. A policy should be formulated and clearly understood by all personnel regarding specials designed to reduce inventory and minimize losses.

COMBINATION SALES

Many opportunities for increased business exist for those willing to focus attention on combination sales. This added effort increases sales and at the same time can prove most beneficial to consumers. For example, hospital arrangements have played an important role in the sales picture for retail florists. A growing number of firms feature weekly or seasonal specials.

They may take the form of potted plants or more likely arrangements of fresh flowers in an attractive and unusual container. The recipient of the gift takes the container home and fills it periodically with fresh rather than permanent flowers.

A second option has not been employed by many retailers. Patients have a great deal of time on their hands during their stay in the hospital and possibly at home. Why not a combination special that features an arrangement or plant with a book? A simple guide to flower arranging might be appropriate for a woman. Pruning trees and shrubs and care of the lawn might appeal to men. A large number of combination specials can be dreamed up for the outdoor and indoor gardener including:

1. Rose clippers with each rose bush
2. Rose bush and fertilizer, insecticide – fungicide combination or peat moss
3. Rose bush and book or bulletin on culture of roses
4. Green plant and slow release or liquid fertilizer
5. Green plant and book on culture of plants
6. Shrubs and tree with pruning clippers
7. Annuals and garden hand tool
8. Grass seed and fertilizer
9. Lawn fertilizer and herbicide as separate products
10. Fresh flowers and preservative

Merchandising-minded retailers continue to look for ways of stimulating sales. Combination sales should be part of your marketing strategy.

CONTAINERS

Plastic containers have become a standard item in the industry for bedding plants. They are cheap, lightweight, and require little room for storage. Clay pots have all but disappeared in many areas. The type of container employed for a particular crop may help a firm differentiate its operation from that of other competitors. Consider the following when opportunities arise in terms of choice of container:

1. Inexpensive containers often break, spilling out plants. The rough edges represent a real danger to the hands of gardeners. Sturdy containers and those without sharp corners should command attention of quality operators.
2. Try to avoid containers that are used by suppliers of mass outlets. It may be difficult to justify premium prices when identical containers have been used by firms focusing attention on inexpensive merchandise.

Attractive and sturdy market pack containers help capture customers' interest and will increase sales.

A few firms have adopted styrofoam units that are sturdy and colorful. It looks and feels like a quality product. The same situation also applies to clay pots. A quality operation will not cut corners in selecting containers. The initial impact can have a bearing on unit price and customer allegiance even though the containers are discarded in a few minutes. Some firms have responded to increased production costs by purchasing inexpensive containers. This practice may backfire for the operator trying to develop a quality image. You must be consistent in all phases of your merchandising program.

COUPONS

Food manufacturers send out thousands of coupons each year to attract the attention of shoppers. Local food stores insert their own coupons in weekly advertisements, often in cooperation with manufacturers. A major manufacturer of hair beauty products has offered $10 worth of coupons simply for sending 25 cents and the label from one of their products.

One may anticipate approximately a 5 or 6 percent return on coupons, providing they offer something of value to gardeners.

Coupons have been and will continue to be big business. Coupons have been used by retailers, producers, and manufacturers for a variety of reasons. A six percent return would be considered a fairly normal coupon return rate. Garden center operators can adopt this practice for one or more of the following:

1. To introduce new products. Consumers often need to be tempted to buy a new product. They have no basis on which to invest dollars in a plant of unknown value. Seedsmen have stated that geraniums from seed will dominate the market by the early 1980s. Aggressive merchandisers might score some points by offering a coupon in which one free plant is given to a customer with the purchase of four units. An alternative approach would involve offering a 25-cent to 50-cent discount on the first plant. A new line of

pesticides might be merchandised through use of coupons, as might early purchase of seed packets or lawn fertilizers.

2. To stimulate sales of "old" products. Coffee manufacturers utilize this concept when introducing a new brewing process or formula. One often has the impression that it is only a tool to capture attention rather than a new and distinctly different process.

3. To measure the effectiveness of advertising. The number of coupons returned to the store helps measure the effectiveness of an advertising campaign. This would pertain primarily to direct mail and newspapers.

The response of consumers partially reflects the advertising medium and its impact along with actual value of the particular item. A coffee coupon provides 50 cents savings while a neighboring advertisement carries a coupon worth 5 cents. Will the 5-cent saving motivate the consumer to tear out the coupon? Relatively small savings may result in low return rates. A second factor deals with the product. Breakfast food coupons probably attract a great deal of attention because of frequent purchases. The same situation applies to soaps.

A coupon for a pack of petunias, especially a new cultivar, should command more attention than one for lobelia. An early season sale of poinsettias could be spurred by a coupon. What do you do if a customer comes in and has forgotten the coupon? Food stores show no mercy. An independent operator might adopt a more flexible position. This is an area that could differentiate the store from large scale competitors. The "I care for you" approach and image is worth much more than the value of the coupon.

DO-IT-YOURSELF

A number of kits are sold containing various types of plant materials. One unit contains daffodils that can be forced indoors. The kit contains pebbles, a container, and bulbs. An enterprising retailer started several the moment they arrived in the store. Customers were stimulated to buy after seeing the ease of handling a colorful product. The display was responsible for many impulse sales and helped decorate the store with plants. Less imaginative managers would have relied on the colorful box to sell the unit. Similar opportunities exist for the sale of amaryllis in mid-winter and starter seed sets in spring. The latter can be employed throughout the year for slow-growing flowers and selected herbs. The added touch marks your operation as a classy and quality outfit. Try making an extra effort to capture attention of buyers. Use your own products and allow them to work for you in generating impulse sales.

Spring flowering bulbs
such as the daffodil can
be started and forced into
bloom to stimulate sales
in mid-winter.

GREENHOUSE

A greenhouse represents one of the strongest drawing cards attracting customers to many independent operations throughout the country. Consumers
often conclude that all plant materials were produced on the premises. One
feels a warm glow walking into a greenhouse in mid-winter and during the
spring season. Everything looks green and healthy. Contrast this picture
and image with that of a discount operation and garden centers featuring
only steel buildings. Independent operators should capitalize on this extremely
important asset. The facility should be maintained in top shape for the convenience of customers.

A growing number of operators have designated one greenhouse to serve
as a sales area. This can be used in the spring and for displaying merchandise
at major holidays throughout the year. The inside of the unit often has been

An attractive greenhouse draws the attention of new and experienced gardeners.

gutted and a peninsula-style bench system constructed for the benefit of consumers.

The emphasis must be on convenience for customers. You can capitalize on the greenhouse only if it is made attractive to shoppers. Then you have a distinct advantage over firms operating without a structure. Promote the fact that you have a greenhouse and that customers can see plants in various stages of development.

INSTANT COLOR

A variety of factors influences the type of plant, in terms of maturity, required by gardeners in your market area. The grower must analyze consumer needs before programming a crop for instant color, a touch of color, or essentially all green.

Apartment and condominium dwellers often procure small quantities of plant materials. They like to see instant color and frequently gravitate to premium quality merchandise. Their entire needs may consist of one large impatiens basket, a super geranium, and possibly a few petunias. They work with a small area and desire a big splash of color instantly. A few green plants will look quite anemic on a balcony early in the season.

All types of gardeners generally require near specimen plants when purchasing materials mid- to late-season. Some growers have produced six-inch sized containers of petunias and marigolds for this special need. The gardener simply does not have time to wait for a seedling or young plant to reach the mature and colorful stage.

Four-inch sized containers featuring well developed and flowering bedding plants have been produced in increasing quantities by growers throughout the country. The consumer must pay a higher price for this commodity in contrast to a pack of four or six units. These superior plants often occupy more space than younger materials. The gardener may need only two good petunias to fill an area normally requiring twice or three times the number of young plants.

An argument can be advanced for marketing plants in the green stage early in the growing season. This would have most appeal to gardeners requiring more than a few plants and not demanding instant color. A green plant normally is much easier to handle. There is less opportunity for injury to occur in transit. The plant can be produced in a shorter period of time which helps keep costs in line. Colored labels, currently used by most quality firms, can help consumers make decisions regarding choice of cultivars. Sample plants forced earlier can serve as examples for the potential of green plants. All parties would seem to benefit from the sale of this material.

The buying public has become convinced that a saleable geranium must have at least one open flower and that a pack of petunias must have color. The emphasis on color has stimulated sale of plants that do not always have the body and substance to continue production of flowers. A single bloom on a geranium plant will disappear in a week or two. What happens if it was borne on a single-stemmed plant? Future blooms will be delayed until the plant grows and develops branches. Contrast this geranium with a multiple-branched plant, perhaps without any color at time of sale. The latter will prove to be much more productive throughout late spring, summer, and early fall.

The rising cost of bedding materials may stimulate some growers to sell plants in the green stage. A lower price for more immature material hopefully will capture attention of the consumer.

There is a legitimate need for plants somewhere between the green and instant color stages. Compact, well branched plants showing a touch of color combine the important assets of green and fully mature petunias and marigolds. The spotlight focuses on potential for rapid development of plants in the immediate future. The touch of color combined with a four-color label should capture the fancy and imagination of most gardeners.

GUARANTEES

A discussion on guarantees can be found in Chapter 8. Some additional comments appear appropriate in this chapter. The philosophy adopted toward customers will have a significant bearing on the nature and extent of guarantees. Those operators suspicious of customers and their complaints will adopt very conservative policies. They are likely to erect signs proclaiming the consumer takes responsibility once the product leaves the premises. A more enlightened view recognizes that consumers are basically honest and some products fail to live up to their expectations. This applies both to perishable and nonperishable products.

Progressive garden center operators try to build a reputation on the basis of product guarantees. Consumer confidence is highly important to any organization and it can be strengthened when consumers learn you stand behind the product without question. The guarantee program can and should work equally well with perishable plants and hard goods. Several success stories testify to this conclusion.

    1.   Retail florists have promoted early sales of the poinsettia plant by guaranteeing them to bloom throughout the holiday season. Knowledgeable retailers

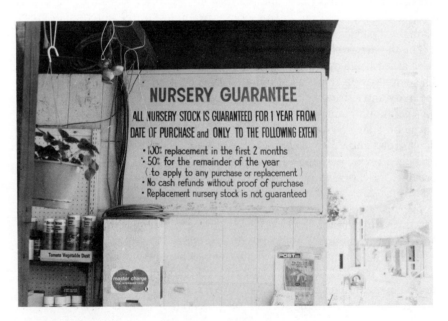

A good guarantee inspires customers' confidence, creates goodwill, and assures return business.

recognize that new cultivars last several months with ordinary care. Requests for new plants or refunds have fallen well below one percent. The guarantee helped one retailer significantly increase sales and to meet sales targets for the month. This one element played an important role in overall strategy adopted by management.

2. A successful garden center operator has guaranteed all plants including spring bedding material. The sales staff has been instructed to fulfill all requests without asking any questions. Staff time is important and management doesn't want a pack of petunias to destroy future sales and a close relationship between customers and the firm. The number of refunds has not exceeded a fraction of one percent.

3. Petunias, a major bedding crop, normally have been hardened by producers before sales at the beginning of the season. The process simply involves gradual exposure to cold temperatures. One operator promotes "frost free" petunias each spring. He has differentiated his product from that of other competitors only in terms of the guarantee and catchy wording.

4. A manufacturer of an inexpensive plastic raincoat printed a "lifetime" guarantee on the plastic wrap. This stimulated one person to buy the unit and then discard the written guarantee. The rationale was that the manufacturer had confidence in the product and thus it wasn't necessary to retain the plastic bag.

Some firms have offered conditional guarantees that provide some protection to consumers. A garden chain operator has placed a fairly large tag on each foliage plant spelling out the store guarantees. It informs you that the operator guarantees only that quality plants have been placed on display tables. The buyer assumes all risks from that point on. The green plant guarantee looks impressive and may convince some buyers to make a purchase. A quick inspection of plants on display reveals that store personnel have been lax in maintaining some items. Some plants should have been discarded and others appear on the verge of departing for the trash pile. Guarantees are good only to the extent that the retailer fulfills his or her part of the bargain. The guarantee tag looks suspicious when products fail to meet specifications outlined in the statement.

Do you still have questions about guaranteeing products? Ask yourself the question, "Why do virtually all manufacturers and retailers, including supermarkets, provide guarantees for a wide range of merchandise?" You can return a steak to most food stores if it does not come up to par. The investment in a loyal clientele is so great that no one wants to risk loss of a customer because of a poor experience with one product. Guarantees tell consumers that you have confidence in your products and services. They represent an important element in helping assure success of merchandising programs.

INFORMATION

One of the best merchandising tools for independent operators relates to information on gardening offered to consumers. The thirst for information seems endless, especially for new gardeners. What can you do to service the multifaceted needs of consumers? A small library can be maintained on the premises for use by customers throughout the year. An investment of $200 can prove highly profitable in terms of customer allegiance to the organization. Garden books can be sold to produce a profit and to serve needs of customers. Some care should be exercised in selecting quality publications to reflect the image of your firm.

Some firms have made available a variety of free pamphlets on various crops and gardening practices. The material may be purchased at modest cost from your local university extension service or the United States Department of Agriculture. These circulars can be reproduced at a local fast copy

Gardeners have an insatiable appetite for information. Be sure your garden center is supplied with books and pamphlets for sale and as a customer service. The more customers know, the more they will appreciate the quality of your operation.

facility without obtaining special permission from the original author or organization. Literature may be produced by one or more talented members of the organization. This material can be reproduced at minimum cost. A number of firms have prepared in-store material to help educate the consumer. These charts and posters should be employed to help answer questions and stimulate sales.

Some organizations have provided speakers for local garden meetings. The extension organization in your area often conducts noncredit classes on various phases of indoor and outdoor gardening. Local speakers from commercial organizations have contributed time in helping teach classes. The "dial-a-garden" tip concept has been employed by a few enterprising operators. This system employs a series of recorded messages made available to gardeners via the telephone.

Store personnel represent one of the major assets attracting customers to a garden center. How knowledgeable are they in responding to most garden questions? Have they been trained to respond intelligently to common questions relating to lawns, flowers, vegetables, and shrubs? "Gardening Illustrated,"[1] written by Lou and Miriam Berninger, was designed specifically to aid garden center operators in training store personnel.

Newspaper and radio advertisements can be informative and help answer many questions coming from gardeners. One operator offers a daily tip on radio and has generated a large audience. Good information and personnel willing to service customer needs can prove highly important in attracting gardeners to a particular outlet. This part of your merchandising program should command special attention from management.

LABELS

A variety of labels has been employed by producers to aid in identifying packs and flats of bedding plants. Some operators have stapled one label to a flat. The simplest approach has been to use a black waterproof pencil to write the cultivar name on the flat or pack. Plain wooden or plastic labels have been inserted by some growers into packs. These efforts involve a minimum cost and contribute little to overall impact on consumers.

A more enlightened approach employs colored labels available from a variety of supply firms. These contain a picture of the cultivar, name, and cultural directions. One label should be inserted into each pack of plants. The four-color labels go against the grain of some cost-conscious operators. They reason that the consumer may discard the label at planting time. "Who cares if they remember purchasing Blushing Maid or Coral Sea petunias?"

[1] Which can be obtained from NASCO, Fort Atkinson, Wisconsin 53538.

Surprisingly, there appears to be a significant number of discriminating gardeners interested in names, and their numbers have been increasing yearly. Attractive and instructive labels perform almost the same function for bedding plants as colorful boxes in selling cornflakes. A distinctive label represents an added touch that distinguishes an independent, quality-oriented firm from one that provides little service to its customers.

The geranium has been one product commonly ignored by producers and retailers in terms of cultivar identification. The industry has pretty much concluded that consumers want only red, white, pink, and salmon colored blossoms. Rarely will you see someone promote a specific cultivar. The sale of red and white geraniums really does little to spark the imagination of consumers. Contrast this philosophy with that of rose operators who coin stimulating names like Samantha. You rarely buy a red or pink rose. These operators spend many dollars creating attractive names and then capitalize on them in their promotional programs.

One might conclude that geranium cultivars have not been named or bear unattractive labels. This is not true. Many geraniums, such as Sincerity, Sprinter, Scarlet Flash, and Carefree, can and will capture attention when consumers have been given an opportunity to request specific cultivars. The opportunity has been there for those willing to capitalize on cultivar names. Labeling geraniums should command more and more attention as

Good labels help answer many consumer questions and in the process save a great deal of time for your staff.

retail prices climb above $1.25 a plant in a 4½-inch pot. This price tag undoubtedly has generated some consumer resistance to geraniums. An attractive label and identification of cultivar should help to stimulate sales and overcome some resistance to price.

PROFIT-ORIENTED MERCHANDISING

Merchandising programs have been hampered by elimination of various products because of limited or nonexistent profits. The florist industry has been adversely affected by the disappearance of many fresh flower crops such as lily of the valley and sweet peas. Fortunately, some flowering plant crops such as primula and cineraria have made a comeback in recent years. The trend had been to eliminate minor crops in favor of only a few select items that seemingly produced the highest profits.

A popular item for many garden center-greenhouse operators in past years involved the sale of decorated urns for cemetery plots. Memorial Day was the signal to roll out urns planted with geraniums, petunias, dracaena and other spring crops. This was regarded as a highly profitable part of the spring business. Three factors have contributed to the decline of urns. (1) Labor has proven to be a major concern for operators faced with a multitude of tasks each spring. (2) An extra effort often has been required to find grave plots. Older help who remembered the exact location of each account have retired. A great deal of time must now be expended in delivering orders. (3) The third stumbling block relates to standard retail prices. They just have not moved up reflecting overall costs for the product and services.

The problem could be solved providing that a creative merchandising program was devised by interested operators. First, delivery time could be modified. Containers could be delivered within a 10-day period around Memorial Day. This would provide more flexibility and remove stress from the seller. High school students can be employed to plant the urns. Inexpensive labor can handle this task in a competent manner. One of the real keys lies in constructing a realistic price schedule for the product and service. This must reflect all costs and a reasonable profit. An aggressive promotion program should be initiated to contact interested parties desiring to decorate a family grave. A system should be devised to simplify the process of finding locations in each cemetery. Special identification tags might be employed in cooperation with cemetery personnel.

This situation has been examined to illustrate the technique that might be employed in solving a problem associated with a particular product or service. Unprofitable items frequently reflect an unwillingness to explore alternatives to the traditional way of doing business.

A real problem arises when large competitors sell merchandise at prices near or below the product costs available to many independent operators. Should you stock merchandise knowing that it will be impossible to earn a profit on selected items? A small volume of a popular item might be stocked purely as a service to valued customers. The retail price may be a compromise between a competitor's and that based on a normal margin for the operation.

Aggressive operators will search for substitutes or other brands of merchandise that can be featured at attractive prices and produce normal profits. This situation often applies to fertilizers advertised for turf. Some independent operators have had sufficient volume to produce their own brand label. Other operators have cooperated in developing and promoting a private label in competition with nationally advertised brands.

Newness

One of the cornerstones of the garden center business has been the introduction of new items to the trade each year. The All-America Award program was conceived by the seed trade as a mechanism for generating yearly publicity for highly rated introductions. The National Garden Bureau, underwritten by seed companies, issues reams of press material about bedding and vegetable plants. Comparable programs have been undertaken by rose and gladiolus organizations.

Newness is one of the truly strong selling points that captures the attention of gardeners. Tell someone it's new and they have visions of it's being superior to existing cultivars in terms of color, aroma, and overall performance. They have an opportunity to be first in their neighborhood and will proudly point out the plant to all friends and visitors. The aggressive operator capitalizes on this merchandising tool. Special signs should be devised calling attention to all new introductions regardless of whether they have or have not been a recipient of an All-America Award. A special table can be placed in a prime location with samples of all new plants and products.

You cannot assume that customers instantly recognize new introductions. Some people arrive on the scene remembering that a new pink rose was publicized in a recent article. Other gardeners forgot the story and their memory must be stimulated to recall the information. A fairly large number of gardeners may not have been exposed to publicity releases about the All-America Awards and other new introductions. You can create a desire right at the moment they are shopping at the store. A good promotional program on the scene demonstrates your enthusiasm with new introductions.

The attention of gardeners can be captured by establishing premium prices for new products. You can justify the price on the basis of higher seed or

Breeders from around the world are bringing forth a wealth of new plants each year. A special effort should be made to promote new items, especially All America winners.

cutting costs. The higher price demonstrates clearly that there must be something unique to warrant the premium. Discount and large chain operations may or may not acquire new introductions each year. A premium price often discourages discount buyers from handling these products. They have some difficulty recapturing costs since little emphasis has been placed on cultivar identification. The pricing schedule calls for one basic price and provides little flexibility to recoup costs associated with new introductions.

Independent operators occupy an enviable position when it comes to newness. They have a great deal of flexibility in establishing prices for all plant materials. Customers really expect to find a little more service in comparison to discount firms relative to new introductions. A premium price for All-America winners almost serves as a status symbol for dedicated gardeners. They may even suspect something is wrong should the price of a new item be at the same level as older introductions.

Open Houses

Gardeners are at a fever pitch during the first warm spell each spring. In fact, they often seem to need just an excuse to start the blood flowing for a new season. Some operators have given gardeners just the right tonic by holding an open house. The event provides an opportunity to see the new "models" of plants for the coming year. This obviously works best when one has a greenhouse.

A free plant, such as a coleus or small marigold, may be given to each person. Some firms have offered a door prize. Visitor names should be kept on file for use in developing a direct mail listing. Large plant materials such as hanging baskets and tree geraniums may be purchased early and tagged for pick-up at a later time. Pansies, an early season crop, may be ready for sale. This is a good time to promote seeds.

The open house substitutes for a garden show in many communities. Customers can bring their cameras and spend many pleasurable hours photographing a variety of flowers. At least one operator specifically features a camera day. Where else in most communities can you take pictures of flowers in late winter or early spring besides a greenhouse?

The open house represents one more effort of promotion-minded merchants to attract people into their place of business. Sure, it takes time and lots of hard work, but how else can you build an image, sales, and profits?

Package Programs

A wholesale producer of bedding plants expanded his operation from a small, part-time operation to a multi-acre facility and a year-round business. The new program was designed to service large discount organizations. A primary concern was the creation of a marketing scheme that would minimize competition from other firms and at the same time insure reasonable prices and profits. There has been something of a cut-throat nature to this business with individuals willing to shave a few pennies off published prices to attract business. The individual in question was shrewd enough to realize that success of his operation could hinge on the actions of a host of competitors. A program was founded providing a unique service to buyers. While it could be copied, the prime ingredients ran counter to the philosophy and actions of most growers. The plan involved the following:

1. Production of quality material
2. Production of a wide assortment and large volume of merchandise insuring that virtually all buyer needs could be fulfilled
3. Erection of display greenhouses on the property of retail establishments serviced by the grower

4. Twice weekly shipments during the busy season
5. Inventory maintained by grower personnel
6. Promotional package including advertising copy and plant materials produced for special sales

Phases one and two are comparable to programs developed by most aggressive firms seeking to attract business from mass outlets. Buyers representing large operations demand a uniform product. They have steadily upgraded quality specifications partially reflecting their own increased awareness of plant materials. The erection of a small display greenhouse has proven to be a key ingredient in the formula employed by this firm. Consumers do respond to greenhouses in a very positive fashion. It suggests a home or locally produced product. Plants can be protected from adverse weather conditions. Their shelf life normally has been extended, resulting in fewer losses and sales of distressed material. Consumers can shop in relative comfort in an enclosed structure. Contrast this with typical displays on a sidewalk or parking lot. The greenhouse structure has been erected at no charge, providing the retailer purchases a minimum volume of merchandise. All of the plant materials have been procured by cooperating retailers from this one supplier.

A variety of common inventory problems has been removed from the shoulders of inexperienced buyers associated with discount operations. The ability to control inventory has played a major role in assuring success and profits for all parties. The creation of a promotional program has provided frosting on the cake. The schedule of proposed advertisements and specials has been based on knowledge of the planting season and desires of consumers.

This case study has been offered as an example of an organization creating a merchandising program to meet specific needs of a consumer group. The strategy devised included elements normally considered outside the activity of wholesale producers. The key to success lies in the fact that competing producers have shied away from special services to mass outlets. Future success can be anticipated because few if any competitors seem inclined to duplicate key provisions of the program. This is a situation where one firm has offered a unique or differentiated product and in reality has gained a near monopoly on some segments of the business.

Pick-It-Yourself

Garden centers commonly run into slow periods during the middle of the summer. This is a slack period occurring after the heavy planting season and before starting new lawns in late summer and early fall. Aggressive operators continue to look for ways of generating income to stay in the black or at least break even. The sale of fresh produce has generated exceptional income during summer and fall months for many roadside marketers. One garden center operator in a northern state contracts with area farmers for fresh produce including sweet corn, tomatoes, potatoes, and pumpkins. Many people started patronizing the operation for the produce and then turned into steady buyers for plant materials and related services.

Another individual started out as a roadside gardener and then moved into the garden center business. A slightly different wrinkle involves a pick-it-yourself operation for strawberries and many vegetable crops. People come from all directions to pick fresh, well grown merchandise. One has the feeling that many urbanites want an opportunity to return to nature.

Some facets of the Christmas tree business also have been based on the desire of many consumers to have closer contact with the land. A number of operations have appeared where you can harvest your own tree. Just think of the joys of tramping around five acres in ten-degree weather looking for the perfect tree! Don't laugh, the program has worked and provided good income to people while satisfying the inner needs of many consumers.

Prices

Independent operators have varied in their philosophy and actions regarding the use of specific prices in an advertisement. Some operators stand toe to toe with discount competitors and slug it out on the basis of price. Other operators seem to be reluctant to post prices. They may list a host of items or focus attention on one or two products.

Two advertisements appearing almost back to back in a local newspaper help illustrate the use and impact of price. One advertisement contained three excellent line drawings of popular plants, good open space, and the words, "20% off regular price." What was the regular price? It's conceivable that the discount, while substantial, really didn't have much value since plants were overpriced prior to the sale. A second firm advertised a truck load sale of green plants at greatly reduced prices. The advertisement contained a line drawing of a truck with all essential information on the side of the vehicle. The retailer identified eight specific plants along with information on pot size, regular prices, and special prices. The reader could see at a glance whether or not the sale contained some really good buys. Posting of the regular price permitted one to compare with those commonly charged by competing firms.

Discount firms have recognized that their appeal often has been based on low, attractive prices. They continually hammer away and support this strong point by posting prices in their advertisements. Independent operators often find themselves at a disadvantage in competing with the giants. They may prefer to compete on the basis of service and quality. There are times when specific prices should appear in print. Special sales lose impact when buyers remain vague about prices.

PRODUCT MIX

Independent operators must focus attention on product mix as a primary means of competing with large organizations. This pertains both to plant materials and hard goods merchandise. Chain operations have frequently focused attention on bread-and-butter items. They tend to minimize risks and losses by handling only those items in great demand by gardeners. This leaves a great deal of room for aggressive, independent operators to maneuver and capture a profitable share of the business.

Seed racks are available from a number of firms and a variety of assortments have been packed by distributors. Popular items dominate most displays including those found in mass outlets. Relatively few, if any, new cultivars may be included in this type of mix. Those operators catering to quality conscious gardeners should request newer cultivars. Unusual vegetables, annuals, and perennial flowers may be included in this type of mix. A special effort should be made to acquire wildflower seeds as an increasing number of gardeners have started growing these attractive and unusual plants.

A small selection of nursery stock generally has been procured by buyers representing some of our larger discount operations. They have focused attention on inexpensive and common items available to consumers. Locally grown nursery stock should be heavily promoted by independent operators. This material should survive the rigors of the local environment. The added cost represents only a minor investment when prorated over a ten-year period.

A special effort should be made to acquire trees and shrubs recommended by your local agricultural extension office. These recommendations, including a listing of vegetables, turf, and some flowers, are publicized annually in newspapers, on radio and television, at meetings and through distribution of brochures.

The development of an attractive lawn is important to many home owners. Quality seed mixes represent the best investment for the inexperienced as well as experienced gardener. The cost of seed accounts for only a small percentage of all expenditures associated with planting and establishing a good stand of turf around the home. You can build a loyal clientele by avoiding cheap products and selling the merits of a recommended grass mix.

A good product mix for rose bushes includes bare root, potted, and those potted and in full flower. The discriminating buyer has a choice both in terms of price and maturity of plant. A good selection would include the latest All-America winners.

Common items such as dahlias, gladiolus, and tulips can be found in most retail stores. One has much more difficulty in locating sources of minor crops such as muscari and anemone. Indoor gardeners have started to force a variety of bulbs such as hyacinths, tulips, and crocus in addition to common items like amaryllis. These people often have had trouble finding plant materials and obtaining recommendations on cultural practices. Extra sales can be promoted in September and October showing gardeners how to force a pot of tulips into flower in late winter. All-America Award programs have been established for dahlias and gladiolas. Your product mix should include new introductions and some of the unusual types such as miniature glads.

Pesticide displays often confuse gardeners. They appear in haphazard fashion and information appears in small print on labels. Some firms carry only popular items offered by many manufacturers. You should check with local pesticide specialists associated with the nearest university or county extension office for their latest recommendations. The materials they recommend to gardeners should be on shelves in your store.

Indoor gardeners often find themselves requiring a variety of products including rooting hormones, containers, peat moss, perlite, vermiculite, and labels. These specialty items will not necessarily yield high returns to the operator. They will help distinguish your product mix from that offered by most competitors.

The product mix should be formulated to achieve a specific image and to satisfy the needs of the group targeted for your operation. Which products will service the needs and bring happiness to gardeners patronizing your garden center? Selection of supplies should be based on the following considerations:

1. Brand recognition
2. Advertising support—nationally and at local level
3. Extent of product line
4. Quality of product
5. In-store display aids

Consumer recognition and quality are important ingredients in handling products from a particular company. A variety of products offered under one label adds to consumer recognition and enhances the value of a brand label. Sales aids assist retailers in stimulating impulse sales. A variety of in-store promotional aids has been made available by many manufacturers to assist retailers. Advertising dollars have been allocated by a number of firms in support of cooperative programs. Retailers should check with manufacturers and their representatives regarding availability of support dollars for local advertising projects.

Easy Shopping

Convenient, one-stop shopping has proven to be an important factor in the success of many mass market firms. This philosophy has been adopted by successful garden center operators. Regardless of size, one can make it easy, pleasant, and comfortable to shop for plants and garden supplies.

A concentration of plants in one area facilitates consumer browsing and encourages impulse sales. The prime thrust has been to make it easy for customers to shop in contrast to providing road maps to direct one to different groupings of material around the property. One or more clerks should have responsibility for restocking displays. It is crucial that a maximum amount of material be on display throughout the day.

Good lighting, protection from wind and rain, and appropriate signs all contribute to the atmosphere associated with a particular operation. The key to success is in making it easy to shop and providing a pleasant experience for your customers.

Public Service

Strong merchandising programs cannot be divorced from creation of unique public service projects. Here are some examples of special efforts in the public service field, all designed to enhance sales efforts of the organization.

1. *Art and craft shows.* A major firm in Toronto has provided facilities to local art and craft organizations for their annual shows. Traffic generated from these events has played a major role in exposing the organization to new consumers.

2. *Clinics.* A number of organizations have held clinics and do-it-yourself sessions on and off the premises. Consumers have had an excellent opportunity to expand their knowledge and to learn unusual techniques in propagation and culture of plants. Some firms have operated in an informal atmosphere and others have constructed mini-theaters. Admission fees have been charged in some instances. Clinics provide an excellent opportunity for introducing new products to your clientele groups. You can combine an educational activity with a merchandising message.

3. *Radio and television.* A willingness to contribute time to radio and television programs of an educational nature can greatly support and enhance mer-

chandising programs. The name of the organization becomes widely known to gardeners when an individual serves as a consultant on interview programs. The demands for this service are heaviest just prior to and during the busy season of the year. This is the time to make hay while the sun shines.

4. *Dial-A-Tip.* A telephone answering service using a recorded garden tip each day can be financed for under $700 a year. This investment can reap many rewards and in the process support merchandising efforts throughout the year.

5. *Tours.* Tours of greenhouses are extremely popular with school children and garden clubs. A visit to a greenhouse during the dreary winter and early spring months helps brighten spirits. Many operators have taken advantage of this situation to build goodwill and to stimulate sales. The aggressive operator not only escourts tours, but sees that school children leave with a small plant. Coleus seems to be a favorite item since it requires relatively little care other than bright light. The rationale behind the gift is that Mom and Dad will ask their offspring where they received the plant. The response may include a mini-sales message regarding all the plants for sale. Just maybe the family will return to purchase some or all of their spring plants. The investment in time does come at a busy period of the year. This also happens to be the best time for whetting the appetites of current and future buyers.

6. *Spring garden shows.* A growing number of communities now sponsor a spring garden show, often in cooperation with a home show. The event has been staged in late winter and early spring. Once again, this coincides with a busy time of the year for anyone involved in the garden business.

Shopping Carts

One wouldn't dream of shopping in a supermarket without first stopping for a cart. You can only hold so many groceries in each arm and then head for the checkout counter. The same situation applies in discount stores featuring nonfood items. What happens when you shop at a garden center? The same needs are there in terms of the consumer. Some operators make it easy to shop while others make it difficult.

One curious operator wondered why his average consumer sales seemingly fell far short of a colleague's in another community. Neither prices nor quality were out of line and a similar product mix existed in both situations. The operator in question encouraged customers to load plants into shoe boxes while his friend used shopping carts. How many boxes would you fill and where would you place them before calling it a day?

Steps should be eliminated and replaced by ramps to provide easy movement of carts. Potential injury to customers also can be avoided by removing obstacles from the sales area. You must make it easy to shop!

Wagons are used by many retail operations to help customers collect material on their shopping expedition.

Shopping carts are a real convenience for customers and facilitate quantity purchases.

Small boxes often limit
sales since shoppers can
hold only a limited
amount of material.

Signs

Consumers can be stimulated to buy on impulse through use of appropriate
signs outdoors and indoors. Do not neglect the condition and appearance of
signs when inventorying the status of the operation prior to each planting
season. Some firms have constructed attractive and well-designed signs in
front of their business. The area will be enhanced by a planting of shrubbery
and flowers. Special banners are appropriate when they blend in or do not
really compete with major signs. The conflict may alter the desired image
of the firm.

One garden center went overboard on signs promoting a host of annuals
and vegetables. Each sign contained a message including available cultivars,
their usage, and prices. So far so good. The signs were constructed by an

amateur. Handwriting was difficult to decipher and lines slanted at a severe angle. A variety of techniques was used in hanging signs from overhead supports. One had the feeling that a class of first graders had been placed in charge of the project.

Bedding Plants Incorporated has developed a series of attractive paper signs promoting a variety of crops. They are color coded and help customers and store personnel locate and identify particular crops and groupings of material.

Special Sales

What constitutes a special sale in the eyes of a consumer? There must be some valid reasons above and beyond the fact that management wishes to unload surplus material. Here are some ingredients that must be considered to insure success of specials.

1. The product must be known to customers. A sale on Scotts lawn fertilizer will have much more impact than that of an unknown brand.

2. The special must provide real value to customers. A retailer complained that an African violet sale failed to ring the bell. The plants featured few blossoms, and broken leaves were evident on many plants. A modest reduction in price, 10 percent or less, will probably capture attention of only those people already planning to buy the product. Significant savings must be advertised to attract large numbers of buyers.

3. A reasonable, if not large, display of merchandise must be visible and on hand for the sale. Customers quickly recognize when they have been had by those managers really interested in selling other products. Should the special be placed at the front of the store or at the rear? Those favoring the rear believe that customers should flow through the entire store and in the process pick up items on impulse. The front of the store site has appeal from the standpoint of making sure customers go home with the special. Other techniques may be employed to assure customer movement throughout the store. Making it easy to find special sale items builds goodwill.

4. The special must be advertised to attract buyer attention. Potential customers also must be made aware of the fact that the store features unadvertised specials on a regular basis.

5. A rain check should be provided customers when merchandise temporarily has been exhausted by heavy sales. The image of the firm must be protected at all times.

6. A good time of the year must be selected for the special. Obviously it would be as difficult to sell lawn fertilizer in December, or Christmas ornaments in July. Specials have high appeal when consumers can use them as soon as possible.

This special sale retains the original price of the pack of petunias. This is in contrast to a reduction to 40 cents a pack. Some operators like the appeal and sound of a 1¢ sale which is quite comparable to that featured in the advertisement.

Objectives.   Why should one conduct special sales? They are a common occurrence in the business world. Special sales should be carefully planned and specific objectives identified to ensure that one receives maximum benefits. A special sale should be targeted to move a given product or service along with:

1. Building store traffic and sales of nonspecial products
2. Increasing sales during slow days or periods
3. Building the image of firm regarding attractiveness of prices
4. Reacting to competitors
5. Reducing inventory of slow-moving items
6. Taking advantage of special purchases'
7. Introducing a new product

The objectives of a special sale should be carefully discussed with all personnel. This must be clearly defined to assure that everyone is pulling in the same direction. Specials should not be scheduled in conflict with major community programs. A foliage plant sale was conducted by one operator on the day of a major football game in the community. Relatively few customers took advantage of the sale.

The evergreen sale offers some real bargains to gardeners. Note the appearance of the regular price which helps convince buyers of the merits of this particular sale.

Some firms have built a reputation of having a special sale once a year, during a particular month or week. The sale loses some of its punch when management conducts the special on an erratic basis. Consumers soon begin to look forward to the annual event and become frustrated learning that one won't be held a particular year. A special sale often attracts new and old customers who have not stopped in for a while. This is your opportunity to show a full line of merchandise. Spruce up the store and make it look alive.

Unique Products

Garden center operators have opportunities to strengthen their merchandising programs by featuring unique products. Just a little extra effort can pay big dividends in the world of plants.

"Trees."   A prominent operator has established an identity through production and sale of tree geraniums. Coleus, fuschia, and lantana plants also have been staked and grown in tree fashion. They capture attention of discriminating buyers.

Chickenwire and similar material has been used to construct display units featuring impatiens. A cylindrical wire "cage" is inserted into a larger pot and filled with a mixture of peat moss, soil, and vermiculite. Young plants are then inserted into the openings and soon root into this soil mix. The display overwhelms gardeners and produces a riot of color on the patio throughout the summer.

An excellent patio item, this impatiens planter will produce a riot of color and attract attention throughout the summer months.

Baskets.   Poinsettia baskets have appeared in small numbers in many areas of the country. A wholesale price of $25 for a quality unit has been quoted by a major southern California firm. Some growers in the Midwest have cut corners by using fewer plants and charging only $15.

Small Pots. The production of bedding plants was associated with wooden flats and small clay pots for decades. Plastic market packs have replaced these units in many communities. A few enterprising retail growers have turned attention once again to producing quality plants in small clay pots. There is a market today for premium quality plants at prices reflecting production and handling costs. Some gardeners want to work with only one or a few plants of a particular cultivar.

Color Mixes. The red, white, and blue theme for 1976 sparked at least one operator to produce an assorted pack of petunias. This individual used one of the special series made available to support the bicentennial theme. Each pack of six plants included two blue, two red, and two white petunias from the Old Glory mix.

SUMMARY

Merchandising strategy embraces a multitude of practices all designed to attract customers and to retain their allegiance to a particular organization. It represents one of the most crucial activities confronting management and should occupy a significant portion of time for key people in an organization.

A simplistic approach focuses attention largely on price. This philosophy assumes that gardeners want to patronize only those operations that offer bargains, regardless of product quality. A wiser view recognizes that a growing number of gardeners have focused attention on acquiring good and unique merchandise in guiding purchase decisions.

Unique products represent a key factor in attracting discriminating buyers to a particular operation. Newness, product identification, and specialty items such as tree geraniums are factors that distinguish quality operations from most retail competitors.

A new generation of gardeners has arrived on the scene in recent years. They have a tremendous thirst for information. Free literature, lectures, and newspaper and radio tips represent ways that aggressive operators can capture attention of new and increasingly discriminating gardeners.

A good product mix will attract attention and help retain loyalty of customers. People like to shop in stores that carry a full line of merchandise. Buying cooperatives have enabled some firms to develop brand names in competition with large discount organizations.

Shopping must be made a pleasant experience for buyers. This includes convenient store hours, in-store promotional aids, pricing, lighting, and ease of finding merchandise.

Your merchandising strategy should focus attention on the strengths of your firm. All weaknesses should be identified and eliminated in the battle to attract attention of buyers. Why should someone shop at your place of business? That question should be asked on a regular basis. The answers should come easily. New customers, competitors, and products continue to arrive on the scene. You must continually revise and modify your merchandising strategy to meet changing conditions and stay one step ahead of the competition.

1. Discuss the role of business philosophy and its impact on the growth of a firm.

2. What factors should be considered in formulating business hours?

3. Define combination sales and offer three examples that have application to garden centers. Support your examples.

4. Discuss the role of guarantees when selling perishable plant materials, bedding plants, nursery products, and turf.

5. What role should labels play in a merchandising program? Can one afford and justify colored labels for geraniums?

6. How do you rate "newness" as a merchandising tool for "mass" outlets?

7. Discuss the pros and cons of independent garden center operators featuring prices in newspaper advertisements.

8. What guidelines can you offer a new operator regarding product mix and its role in developing an aggressive merchandising program?

9. Public service programs can enhance the image of a firm. Identify and discuss three types of projects that could be adopted by most garden centers.

10. What constitutes a special sale? Discuss.

11. What are the benefits of conducting special sales? Discuss.

12. Unique items attract attention. Discuss opportunities for increasing sales and attracting store traffic through sale of unusual items.

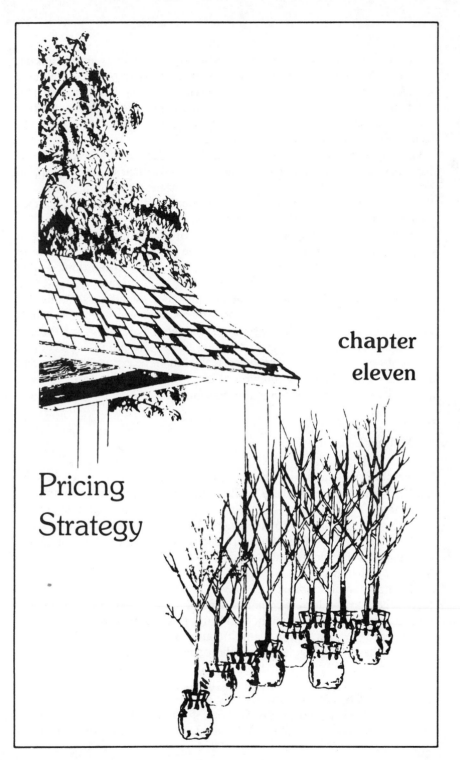

chapter
eleven

Pricing
Strategy

What price are you going to charge for a pack of petunias and geraniums this year? Successful operators focus significant attention on the art and science of pricing their products and services. Pricing is not a game for amateurs, nor can it be pushed aside by those who prefer to focus attention on other topics and concerns. Those who develop a sound pricing strategy continue to expand and record reasonable profits.

Growers and retailers no longer can enjoy the luxury of allowing outside forces to formulate and guide pricing practices for their organization. This practice, often known as "follow the leader," has persisted for many decades. Rapidly rising operation costs require individual operators to formulate their own pricing schedules after careful analysis of all costs.

There is a sign that appears in a number of greenhouses throughout the country. The words vary but the theme is the same. It identifies the tons of coal or gallons of fuel oil, labor, and everything else you can think of that goes into the operation of a greenhouse and the production of fresh flowers, and potted and bedding plants. The key line goes something like this: "If customers only knew how much it took to produce a geranium, they would not argue about price or think prices are too high." Baloney! A trip through an automobile plant would probably have little bearing on the reaction of a buyer to the sticker price. Consumers really cannot be expected to appreciate all the costs involved in production of any item. They only focus on price and the value it represents to them as consumers.

COMMON LANGUAGE

Wholesale price quotations for a 4½-inch geranium have varied in some markets from a low of $1.00 to $1.25. Retail prices for the same commodity have ranged from $1.50 to $2.00. The situation can be quite puzzling to new operators and perplexing to consumers. There must be valid reasons why this situation exists. The failure to clarify the situation can only prove damaging to the industry and especially to those individuals producing quality merchandise.

The spread in prices often leads buyers to press their advantage and try to force sellers to the lowest common denominator. An operator seeking to retail a geranium at $2.00 might buckle upon seeing an advertisement from a competitor marketing the "same" item at $1.50. Relatively few, if any, pressures have been applied from the opposite side of the fence. Buyers have no reason to suggest to sellers that they raise their prices. The strategy always has been to force sellers to reexamine their position in light of lower prices offered by competitors.

Valid reasons do exist to justify most, if not all, price spreads occurring at both wholesale and retail levels. Focus attention on the 4½-inch geranium.

This common and important plant has been sold in a pot measuring approximately 4½ inches in diameter. The "descriptive" language tells the buyer nothing about the size or overall quality of the plant. A grower has the option of spacing geraniums 6×6 inches, 6×4 inches, or 6×8 inches with minor variations. The first spacing permits four pots to be placed in a square foot of bench space. It has been the recommended spacing for a number of years. A 6×4 inch spacing crowds six plants into the area and generally reduces the quality of the geranium. The last spacing normally produces a superior product with only three plants in one square foot of space. Production costs vary considerably as you go from three to six plants in the same area of bench space. This fact should be and has been reflected in costs established by many operators.

The real crime has been that relatively few producers spell out the quality of product identified as a 4½-inch geranium. This also applies to retailers who continue to feature the diameter of the pot. Someone might ask whether the industry has been selling pots or plants.

One unwritten specification exists when marketing geraniums. The plant should have one open cluster of flowers. Consumers have avoided "green" plants like the plague. Retailers often have rejected shipments they considered unsaleable because of the absence of blossoms. The $1.00 geranium undoubtedly contains one bloom. The cluster looks down on small leaves and one main stem. This plant was crowded on a bench and undoubtedly started just a month or so before selling time. Look carefully and note the absence of roots anchoring the plant to the soil mix. Regardless of quality the plant still qualifies as a 4½-inch geranium.

Let us turn to a pack of petunias. What does the term "pack" mean to you? It could contain four, dix, eight, or a dozen or more plants. This is another example of poor, inexact terminology employed by today's garden center industry.

One garden center operator moaned recently that his packs were not selling at $1.25. A discount competitor down the street was advertising packs for 65 cents. The higher priced item contained twelve healthy petunias while the competitor offered a pack with six average quality plants. The situation should have been reversed, with consumers recognizing a better buy with the larger pack.

Communications between buyers and sellers in the garden center industry have often been backward and out of date. A simple language has been adopted to describe many of our products. This lack of precision has penalized many operators, especially those trying to get top prices. A major effort should be made by the industry to adopt a meaningful language to describe potted and flatted material. Individual operators can help improve the current situation by avoiding simple terminology that fails to describe plant materials accurately.

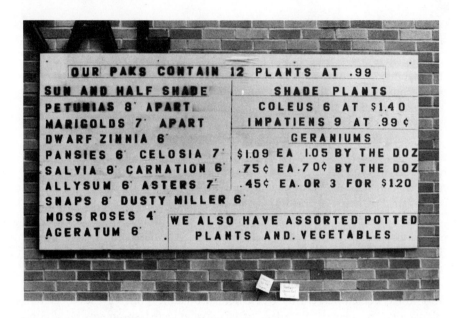

This attractive sign spells out quite clearly the number of plants in each container along with price of each unit.

Pricing strategy begins with employment of precise descriptions. The system becomes chaotic with the use of meaningless terms such as 4½-inch geraniums. This practice deceives buyers and is not in the best interests of consumers. Neither will it support the growth objectives of profit oriented and aggressive firms.

FOLLOW THE LEADER

A common practice in the garden center industry has been that of following the leader in establishing prices. Large firms generally wield a great deal of power. Smaller operators look to the giants for leadership in developing price schedules for garden products.

One producer told of waiting for the dominant firm in his market to issue prices before setting his own. He then cut prices established by the leader by 10 percent. This practice was defended on the basis that a smaller firm operated more efficiently than the larger. While the justification is debatable, it occurs frequently and does present a good picture of industry practices.

You can appreciate the frustration of the leader upon finding that many followers cut prices and continually offer a more attractive package to buyers. Prices may remain at a plateau for a number of years simply because the leader wants others to reach his or her level before initiating a price hike. The leader often has been given the responsibility of accurately determining production and selling costs. It has been assumed by many followers that bigness goes hand in hand with knowledge regarding costs of operation. This often has been the case, but there is no guarantee that the leader has all the answers.

USING LAST YEAR'S PRICES

Prices established the previous year often serve to guide operators in preparing strategy for the coming year. Rising costs may stimulate some operators to increase prices 5 or 10 percent. There is the assumption that prices from the previous year accurately reflect cost of raw products and services. This has not always been the case as one examines the pricing strategy of some firms. Some operators have been prone to absorb minor costs over a period of years before suddenly realizing that their firm was trading dollars. A sharp increase stuns buyers and builds a wall of resistance to new prices. Wholesale commission rates for floral products in one market rose from 20 to 25 percent one day. This substantial increase just about wiped out all profits of growers shipping on consignment to that market. A gradual increase would have been much more tolerable.

Pricing strategy should be reviewed annually and formulated on the basis of current conditions. Increases in input factors such as fuel and labor, especially those caused by inflation, should be reflected immediately in the new price structure for a line of products. Aggressive operators rarely remain content to absorb minor increases in product costs. They recognize that this endangers their profit position.

COMPETITOR'S PRICE

A common technique employed by buyers has been to quote prices offered by a competitor. "I can buy the same item from Joe down the street for 25 cents less a pot." The best answer to this line should be, "Do yourself a favor and buy from Joe." A small chrysanthemum operator handling 6-inch pots started to panic when a buyer from a large chain reported that the crop was becoming a drug on the market. One operator reportedly had an inventory of 1000 plants in comparison to a norm of 300. Prices were falling rapidly and the grower was advised to trim 50 cents off of the normal $3.50 price for this crop. The small operator caved in as he had visions of not selling the 100 plants in flower on his benches.

The truth of the story was far different than the line given to the small grower. The excess inventory already had been worked down to near normal levels at the time of the conversation. Smaller pots, namely 4½-inch units, had dominated the glutted market. A shortage was beginning to develop for larger units. The grower was conned into a price reduction when the facts probably warranted a better than normal price.

Prices often fluctuate at farmer's markets which have become popular in many communities in recent years. Word was received in one situation indicating that a competitor had chopped his price of hanging baskets in half. The pressure was on to take similar action. The special price applied only to small baskets and not those commonly handled by other sellers in the area. A large sign was employed, calling attention to baskets priced at $3.99. It was unfortunate that the seller failed to mention container size, misleading many buyers.

Whether you are in the retail or wholesale game, be on the lookout for these buyers telling you what someone else is charging for a product. Investigate the situation before taking any action. You will probably find good reason for the attractive price.

FORMULA PRICING

Most retailers price merchandise on the basis of a particular formula. It is not uncommon for some to talk about a two to one system based on product cost or a markup of a fixed percentage. Some operators have used margin and markup to mean one and the same thing. There is a significant difference between these two systems that could dramatically influence real profits.

Selling price should cover all costs of merchandise plus net profit. The price is always 100 percent since it represents the total amount of money coming into the firm. All costs will be represented as a percentage of net sales. Margin is always figured on the selling price. It is a percentage of sales. Markup is a percentage of cost. A firm buys an article for $2.40 and retails it for $3.20. This provides a margin of 80 cents or one quarter (25 percent) of the selling price. A markup of 25 percent on a product costing $2.40 yields a selling price of $3.00. One quarter of $2.40 comes to 60 cents. This figure is added to cost ($2.40), bringing the total to $3.00.

There is a 20 cent difference in selling price when computing a 25 percent markup and margin on a product costing $2.40. The differential could very well wipe out all profits on the product, if you were to work on a markup rather than a margin of 25 percent.

Let us assume you want a gross profit of 40 percent and the wholesale cost of a geranium is 75 cents. The selling price should be $1.25 to assure a gross profit of 40 percent. To test this answer take 40 percent of $1.25. This comes to 50 cents and leaves 75 cents to cover product costs.

EXAMPLES OF PRICES AND MARGINS FOR INDEPENDENT GARDEN CENTER OPERATORS

Item	Cost	Selling Price	Margin (%)
Geranium	$1.10 pot	$ 1.98	44
Bedding plants	6.50 flat	10.85	40
Hard Goods	3.00	5.00	40
Flowering and Green Plants	1.80	5.40	66
Nursery Material	3.00	7.50	60

Some confusion enters the picture when retail florists talk about a three to one markup. A retailer would charge $3 based on a cost of $1 for a particular item. This sounds like robbery in comparison to a margin of 40 percent. In reality, the retail florist has worked on a margin of 66⅔ percent.

$$\frac{\text{Selling price—Cost}}{\text{Selling price}} = \% \text{ margin}$$

$$\frac{\$3.00-\$1.00}{\$3.00} = \frac{2}{3} = 66\text{-}2/3\%$$

Manufacturers and distributors may or may not provide suggested retail prices for their products. Greenhouse and nursery producers tend to avoid suggestions regarding retail prices. Suggested prices often have been based on a formula allocating 40 percent of the retail prices to cover profits and all costs above and beyond the basic product and delivery charges. This often has been referred to as the margin required to yield a fair profit.

Rigid formulas must be employed with care and with one eye on your competitors. Aggressive retailers often think in terms of how much they can command for a product reflecting value to the buyer. Small firms often operate at a disadvantage when competing with large volume stores selling nationally advertised products. The suggested margin may be in the vicinity of 40 percent. Volume discounts often permit large buyers to retail at a price equal to or just above the wholesale price paid by smaller scale operators. The former may still command a 40 percent margin although this will be applied to a lower acquisition price. The small operator often must choose between fewer sales or possibly trading dollars on selected items.

Focusing attention on gross profit helps simplify the process of controlling product costs and expenses. You have full visibility regarding product costs and the extent to which they remain within stated guidelines. Attention will be turned to operational costs when problems arise relative to profits and one has maintained control over gross profits. Utilizing a formula helps retailers achieve reasonable profits. The formula should not be so rigid as to preclude modifications reflecting quality.

Comparing Products and Services

Shrewd buyers, whether at the consumer or retail level, will compare prices before accepting a particular offer. This process helps convince buyers that they made the right move and have not been taken to the cleaners by sellers.

Terminology. Most large outlets, especially discount stores, have featured 4½-inch geraniums. A picture of a good quality geranium often is used to attract the attention of consumers.

A top quality geranium features numerous branches and several clusters of flowers. It can easily be identified as a "giant" as distinguished from small- to medium-sized plants in 4 ½-inch containers.

An aggressive garden center operator found himself competing with at-tractively priced geraniums in 4½-inch pots. What action was required to break down barriers to the top price he felt was justified for a quality geranium? The first step was to drop all reference to pot size and to initiate other descrip-tive, and more meaningful, terminology for his merchandise. The operator marketed geraniums in 3½-inch, 4½-inch, and 5½-inch containers. A shopping expedition in a local supermarket brought him face to face with the display for laundry soaps. The three words that captured his attention were: Regular, Giant, Economy. Why not apply those terms to his three sizes of geraniums? The primary competitor did not employ that language nor did other independent operators in the same market area. This operator gained some valuable distance in distinguishing his product from that of the local discount firm.

Cultivars.   The second step was to start advertising and identifying the proper cultivar of all geraniums. This was in contrast to the simple task of calling them red, white, pink, and salmon.

An extra effort must be undertaken by those seeking top prices for their products. Sometimes it involves handling a slightly different product and capitalizing on its uniqueness. Often it simply involves good common sense in trying to make your products look different from those available at competing stores.

Providing an Option

Aggressive sellers have learned the value of providing buyers with some choices or options when purchasing products and services. This permits the buyer to go up or down without fear of being embarrassed when turning down a proposition or single price. This technique has been employed by some bedding plant operators and retail florists. The geranium provides us with one more example of what can be done to sell quality, high-priced merchandise in the face of strong competition from discount firms.

A typical geranium crop consists of some high quality plants, a comparable quantity of low grade plants, and the bulk in the average category. The break-down of a crop into three grades will be influenced by space allocated to plants on the production bench. Some growers sort merchandise prior to shipping. This is rather rare, as most orders are picked on a bench run basis. When sorted, those plants without blossoms and obviously well below par are eliminated from the shipment. All other plants ranging from just below average to superior would be included in the order. Growers shipping on a bench run basis normally take everything including blossomless and poorly developed plants.

A retailer essentially has two choices. The plants can be displayed in one area and all offered at the same price. This involves little or no effort other

Extra-large geraniums were sorted out from average-sized plants. The higher quality plants commanded a premium price, yielding a higher return to the retailer.

than unpacking and placing them in the selling areas. The second option involves sorting the product into two or more categories. This technique can be employed in the presence or absence of strong competition. The concept has merit on the basis that shoppers are given a choice.

Some operators prefer to take advantage of their customers and hope to sell everything at top price. Their success often is dependent on the volume and appearance of lower quality plants. A growing number of buyers have learned to bypass junk or poor quality merchandise. They leave plants that obviously should have been reduced in price. The operator often must dispose of unwanted plants at a ridiculously low price at the end of the season. These plants also required extra care because of the long time on the sales bench. The geranium display looks worn out from the stragglers who could not find a home.

Sorting products has been employed by some operators as a means of competing with low-priced discount operations. An attractive price can be placed on a small quantity of below average merchandise. This technique effectively removes low quality plants from the display featuring top prices and premium merchandise. The consumer then has the option of selecting an inexpensive geranium or the quality product. The choice is up to the buyer. You have provided a valuable service and one not available from the discounter.

The potted or flowering chrysanthemum has been another popular item sold throughout the year by garden center operators, retail florists, and discount firms. It has great appeal because of color display and long shelf life. A Canadian retailer tells the story of his efforts to compete with a neighboring supermarket in capturing attention of consumers relative to the pot mum. The competition was selling a poor quality chrysanthemum for $4.99. His cash and carry price was around $8.99. There was a significant difference in quality of the two products. The retailer visited his friendly supermarket and purchased four plants. He displayed them in his store with a prominent sign that read in part, "This is the product sold by M & M Supermarket for $4.99. Compare it to my quality plants at $8.99."

A friend operated the supermarket and within a few hours he was in the store complaining about the sign. The retail florist offered to soothe his friend by placing four free plants in the supermarket. A sign would be constructed with similar words advising supermarket shoppers of the price and quality of plants available from the florist. Needless to say, the offer was not accepted.

A significant point should be recognized in the above illustration. The retail florist was giving consumers a choice and helping them compare two levels of quality. It is highly important to provide buyers with an option both in terms of quality and price.

Value to Buyer—Justifying Price

How much effort have you made or will you make to justify a particular price for a product or service? Are you willing to help the buyer convince himself or herself that they are making the right decision? Seed geraniums have slowly been taking over a larger percentage of the geranium market. The early cultivars generated little enthusiasm from growers because seed had to be sown in early January in order to have flowering plants by mid-May. It was difficult to justify the longer production period, the problems associated with a new crop, and still charge traditional prices for the geranium. This new item often failed to stimulate retailers because some growers offered plants in the green stage. This practice was designed to cut production costs, as seeds were not sown until much later in the spring. Gardeners frequently did not see any color until July and reported their displeasure to retailers. A significant point was overlooked by growers and retailers. No one seemed to recognize that good quality seed geraniums outperformed many vegetatively propagated plants. Those started from seed normally flower much later into the fall. They occupy much more space in the garden. In fact, three good plants often will outproduce four geraniums started from cuttings.

The economics of this situation was ignored by many operators. Four geraniums priced at $1.75 comes to an expenditure of $7 for a gardener. This means that a seed geranium could bear a price tag of $2.33 and still total only $7 for a comparable display of color. The higher retail price should be reflected in a higher wholesale price. On the basis of a two to one markup, the geranium started from a cutting would wholesale for 88 cents while one started from seed should go for $1.17. The 29-cent difference would have easily covered increased production costs for the seed geranium.

A second illustration occurred recently when the author went to purchase a set of tires. The object was to buy a good set at the lowest possible cost and avoid spending too much time dickering over price. A visit was made to a local dealer. I requested to deal with the sales manager. This was probably a mistake since he had years of experience in dealing with "shrewd" buyers.

He was pleased to sell me a set of tires and provided assurances that the offer would prove very attractive. First though, he had some questions.

Question: How many miles a year do you drive?
  Answer: 25,000

Response: That's a great deal!

Question: Are you married?
  Answer: Yes

Question: How large a family?
  Answer: Four children
Response: You sure want a good set to protect that family. I think you really need our top line of tires.

The technique employed was smooth, sound, and designed to help the buyer as much as the seller. I was given the opportunity to reevaluate my own needs. The information helped the seller identify my real needs. The discussion moved away from the topic of price. We returned to price only after identifying needs and discussing the attributes of the product.

A third illustration will reinforce the need to avoid total emphasis on price when trying to market quality products. A producer of green plants received a long distance call one day. The caller identified himself as a buyer for a discount organization. He wanted a price quotation for a particular sized rubber plant. The grower hung up the phone. The buyer replaced the call, and again identified himself and the desire for a price quotation. The grower again hung up the phone. A third call was made and the buyer was getting a little hot under the collar. He concluded that the grower had deliberately hung up the phone each time. Why this treatment? The grower calmly responded that he did not begin a conversation with the emphasis on price. The firm offered quality products and the buyer should look elsewhere if he really was interested in bargain basement prices.

It is interesting to note that a deal was arranged for shipment of rubber plants. Why did the buyer start the conversation with price when in reality he was willing to buy quality products at top prices? This is a standard technique utilized by most buyers including yourself. Aggressive buyers like to put sellers on the defensive. So you begin a discussion asking directly or indirectly for a low price.

The seller must play the game and adopt his or her own rules. The primary effort should be to shift emphasis away from price to service and the plus features of the product. Weak sellers buckle and play the wrong game.

PRICE INCREASES

How can you justify a price increase to your customers? Do you have to justify a price increase? Growers often argue that an increase in production costs should be reflected in higher wholesale prices. An examination of wholesale prices, for example those for fresh flowers, will show that they have remained relatively stable over the last two decades. Higher fuel costs finally have moved some items upwards, but not without a struggle.

It has not been easy to ask for and obtain a price increase for floral products. Buyer resistance often counters or slows down the upward movement of prices. Retailers and growers should experience relatively few problems in raising prices when offering a unique or differentiated product. A floral arrangement rarely can or will be duplicated by competing florists. The designer has an option of working with a variety of flowers and foliage items, varying count of blooms, selecting from a variety of containers and employing different design techniques. All these factors can be manipulated when quoting prices for a particular arrangement. The consumer simply selects a price from one quoted by the retailer. A rise in costs of any one input factor can be offset by altering other ingredients. The range of prices can be spread out from $10, $12.50, and $15 to $10, $15, and $20. The consumer has a choice and yet will not be in a position to compare prices with a competing firm.

Potted flowering plants must be considered in the same framework as selling loose, unarranged fresh flowers. The retailer does not engage in a manufacturing process comparable to the sale and creation of arrangements. A firm can distinguish itself from competitors when handling pots and loose flowers by uniqueness, quality, and extra service such as special wrapping, credit, and delivery. These services will distinguish a traditional retail florist from supermarkets and similar operations.

Special services may accompany some garden products. Trees and shrubs may be planted free of charge providing the order exceeds a minimum amount.

Free landscape design services also can be provided when plant materials have been purchased from the firm. These services help justify and command premium prices.

What can you do to command top prices for geraniums, and potted bedding plants? Few, if any, special services accompany these products. This situation applies to wholesale producers along with garden center and other independent operators. You must identify characteristics of the product that are meaningful to buyers. The illustration of the seed geranium earlier in the chapter focuses attention on one important factor. The consumer could buy fewer plants and ultimately have a bigger display of color than buying vegetatively propagated plants. Spend a few hours analyzing your products and listing unique features that can attract attention of buyers.

Newness. A tremendous opportunity exists for producers and retailers to soften resistance and to move prices upward gradually through introduction of new cultivars each year. This concept also serves as an excellent merchandising tool in helping firms command attention and building a strong, positive image. Blushing Maid, a double petunia, was designated as an All-America winner for 1977. Wholesale seed prices were exceptionally high and reportedly the highest ever charged for a petunia. Could growers afford to produce this new introduction?

Some growers traditionally have shied away from cultivars bearing an expensive label. They have worked with older, more inexpensive selections. Why change to something new when the seller does not have the courage or feels that new cultivars warrant top prices? This position was adopted by a large number of firms hoping the price of Blushing Maid would fall to more competitive levels with other double petunias. The advance guard, generally few in numbers, always have been willing to stick their necks out regardless of the price tag. They have enjoyed an excellent reputation and one associated with firms annually introducing new materials to retailers and consumers.

Most operators have absorbed higher seed costs and spread them out over the entire petunia or bedding plant crop. The extra effort employed to obtain a premium price for selected items rarely seems justified to these operators. A golden opportunity often has gone down the drain when producers and retailers fail to capitalize on newness. Blushing Maid carried the unique label for only a year or two. Then, it faded from the spotlight and was replaced by another outstanding petunia. The basic concept of the All-America Awards program has been to introduce three or four new annuals each year. Seed companies also release a number of new items even though they failed to capture a special award. Blushing Maid represented an opportunity for progressive growers to recapture their investment in seed and to

NEW VARIETIES

Available from
your seed supplier

Newness is the theme of
this piece of promotional
literature prepared by a
major breeder of flowers
and vegetables for the
home gardener.

program buyers for some increases in prices the following year or two. A premium price should have been charged for this new introduction and applied the first year it appeared on the scene.

A separate price structure for this double petunia also calls attention to the particular cultivar. Discriminating garden center operators will want to know what's so unique to command a $1 or more premium per flat of plants. Some buyers will want a few flats for their special customers. They in turn will ask another 25 cents a pack to cover high wholesale prices. Consumers will come face to face with Blushing Maid and repeat questions regarding its price tag. What is so special about this petunia? The award helps justify a higher price, and stamps this petunia as being different and unique. A number of gardeners continually look for new items and want to be identified as a leader in their club and community. They might have paid a premium price for Blushing Maid. The beauty of the system lies in the fact that the higher price for one sets the stage for some increase the following year or two. Your premium price in 1983 can become the base price for established cultivars in 1984 and 1985.

Some groups within the flower business have encouraged and capitalized on newness. Seed distributors obviously have taken advantage of the situation. A second group has been the hybridizers introducing chrysanthemums, poinsettias, and most other ornamental crops. Take a good hard look at catalogues coming from these firms and their representatives. Producers must pay a royalty or premium price for all new introductions. Why don't growers take advantage of the same situation? One of the best illustrations of the traditional reaction of most industry people goes back to the 1960s when the Paul Mikkelsen poinsettia was introduced to the trade. Poinsettia cultivars prior to this breakthrough commonly lost their leaves and bracts before the beginning of the new year. It was a real headache for growers and retailers working with standard cultivars available to the trade. The new introduction initially received the "thumbs down" award from many people in the business. It featured a small bract that just couldn't compare with established selections. One large grower openly apologized for this fact of life and begged retailers to try a few plants. The firm introducing the new selection fortunately charged a royalty for each cutting. Growers handling the product were faced with the perennial challenge of absorbing costs or passing them on to retailers. Most firms opted for the former, since they really could not see much value in the new introduction.

Consumers played a major role in upsetting the apple cart. Some plants managed to find their way into homes throughout the country. Retailers were astonished at the positive reaction of consumers and suddenly pounded on doors for this new, marvelous plant. No longer would they have to refund or replace plants. No longer would they have to respond to questions and more questions regarding leaves and bracts dropping from plants.

A few aggressive growers recognized early that this was a great opportunity to move poinsettia prices up to a more realistic level. Wholesale prices had stagnated in many markets for a number of years. They took advantage of it while others apologized for newness. The illustration tells a great deal about this industry, especially producers. It is no wonder that growers continually lament about poor and stagnant prices when they fear to take advantage of tools on the work bench.

Cultivar Identification. Buyer resistance to premium prices can be tempered to some degree by promotion of cultivar names. This represents another reason to be offered buyers when trying to convince them to invest in a higher priced commodity. Test your own reaction to the following:

1. Sprinter or red geranium
2. Samantha or red rose
3. Blushing Maid or red and white double petunias
4. He Man or red tomato

Which title adds glamour to the product? Which of the above would help to distinguish a firm from its competitor? Which name will help command a premium price?

The job is made much easier when breeders coin attractive and enticing names. It is difficult to promote C-1 as an exciting new poinsettia cultivar. Rose breeders continually hit the jackpot, coming up with exciting names for their products. We should take a lesson from them in designing appropriate and mouth-watering names such as Samantha for all new plant materials.

Some members of the greenhouse business have proven to be their own worst enemies. These individuals faithfully attend open houses and devote valuable time and space toward evaluation of new plant materials. Then they turn around and sell geraniums as white, pink, salmon, and red. Roses travel through the florist marketing system unlabelled. New petunias come to market in poorly labelled packs and flats. It is no wonder that buyers resist higher prices and cannot understand why growers want to raise prices.

Take a tip from our auto manufacturers. They go out of their way spending thousands if not millions of dollars coming up with the right name for each new model. Advertising people capitalize on names and everyone works to see that consumers can identify with the new product. We have new products coming out every year. Let us take advantage of the opportunities to command reasonable prices by promoting cultivar names.

HE MAN
This year don't grow a boy or a girl to do a HE MAN'S JOB. Try Goldsmith's highly productive mid season, large fruited variety HE MAN. Vigorous, indeterminate plants are loaded with large, smooth, uniform ripening bright red fruit from about 70 days after planting until frost. Tolerates Verticillium and Fusarium wilts. One of the highest yielding tomato varieties.

SWEET 100
This unique new cherry tomato is reported having outstanding results in trial gardens across the United States and Canada as well as in many European countries. Sweet 100 produces amazingly high yields of 1 inch diameter fruit, very high in vitamin C. Sweet 100 plants produce several long, multiple branched clusters containing up to 100 or more fruit on each cluster. Fruit is very sweet and flavorful and is perhaps higher in vitamin C than any other tomato variety now on the market. Sweet 100 is an early variety, of indeterminate growth habit that continues producing heavily until frost.

BRAGGER
Extremely large fruited "beefsteak" type tomato. This is the variety for the gardener who wants to produce the biggest tomato on the block. Oblate shaped fruit over two pounds in size are more resistant to cracking and splitting than other beefsteak types. Excellent flavor, deep red color and meaty interior. Indeterminate growth and early maturing for this type (75 to 80 days). Almost every home gardener wants to plant a "beefsteak" tomato. Why not give him one he can really "brag" about?

He Man

Bragger   Sweet 100   Litho in U.S.A.

GOLDSMITH SEEDS

These new tomato introductions are bound to capture the fancy of new and old vegetable gardeners.

Product Maturity.   Price should reflect stage of development and overall quality of our products. This fact often has been overlooked by many operators. Possibly some have assumed that consumers automatically distinguish between or are aware that independent firms featured higher quality products than those found in mass outlets. This assumption does not float and contributes to many sad experiences and frustrations.

Supermarkets often feature inexpensive daffodils each spring. They may come from outdoor farms in southeastern states and often appear wide open on display tables. A much higher quality product, generally still in the desired bud stage, has been procured from local greenhouse operators and northwestern states by most retail florists. The bud stage insures the flower will provide several more days of color for the consumer than a wide open bloom. This is a good reason why "tight" flowers command premium prices.

Some potted plants like the azalea and cineraria may be sold by discount firms in the wide open stage. This product will have a short life in the home. Contrast the wide open plant with one featuring a large number of buds in various stages of openness. The presence of buds on many of our flowering plants assures the consumer of several weeks or longer of color. Surely, this products warrants a higher price tag than that associated with wide open plants.

The condition of plants and fresh flowers and how they have been maintained in a store should be reflected in the final price. Plants allowed to wilt periodically, crowded, and exposed to poor light conditions, often must be sacrificed at bargain basement prices. A shrewd retailer will put his or her best foot forward in calling attention to all processes employed in maintaining plants and flowers in top condition.

Attractive Prices.   A retailer embarking on a program to develop impulse sales for fresh flowers must give serious consideration to the range of prices that will attract attention. Three carnations might be marked for 99 cents, six for $1.99 and a dozen for $3.79. The 99-cent figure appears attractive in terms of generating impulse sales. It requires relatively little thought to put a dollar bill down on the counter. Step up the price to $2 and some customers will walk on after pausing for a few moments. It requires just a little more consideration than a 99-cent purchase. Much more resistance can be anticipated at and above the $3 level. This price could sabotage a program designed to promote impulse sales. Prices might be thought of in terms of consumer reaction and the resulting impact on sales.

Establishing Prices

Two general approaches have been used by business people in establishing prices for a commodity. The more common approach discussed earlier in the chapter begins with an existing wholesale price for a product. A formula may be utilized to achieve a specific gross profit, thus indirectly arriving at a retail price. A second approach begins with an analysis of consumer wants and needs. What price or range of prices will appear attractive to our targeted consumers?

Product Value. This sophisticated approach tries to mold a product to the desired price. The technique essentially was used by many discount firms to price for bedding plants several years ago. Wholesale and retail prices for a pack of twelve bedding plants rose to the point where they met some resistance from buyers. Representatives from mass outlets promoted the idea of six packs. This cut the wholesale price virtually in half and permitted discount firms to feature the item in the vicinity of 50 cents. Retailers avoided the necessity of going over $1 for a pack of petunias.

It is interesting to note that the shift from a twelve to six pack was made with relatively little fanfare. In fact, consumers were not really informed in any significant manner of the change in plant count. The lower price tag captured attention and helped spur sales of bedding plants through mass outlets. A similar technique has been employed with other crops, specifically geraniums.

Magic Numbers. There always has been discussion about magic numbers like 99 cents in preference to a dollar. Some people feel that 79 cents commands as much attention as 75 cents. It has been argued that one should move from 79 cents to 99 cents without pausing at the 89-cent level. This is based on the belief that little resistance will be encountered from consumers as you move above 79 cents on to the $1 level.

Flexibility. Some flexibility in pricing may prove helpful in balancing accounts over a period of time. The retailer may take a beating on some items that had to be adjusted downward to reflect quality. Higher than projected prices would provide revenue to cover those misfortunes that periodically occur in any business. A rigid formula could rapidly destroy the image or reputation of a firm.

The relationship between price and quality also applies at the wholesale level. Cost-of-production figures often have influenced growers when pricing their products. A grower may feel that he or she needs 75 cents for a plant in a 4½-inch pot to realize a modest profit. What happens when a cultural problem arises reducing the quality of the crop? Should he still charge 75 cents? Does the quality of the product warrant the listed price? Can a retailer make any money paying 75 cents and then being able to charge only $1 for the plant?

Services

Consumers often have difficulty recognizing that services such as credit, special wrappings, delivery, and planting all must be reflected in prices. These services must be identified to insure that consumers do not come to inaccurate conclusions regarding prices associated with independent and service-minded firms. Some operators have broken down costs offering consumers the choice of purchasing undecorated plants and buying on a cash and carry basis. This technique has helped retailers post more attractive prices and become more competitive with large discount firms. Some garden center–nursery operations offer a planting service with shrubs and trees. The cost of employing a planting crew has risen considerably in recent years. The cost must be recaptured and reflected in the retail price or applied as a separate fee. Special services bear a price tag and consumers must be advised when retail prices include them along with basic cost of the product.

Special Prices

Mass merchandisers often advertise a slight break in price when purchasing two or more units. This practice has been adopted by some wholesalers and retailers marketing geraniums. A single geranium might retail for $1.75. The price for a dozen could be set at $17.00 rather than $21.00. Some consumers can be tempted to buy a larger volume because of the reduction in price. Special prices must be constructed with the recognition that they will have an impact on gross profits. The price may be justified on the basis of increased store traffic even though the store ends up trading dollars on the particular item. Price reductions made on the spur of the moment and without any real thought can seriously impair the profit position of a firm.

Posting Prices

Exclusive stores often have the reputation of displaying unpriced merchandise in windows and display counters. Many shoppers shy away from retail stores adopting this practice. Unpriced merchandise also has the same impact on some people as waving a red cape in front of a bull. It suggests that the seller plans to gouge the buyer. This, in fact, often has been the situation, with sellers trying to capitalize on unsuspecting buyers. One garden center operator freely admitted that prices varied according to the dress of the customer.

There is no excuse to mask the price of plant materials and related items. The practice suggests that someone is consciously trying to deceive or simply does not understand the needs and wants of consumers. Customers have been forced to ask untold numbers of questions of store personnel in situations where prices have not been clearly posted. Valuable time has been sacrificed by clerks responding to questions that might have been avoided. The desired image of the organization can be distorted through failure of management to price merchandise. Carefully consider and relate all aspects of your pricing programs to overall goals and image of the firm.

Profits

A primary goal of your pricing strategy should be to record reasonable profits at the conclusion of the year. Profits provide the means for growth and replacement of deteriorating structures. A good profit record insures that some day the operation will prove attractive to buyers. The ability to generate loans often hinges on the record of the firm in recording a reasonable return on investment. A poor record, often reflecting archaic pricing practices, cannot stand the test of examination by those handling bank loans.

Pricing strategy must become more sophisticated to help counter dramatic and sharp increases in product costs and labor. The era when managers were content to average profits from the entire product mix has drawn to a close. Well-trained business people have entered the industry and focused increasing attention on analysis of costs for each and every item offered to buyers. They have demonstrated clearly that producers, for example, have lost money on some items and traded dollars on many other products. Prices must reflect costs, value to consumers, and a fair return on investment. Retailers as well as producers must continually analyze their pricing strategy to insure that it accurately reflects current conditions and assures a reasonable profit.

SUMMARY

Pricing strategy is an art and a science. Sellers must analyze a product or service in terms of its value to buyers. Careful controls must be exercised to insure that the organization will stay in the black and record a fair return on investment. A variety of techniques may be employed including one or more formulas in achieving stated goals. Often, this involves identifying a specific gross profit percentage that represents an important step in assuring a reasonable profit.

Sellers must recognize that buyers continually look for and capitalize on weaknesses to drive prices down or maintain the status quo. The absence of a common language often has worked against the best interest of sellers. The 4½-inch geranium illustrates this dilemma clearly.

Some operators have adopted the simple strategy of follow the leader. They hope and pray the leader has full knowledge of costs and reflects them in the pricing schedule.

Consumers should be given the option to compare products and have an opportunity to choose inexpensive, moderate, or high priced merchandise depending on their needs. Buyers respond favorably when offered a choice.

Innovation and cultivar identification represent two important weapons in the arsenal of producers and retailers to command premium prices. Garden center operators are virtually assured that seed companies will offer a host of new selections each year and for many years to come. The All-America Awards program has been created to attract publicity to three or four new flowers and a comparable number of vegetables. New introductions provide a mechanism for firms to raise prices gradually and differentiate their operations from competitors. Prices should be clearly posted on all merchandise.

This practice reduces inquiries from consumers and avoids the possibility of projecting an image of an "exclusive" organization.

The art of pricing often involves a special touch to anticipate consumer responses to one cent sales and magic number prices. Impulse sales will be stimulated when consumers do not have to stop to think whether they can afford a product. A real test of management ability lies in its skill at overcoming buyer resistance to higher prices. Your pricing strategy should strengthen and enhance the image and profit position of the organization.

1. Discuss and provide examples of the nature and extent of a common language employed when describing bedding and related plants.

2. Compute the selling price on an item costing $2 and having (a) a 40 percent margin and (b) a 40 percent markup.

3. What might be the advantages and disadvantages of the role of price leader?

4. How should one react to news that a competitor is selling a particular item at an extremely low price?

5. What are the advantages and disadvantages of providing options in terms of low, medium, and high quality products?

6. How can you justify a particular price or an increase in price?

7. Provide examples of and discuss merits of attractive prices and magic numbers.

8. Outline a product and price situation in which the seller has molded a product to meet specific needs of a clientele group. Discuss philosophy of this project.

9. What are the merits of a one-cent sale vs. a two-for-the-price-of-one sale?

10. Why should prices be posted clearly for all items displayed in a store?

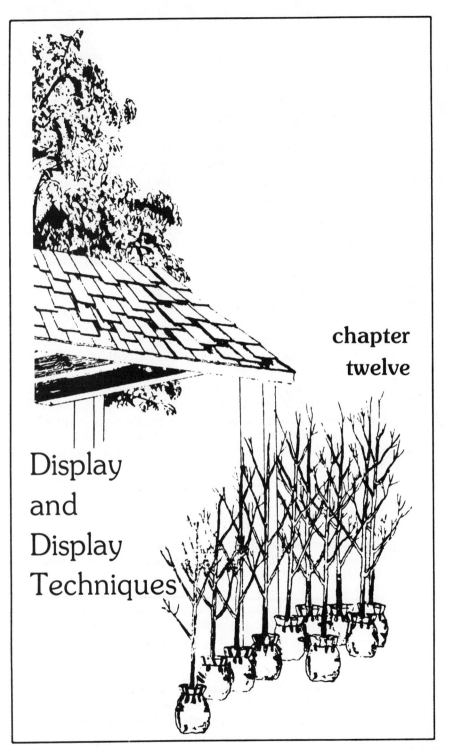

chapter
twelve

Display
and
Display
Techniques

Good display techniques stimulate sales and minimize injury to plant materials. Customers like to shop in well-lit areas and where they can easily reach plants and supplies. Narrow aisles, crowded displays, slippery walks, and dimly lit rooms counter all the natural attributes of garden center products.

Warm weather signals the beginning of spring and a new selling season. The rush is on with gardeners anxious to landscape their property and start a vegetable garden. The pressures become so great that one simply doesn't have time to practice all that one hears about good display techniques. Surviving each day becomes the primary objective for management and workers.

The real key to good displays lies in planning and preparation well before the start of each new season. January and February traditionally have been slow months for many garden store operators. This is the time that one can review traffic flow patterns and create special displays. Signs can be fabricated and tables repainted to provide a new look to the operation.

A simple technique can help you prepare for each new season. Ask a friend to join you and an employee in taking a good hard look at your operation. This could be done individually or as a team. The process starts even before you enter the store. Travel by the garden center in a car. How do the approach signs look, as well as those in front of the store? Are the front windows dead or alive? Does the front need a new paint job? If so, put it on the calendar for a summer activity or just before the spring rush. Now, it's time to pass through the front door. What do you first see? Does it spark some excitement? Are there signs directing people to different areas of the store? What kind of traffic flow pattern have you established with display units? Look at your displays through the eyes of customers. Would you want to shop in your own store? Why?

DISPLAY UNITS

Bedding plants and small potted materials capture attention when customers can look down on them rather than up. This provides an opportunity to view the blossoms fully. Placement of packs and small pots on the ground has been commonly practiced by many mass outlet operators and some independent managers. This location insures that customers can view plants in a near normal setting. It does require that customers bend a great deal to reach the units. The long reach may discourage some people from browsing and shopping for extended periods of time.

An alternate solution has been to construct display tables approximately 24 to 30 inches above ground level. Plants are within easy reach of consumers. They can browse in comfort and not exert a great deal of energy in examining bedding plants. One operator has effectively used two levels of apple crates

Customers must bend a long way to reach bedding plants that have been displayed on the ground. There is always a possibility that plants will root through into the soil.

Low display tables provide easy access by shoppers, and plants receive adequate light to avoid stretching and leggy growth.

to construct display tables. These units have been available in spring and then put to use handling apples in the fall, simplifying storage problems of a bulky unit.

A third method has been construction of tiered shelves. The unit may be designed in the form of an inverted V to display materials on two aisles or from one side. The shelves are approximately 12 inches wide and capable of holding flats and individual packs as well as pots. Tiered shelves help minimize plant injury in contrast to customers reaching into the center of level benches for choice plants. There is something extra special about the appearance of the display when plants have been neatly arranged on these shelves. The feeling also is created that the display tables hold much more material than actually on sale.

The lowest shelf can be placed approximately 6 to 12 inches above the ground. The upper shelf might be about 5 feet from ground level. All plants should receive adequate light with this arrangement of shelves.

Tiered shelves provide maximum and orderly plant display, in addition to facilitating access by customers and minimizing injuries to plants.

Several operators have displayed plants on shelving comparable to that used by supermarkets. Each shelf blocks light from plants displayed on a lower shelf. Plant quality declines rapidly unless market packs and pots are rotated and stay only a day or two on the premises.

Large, bulky nursery stock normally has been displayed on the ground, since one does not move such plants for inspection as easily as geraniums and tomatoes. A special effort should be made to maintain and display balled and burlapped (B & B) and container stock in an attractive manner. Care should be taken in placing an attractive mulch material around plants in well-defined sales beds.

Special racks can be utilized for display of roses and some packaged nursery stock. Ideally, customers will be looking down when viewing this material. Rose bins have been constructed so that the base stands approximately 30 inches above the ground. Customers can easily reach and examine packages without having to bend over into an awkward position. Racks for nursery stock may be much closer to ground level and dependent upon overall size of plant materials.

This cart can be moved indoors in a matter of minutes at the close of each day. Plants in the center and on the lower shelves may have a tendency to stretch when not exposed to more adequate light conditions.

Large foliage plants should be displayed in a natural setting. Their overall size normally requires that they be displayed close to the ground. Some operators have created gardens similar to what you might see in a large conservatory such as Mitchell Park in Milwaukee, Wisconsin. Plants of varying heights and foliage patterns can be grouped together in these informal displays. Low display tables like those used in homes can be used to merchandise effectively medium sized green plants. Small green plants should be displayed within easy reach of customers. They can be placed on tables about 30 inches high. A two or three tier recessed shelving arrangement can be placed on top of the table for maximum display of plants.

Flowering plants vary in size from African violets to poinsettias. The customer sees the maximum display from the Christmas poinsettia plant by looking down on the bracts. Typical supermarket display units do not show off plants in an ideal fashion. Those displayed on the top shelf often have been out of sight for most customers. Floor displays are acceptable if customers do not have to bend over continuously to shop for merchandise.

A recessed, tiered arrangement of shelves also provides maximum flexibility in displaying a wide variety of flowering plants. Shorter plants can be placed within easy reach of customers. The top level works well for low growing plants such as the African violet while lower levels can feature taller growing items.

Balled and burlapped trees and shrubs should be set in mulch material to provide an attractive display and prevent root damage.

Saw-horse racks provide excellent displays for packaged nursery stock.

SIGNS AND POSTERS

The great garden boom of the 1980s has been spurred by many new and young gardeners. People who never planted a seed before suddenly became captivated with a patio tomato, a hanging basket, or a single geranium plant decorating a sunny window. These enthusiastic and budding gardeners still desire a wealth of information. They never cease to ask questions of anyone willing to stop and chat for a few moments.

Colorful signs have become an essential ingredient for successful garden center operators all across the country. They have been used to attract attention and present information on prices and cultural requirements of plants. Common questions often can be answered without tying up valuable time of sales personnel. Attractive posters often provide consumers with suggestions on planting combinations and plants suitable for different locations. These sales aids have proven highly beneficial to new gardeners.

Too many signs can clutter the entire landscape. This tends to detract from saleability of colorful plants. Haphazard sizes and materials used in constructing signs often suggest that the operator is amateur and reflects poorly on the image of the firm. Excessive and illegible information won't be read even by interested gardeners.

Good display posters should be legible and answer most of the questions that customers have about the product.

Colorful posters focusing attention on trees, shrubs, garden roses, green plants, and garden flowers have been available from a variety of suppliers and commercial printers. This material can be used to help customers make purchasing decisions. Care must be exercised to display them neatly and not overpower a particular sales area. The unit on green plants should be displayed in the vicinity of the foliage sales area and other signs in similar fashion near various plant materials.

Hand-lettered signs should be prepared by someone who has talent with a magic marker. Uneven lettering and misspelled words reflect poorly on management. Colored posters have a tendency to fade after being exposed to direct sunlight. Old posters should be removed to avoid giving the impression that your operation is handling outdated products.

Manufacturers of herbicides for lawns have developed colored posters helping gardeners identify weeds. This material should be displayed adjacent to the display of pesticides. A series of colored posters was prepared by the University of Wisconsin–Extension several years ago, focusing attention on common garden problems. Each poster contained close-up views, an appropriate title, and brief description of the problem. The garden center operator was directed to use a grease pencil to list available and recommended products for control of each pest. Gardeners were able to identify their own problems and select products to control the appropriate insect or disease organism.

Planting Guide for Annuals

Variety (Annual Flowers)	Space Plants (inches)	Height (inches)	Flower Beds Borders	Bas Boxes Planters	Hanging Baskets	Cut Flowers	Pots	Packs	Sun/Shade
ALYSSUM	7"	4"	•	•					
AGERATUM	8"	8-12"	•	•					
BEGONIA	6-8"	8-10"	•	•	•				
CELOSIA	12"	6-30"	•	•		•			
COLEUS	12"	8-10"	•	•	•				
GERANIUMS	18"	20-24"	•	•					
IMPATIENS	12"	8-12"	•	•	•				
MARIGOLD, Dwarf	9-12"	6-15"	•	•					
MARIGOLD, Tall	18"	18-36"	•			•			
PANSY	6"	6"	•	•		•			
PETUNIA	12"	10-14"	•	•	•	•			
PORTULACA	6"	6"	•	•		•			
SALVIA, Dwarf	12"	10-16"	•	•					
SALVIA, Tall	18"	18-30"	•						
SNAPDRAGON, Dwarf	12"	12"	•	•		•			
SNAPDRAGON, Tall	12"	24-36"	•			•			
VERBENA	12"	8-15"	•	•	•	•			
VINCA	10"	10-12"	•	•		•			
ZINNIA, Dwarf	8"	6-12"	•	•		•			
ZINNIA, Tall	12"	18-36"	•			•			

Vegetables / All Sun	Spacing In Rows	Inches Between Rows	Days to Harvest	Pots	Packs	Comments
Tomatoes	24-30	36	45-80			
Peppers	18-24	18-24	65-80			
Cabbage	18	18-24	70-90			
Cucumber	12	48-60	30-45			
Cantaloupe	12	48-60	60-75			

Culture:
1. Rake flower bed to smooth, even surface
2. Water plants thoroughly
3. Remove plants carefully, do not injure roots
4. Press soil firmly around root ball
5. Water to settle soil - do not let soil dry out
6. Feed the newly set plant to hasten rooting
7. Shade plant first day or two if 75° or above
8. Water slowly but thoroughly - 6 inches deep

This planting guide contains a wealth of information on the culture of popular annual flowers.

TOMATO VARIETIES

hybrid	days	size	
Sweet 100	45	mini	
Early Girl	60	med	good early
Fantastic	65	med	high yield
Earliana	65	med	
Early Giant	65	large	high yield
Spring Giant	70	large	high yield
Patio	70	med	for containers
Better Boy	75	med	high yield
Marglobe	75	med	
Heinz 1350	75	large	high yield good canning
Golden Jubilee	80	med	low acid · yellow
Bragger	90	large	pink fruit
Oxheart	90	large	pink low acid
All Season Mix	best early medium & late selection		

This garden center features an excellent selection of tomato varieties and provides gardeners with desired information regarding fruiting season, yield, and type of fruit.

239

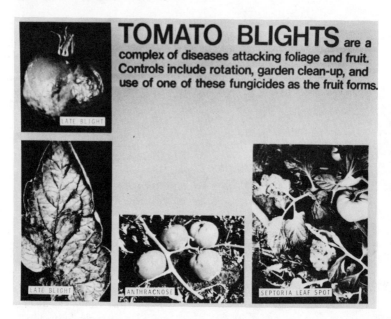

This poster was created to help garden center operators sell pesticides and answer questions concerning a host of garden problems. (Source: Originally produced by University of Wisconsin—Extension, Madison, Wisconsin.)

SPACING

Customers shy away from areas when they can't have an opportunity to turn plants around or see them from all sides. Crowding nursery stock, annuals, perennials, and indoor plants results in excessive breakage and injury to stems, leaves, and flowers. Plants cannot be displayed like boxes of corn flakes or even oranges and potatoes. A typical geranium plant in a 4½-inch pot will have a spread of approximately 6 to 8 inches. You must allocate a minimum of one quarter of a square foot to avoid injury and to stimulate rapid turnover.

Nursery stock in containers and B & B should be displayed so that foliage is not overlapping from plant to plant. There is no other way to determine the symmetry or shape of a plant. An orderly and neat display captures attention and stimulates sales. Package roses often have been displayed tightly. This can be accomplished with minimum injury providing new growth has not started to spread. Customers can cause serious injury by digging into displays for that choice plant, especially when new sprouts have appeared on canes. Injury to roses can be minimized by storing bushes in a cool location to prevent sprouting. Bushes should not be stacked ten deep but rather in an upright position and in only five or so layers.

Disorderly displays detract from the appearance of unsold plants and give customers a bad impression of your business.

Remove plants from shipping cartons before displaying them to customers. Close spacing damages plants and hinders examination.

241

SHOPPING ENVIRONMENT

The sales area environment plays a major role in helping attract customers and maintaining plants in top condition. Spring weather conditions are highly variable and often feature sun, wind, and cool temperatures. Gardeners like to shop in convenient and pleasant surroundings even though most plants are destined for the outdoors.

Nursery stock must be protected from strong winds. Excessive drying conditions can result in wilting and decline of the root system. Young growth may suffer and fail to survive periods of extreme water stress. A wind barrier helps reduce water loss and maintains plants in good condition.

Some trees and shrubs can tolerate partial shade. Fruit trees and some stock sold in bare root or packaged form can benefit from reduced light intensity. Lath structures break or reduce intense rays from the sun. Customers can browse in more comfortable conditions and often receive protection from light rains.

Bedding plants often are displayed outdoors. Mother Nature can be especially hard on young, tender plants. Low night temperatures can set plants back and occasionally destroy tender annuals. One enterprising operator has placed wire frames bent into a semicircle over his bedding plant displays. These are designed to hold up plastic used to cover displays on cold nights. The covering can easily be pulled over in a few minutes. The

A lath structure protects plants and provides customers with comfortable browsing areas.

purchase of hardened plants helps minimize losses caused by unusually cold nights. This material has been slowly exposed to cold temperatures by knowledgeable growers.

A greenhouse provides an unusual and often ideal shopping environment. Customers can browse in comfort and often discard heavy coats. Plants never have that weather-beaten look and seem to have extra appeal under a glass or plastic roof. Gardeners can shop throughout the day without fear of winds, rain, or snow. Some operators have reported that their best sales often have occurred on nasty days and only because gardeners couldn't work outdoors. The greenhouse turns out a welcome haven for the impatient gardener.

Mass Displays

Solid blocks of color capture much more attention than hit-and-miss displays featuring several colors as well as several types of plant materials. One operator lined a whole wall of his sales area with red geraniums. A second and somewhat shorter area featured pink cultivars. The sight was almost overwhelming to shoppers who couldn't resist taking home a few plants.

Limited space requires that you operate on a small basis when grouping plants. Six petunia cultivars were placed in neat fashion on a 4 by 12 foot peninsular bench. The orderly approach gave the impression that much more merchandise was on display than was really there. Customers were attracted to the neat color display and could easily compare cultivars.

Nursery stock should be displayed in the same fashion as just described for bedding plants. Large blocks of uniform plants capture much more attention from shoppers than sloppy displays. Ground covers must be grouped together just as you would locate foundation plants in a separate part of the sales area.

All shade-grown material grouped into one sales area permits shoppers to carefully and easily choose among recommended items. Signs should indicate that these materials have been selected for shade. Sun-loving plants also should be identified according to their cultural needs. Shade trees scattered on a hit-and-miss basis requires a great deal of walking on the part of store personnel and customers. Orderly displays based on customer needs simplify the selling process and in the long run stimulate sales.

Perennials as well as annuals should be assigned specific areas based on physical size and amount of dollars grossed per square foot. One new operation began with vegetables mixed in with annual and perennial flowers. Customers got very angry trying to find tomato cultivars among the petunias.

"The Vegetable House" appears on a sign hung above the doors of a small plastic structure on the premises of a garden center. Customers can find all their vegetable plants in this area. Tomato plants ranging in size from two feet, planted in a large tub, to a pack containing six young plants, all appear in this area. Convenience has been the theme of this particular operation.

Bench Coverings

Many potted plants have been sold direct from greenhouse benches. The production area quickly becomes converted to a sales area with the beginning of the bedding plant season. Placement of pots directly on soil often leads to roots penetrating into the bench soil. Roots seek a source of water and move out through the drainage opening and down into soil or a layer of sand appearing on the surface of the bench. Consumers find it difficult removing plants and in the process often injure roots. A mass of roots may still protrude from the drainage opening, making it impossible to rest the plant on a level surface. Many growers have used a layer of black polyethylene or a wire-meshed material to prevent roots coming into contact with soil. This provides the consumer with a cleaner pot and a healthier plant.

Roots quickly grow through the base of small pots and into soil. Some form of barrier must be used to restrict root growth to the interior of pots.

Special Displays

Garden center operators often find themselves short of display space in the spring. This partially explains limited utilization of special tables featuring:

1. New items
2. Combination sales
3. Half-price specials

New introductions often become lost in the shuffle during the busy spring season. Some gardeners have been exposed to All-America selections and then can't distinguish them from other selections when browsing in a garden center store. A special table near the entrance can be employed to show representative samples of all new plant materials for the year.

Aisles

Narrow aisles, a common occurrence in many greenhouses, play a major role in limiting sales each year. Customers risk injury to clothing and must

A narrow aisle restricts traffic and often means customers' clothes may be soiled or torn.

work to inspect plants. One person shopping in an aisle limits other customers from browsing in the same area. You simply cannot pass by another person when the diameter of an aisle ranges from 18 to 24 inches.

A peninsula system provides sufficient aisle space for maximum customer population in a given area. The aisles are relatively short and often two people can pass by each other with a minimum of effort. A wide center walk permits the use of shopping carts to facilitate purchase of large quantities of plants.

The peninsula benching system features a wide aisle and permits one to push shopping carts without concern for blocking the traffic pattern of other shoppers.

Greenhouses do attract attention and customers like to see plants in this environment. Shoppers must be protected from splinters, algae growing on wooden benches, and wires holding up interior racks and containers. One of these could destroy good clothing in a matter of minutes. Broken glass often becomes a hazard in older structures. Panes slip out occasionally and splinters fly in all directions.

Walkways should be black-topped or covered with concrete. They can become very slippery when moisture comes in contact with a soil base. One often has the feeling of treading on an oil slick. Outdoor aisles should be wide enough to permit easy flow of customers. They should permit two people to pass by without rubbing shoulders.

Normal greenhouse

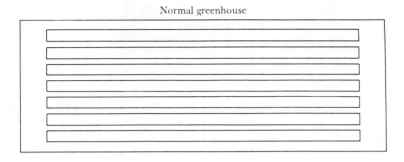

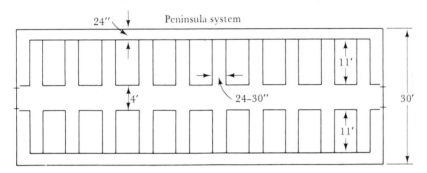

Long aisles outdoors, in the greenhouse, and in the garden shop should be avoided for the benefit of sales personnel and customers. Supermarkets used to force customers to walk several miles, traveling up and down aisles from the front to the rear of the store. Modern stores now have crosswalks permitting short cuts. A good mulch material, such as bark, can be employed on outdoor walks to aid customer safety. Slippery spots can be avoided and in the process mud will be kept from discoloring shoes.

A new type of concrete, known as porous concrete, can be used for flooring in garden centers and greenhouses. This is especially beneficial in those areas where plants are maintained and water settles on the floor. The porous concrete allows water to pass through. Customers can move through the area with little or no threat of slipping and subsequent injury.

Chemicals

What happens if someone knocks over a bottle of an insecticide and it crashes onto the floor? Are you prepared to wipe up the liquid quickly before the material spreads and the odor drives customers from the store? How should you clean up a pesticide? A supply of mops and paper toweling will do a poor job in quickly soaking up potent chemicals. You really need something that will soak it up in a few seconds. A supply of sawdust or ground

The material used under the benches is known as porous concrete. Excess water drains rapidly and surfaces dry shortly after each watering.

corn cobs can be applied to a wet floor. These and similar products will soak the unwanted materials up rapidly, returning the floor to its normal condition.

Sample Plants

Consumers like to buy bedding plants like petunias in full color. Producers and many garden center operators prefer to sell them in the green stage or just starting to show a little color. A green plant generally doesn't occupy as much room as one in full flowei. Customers often receive a better buy in terms of receiving a well branched and compact plant ready to burst forth with a riot of color. An aggressive operator solved the problem by constructing a special rack adjacent to the petunia display. It contained pots of all the cultivars that were being sold in market packs. Each pot was labeled and in full color. Customers could quickly view this unique display and choose from among thirty different petunias for their garden.

Potted materials coming into early bloom have been handled by many operators for customers wanting a premium plant for a cemetery planter, hanging basket, or window box. These plants have been started earlier than those in packs and come into full bloom at the beginning of the season.

End of Season

Many garden centers and greenhouses look like disaster areas near the end of the season. Plants often have been allowed to wilt and it's difficult to separate out saleable material from that destined for the trash pile. It takes a special, and sometimes superhuman effort to maintain displays in reasonable condition toward the end of the season. You must make this effort if you really want to sell merchandise at this late date.

Wilted and sick plants are unsalable and should be removed from display areas. This is a common sight at the close of the traditional bedding plant season and on busy days.

Some operators have acquired fresh merchandise for late sales. This material is healthy, stocky, and looks as good as those plants sold on opening day. A growing number of producers have planted a late crop specifically for this business. Reordering nursery stock in late spring depends to a large extent on your summer and fall plans as well as availability of stock. A landscape contractor requires many items right up until frost. The ability to overwinter stock often influences size of purchase orders. Poor or inadequate facilities may discourage extensive late deliveries. Good winter facilities including plastic structures provide an insurance policy. The operator can buy confidently knowing that material will be available for sale the following season.

Mass outlets and some independent operators have conducted business during a relatively short period of time in the spring. Most nursery stock will be ordered well in advance of the new season with one or two deliveries coming just prior to the main rush of business. There has been little time for reordering during the short, concentrated selling periods. Late deliveries can create many problems as management begins to fold the tent in favor of other store activities.

Close-out sales, while a necessity, should not be required to move unusually large volumes of unsold merchandise. It would be wise to avoid the temptation of late purchases. The smart operator has learned to be content with hanging up the "Sold Out" sign when unprepared to handle nursery stock throughout the summer months.

Haphazard Displays

Have you ever walked into a garden center or any retail operation and wondered who the clown was that set up and maintained displays? Some operators make it a chore to separate out recently acquired plants from those that should have been junked months ago. Here are some pet peeves:

1. Pots allowed to remain on their side due to an uneven or unstable base.
2. Indoor plants mixed with outdoor and sun-loving plants.
3. Impatiens displayed in one greenhouse and other shade-loving materials in distant areas.
4. Different size pots on the same bench and only one price tag obviously for one size unit.
5. Dead plants left on the bench.
6. Weeds growing under benches.

The rush of business often has been identified as the primary reason for rundown displays. While this often has been true, poor planning ranks as a most significant factor in management's inability to maintain displays in top condition.

Quantity on Display

People seem to be suspicious when only a few items remain for sale. Large displays, on the other hand, capture a great deal of attention. Restocking your selling area is an important marketing task that cannot be relegated to an inferior position. Try to arrange mass displays and keep them well stocked during the busy season. Most customers like to browse and choose the best plant from among a good selection of merchandise. They often will discuss the item with neighbors and friends whether it's an indoor plant, a tree, shrub, or geranium. The purchase reflects on their taste and good judgment in selecting a quality plant. The decision making process becomes much easier when the buyer has been presented with a number of choices (more than six). One plant on display, unless unusually attractive, leads to the conclusion that it represents the bottom of the barrel. The decision not to buy becomes easier.

Display Gardens

Gardeners want to beautify their property and homes with goods and services offered by garden center operators. They receive some ideas from magazines and other gardeners. An excellent source of ideas often has been those available from garden centers and specifically display gardens constructed for benefit of the public.

An elaborate planting of spring flowering bulbs graces the perimeter of one rapidly growing garden center just outside of Milwaukee, Wisconsin. All cultivars offered for sale have been planted in a number of beds along with trees and shrubs. Special emphasis has been given to color combinations and season of bloom. A small planter around an attractive sign in front of an establishment can stimulate ideas. Some spring flowering bulbs followed by a planting of petunias or fibrous-rooted begonias can trigger many purchases.

A major landscape contractor recently expanded his operation to include a full-fledged garden center. A large area for a display garden was available to this operator located on the outskirts of a medium-size community. The contractor carried an extensive line of decorative stone mulches, concrete patio blocks, and railroad ties for retaining walls and steps. He proceeded to put these materials to work in showing customers how they would look in actual settings.

Some people can create mental pictures from small samples, and others have to see the complete picture. The patio and mulch displays left few questions regarding usage and role of each product.

A return trip to this landscape contractor some years later proved disheartening. He had deemphasized many facets of the garden center business. Customers were still invited to choose nursery stock and select mulches and related materials. Virtually all displays had been allowed to deteriorate. Patio blocks had turned to dust and weeds covered the once attractive displays. This pathetic display was working against him as customers could see some of the future maintenance problems they would have with their gardens and patios.

An attractive sign and a small bed of flowers welcome gardeners to this retail operation each spring, summer, and early fall.

Display gardens aid sales—but they must be maintained. Poor upkeep will destroy customer appeal.

Display gardens can be a positive marketing tool. They must be carefully designed and then maintained in top condition. Tear them out and sod the area when they have outlived their usefulness. Don't let them deteriorate right in front of potential customers.

Color

Color is a major weapon in the hands of garden center operators seeking to attract customers. Manufacturers of foods and most other products have devoted valuable resources toward creation of colorful boxes and wrappings for their products. Sometimes we take for granted that our products are colorful and require few if any skills in making them attractive to customers. Good color grouping adds to the environment and spurs sales.

The impact of color was dramatized recently during a visit to two small Quonset greenhouses. They were identical units that had been set up on a temporary basis on parking lots and separated only by a distance of less than one mile. One unit was maintained by part-time clerks working for a large outlet. The interior appearance was ugly. A retail florist maintained the second unit. It was a riot of color and truly beautiful. Each greenhouse had been supplied with the same assortment of plants. One individual knew how to use color and the other neglected it entirely.

Central Sales Area

Garden center–greenhouse operations frequently have been noted for selling plant materials over a wide area of space. Vegetable plants may be located in House 7, petunias in House 1, and geraniums somewhere in the back forty. Customers and sales personnel have walked many miles to select plants.

A better approach has involved concentration of plant materials into one central location. Sufficient stock of all saleable merchandise has been brought to this area. Customers can choose plants with a minimum of effort. A few clerks may be employed in addition to those at cash registers to answer customer questions. It is important to stock this area continually to discourage customers from wandering into other greenhouses. This is likely to happen when the geranium supply has been depleted. You may need to assign a person the task of refilling sales tables throughout the day.

Light

Light is one of the most important environmental factors in capturing the attention of potential customers. Poorly lit areas repel and bright areas attract. A part-time operator tried to display bedding plants on typical retail racks in a relatively dark area and under fiberglass. The plants stretched and stretched because of low light intensity. Customers even had a hard time finding materials.

Excessive light in the summer, associated with heat, can make it unbearable to shop in greenhouses. Some shading compound becomes necessary to improve the sales environment.

Many garden center operators have unknowingly made it difficult for customers to shop by providing minimum light intensities on displays throughout the store. Good lighting is a key ingredient in increasing sales and profits. Purchase a light meter and record readings just on top of merchandise throughout your store. Make sure you provide the recommended intensities in foot-candles for the following key areas:

Foliage and flowering plants	200 f.c.
Self-service areas	100–200 f.c.
Showcases	200–500 f.c.
Special display tables	150–250 f.c.
Small conference or reading room	150 f.c.
Show windows	200–400 f.c.
Cash register area	Min. 70 f.c.

Very high output fluorescent lamps have been used to light this foliage display room. The cathedral-type ceiling gives a feeling of spaciousness and a more natural atmosphere for the sale of green plants.

A special effort must be made to balance light intensities to avoid drastic changes as customers move from area to area. The eyes can tolerate only minor variations.

Take a walk through the store and carefully examine each area including the ceiling and walls. Here are some problems that you should always attempt to avoid:

1. Shadows from improperly placed fixtures, suspended signs, and vertical displays. Remember that merchandise always looks dead when located in a shadowy area.

2. Glare from unshaded light bulbs and reflections from merchandise and display tables can prove irritating to eyes.

3. Distorted colors such as dark purple roses and poinsettia bracts coming from use of cool-white fluorescent lamps.

4. Poor decor on lamp fixtures.

5. Failure to adequately highlight display tables. You can use spotlights for accent lighting.

Don't confuse good lighting with high light intensity. Some merchandise, like plants, requires unusually bright conditions. Typical displays of pesticides often require only half the light intensity.

A rule of thumb to follow is that the distance between light fixtures should be just less than the distance from the floor to ceiling. A 10-foot ceiling would suggest that 4-foot fluorescent light fixtures be spaced no more than 8 to 10 feet apart. Mercury vapor lights have become increasingly popular for lighting in some retail stores. This source of light works especially well when the ceiling height is about 14 feet above the floor.

The light source can distort or aid the true colors of the products you have for sale. A combination of warm and cool-white fluorescent tubes can provide a balanced spectrum for good plant growth. The units must remain on 10 hours a day, for 7 days a week.

Cool-white fluorescent tubes give off large quantities of blue light. They have been used extensively for general lighting in stores. People and clothing do not show as well under this type of light. Warm-white bulbs emit light in the red spectrum. This light brings out red colors and is also good for foliage plants. This is a good choice for efficiency and color tone. Deluxe warm-white is less efficient than warm-white, but people and clothing appear to advantage under this light.

The following information, compiled by Dr. H.M. Cathey, USDA Research Horticulturist, and Dr. L.E. Campbell, USDA Research Agricultural Engineer, Beltsville, Md., helps answer questions on how light sources affect color:

LAMP Fluorescent	GENERAL APPEARANCE ON A NEUTRAL WALL OR SURFACE	SKIN COMPLEXION
Cool White (CW)	White	Pale Pink
Warm White (WW)	Yellowish	Sallow
Gro Lux (GRO)	Pink white	Reddish
Gro Lux-WS (GRO-WS)	Light pink white	Pink
Agro-lite (AGRO)	White	Pink
Vita-lite (VITA)	White	Pink
Discharge		
Mercury (all types) (HG)	Purplish white	Ruddy
High pressure sodium (HPS)	Yellowish	Yellowish
Incandescent (INC)	Yellowish white	Ruddy
Note: Incandescent is the regular household lamp.		

ATMOSPHERE (The effect or general feeling of the room)		FLOWER COLOR (Colors improved or strengthened)	GREYED (Undesirable)
CW	Neutral to cool	Blue, yellow, orange	Red
WW	Yellow to warm	Yellow, orange	Blue, green, red
GRO	Purple to pink	Blue, red	Green, yellow
GRO-WS	Warm	Blue, yellow, red	Green
AGRO	Neutral to warm	Blue, yellow, red	Green
VITA	Neutral to cool	Blue, yellow, red	Green
HG	Cool	Blue, green, yellow	Red
HPS	Warm	Green, yellow, orange	Blue, red
INC	Warm	Yellow, orange, red	Blue

The task of properly lighting a store often requires the services of a trained lighting specialist. Proper lighting should be treated with the same concern as selection of display tables and even the product mix. You simply cannot sell merchandise unless it appears attractive and can easily be viewed by your customers.

Pesticides

Many if not most gardeners have experienced difficulty in finding and selecting recommended pesticides. Part of the frustration begins with their own inability to diagnose a problem. They may have difficulty in accurately describing it to store clerks. Inexperienced sales personnel may not be able to distinguish a fungicide from an insecticide. The problem has been compounded by displays containing all types of pesticides arranged in haphazard fashion.

A carefully designed pesticide display can help eliminate many frustrations and in the process insure customer satisfaction. This task requires time and planning on the part of management. The process begins with a simple sorting of chemicals into at least three groupings:

Pesticides should be sorted into appropriate groups such as "controls for sucking insects" to facilitate choice and prevent errors by customers or sales personnel.

1. Insecticides for control of insects
2. Fungicides for control of diseases
3. Herbicides for control of weeds

Good attractive signs that describe the basic pest category should be placed above these three groups to insure that customers do not leave with the wrong material.

Subgrouping would further aid the consumer and sales personnel in selecting the right product for a specific problem. Those materials controlling sucking insects should be displayed in one section. Chewing insects require a separate and distinct grouping of compounds. Leaf spot diseases can be distinguished from problems attacking the root system, seeds, and stem.

A number of common problems arise every year. A special display or colored tags can be placed on products designed to control:

1. Crabgrass

2. Dandelions
3. Aphids
4. Grubs
5. Mildew on roses
6. Black spot on roses

The pesticide display area can be arranged in systematic fashion according to particular pests or groupings of pests. Make it simple to buy recommended products and in the process guarantee satisfied customers.

PRODUCT LOCATION

Small shops limit flexibility of management in selecting the best area for each product. You must try to avoid the cluttered look and still stock as much material as possible in the store. Limiting product lines may become a

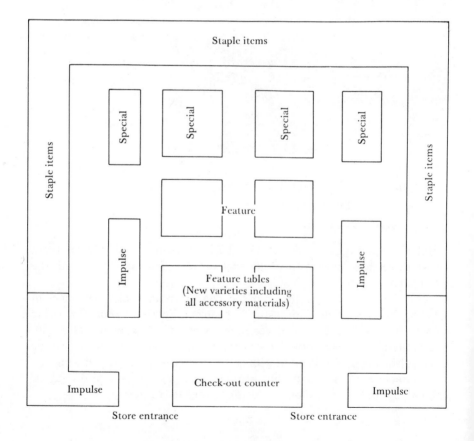

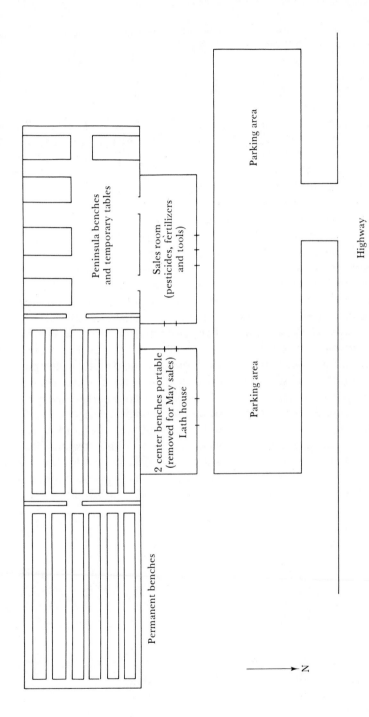

necessity to insure displaying an adequate volume of each product and providing room for customers to browse.

Pesticide displays can capture a great deal of space because of the number of products and manufacturers. You can save space by selling products from only one manufacturer except in those instances when the firm does not handle an important item.

Store managers have room to maneuver when larger areas become available for indoor display of garden products. Returns per square foot of floor space often serve as a good indicator of space allocation and location of each product within the store. Prime space cannot be given to slow moving and bulky items. Quick turnover items often occupy more expensive space near the front of the store.

Where do you locate the pesticide display? Pesticides fall into the necessity category and are rarely subject to impulse sales. A common practice has been to locate these products near the rear of the store. This assumes that they will have some visibility and consumers know that you stock the merchandise. Customers must move to the rear of the store passing numerous displays to acquire the desired item. There is always the hope that they will pick up some impulse items along the way and thus help increase sales.

The route taken to the rear of the store may be direct or side to side as customers pass by numerous displays. The latter forces them to see a great deal of merchandise that they might miss moving directly to the rear of the store. Too many obstacles can frustrate customers. The challenge becomes one of trying to maximize product display without antagonizing shoppers.

Directional signs at the front of the store can help customers find desired merchandise. Supermarkets have effectively utilized overhead signs to guide people throughout the store. One firm has a unique structure with three wings coming off from the center sales area. A large sign informs customers that pesticides and fertilizers can be found in one section, indoor plants are located in a second area, and books and tools in a third section.

SUMMARY

Good, exciting displays help sell merchandise and stimulate impulse sales. The care and intensity with which one approaches the task of creating attractive displays ultimately will be reflected on the bottom line. Profits tell a great story about how well management prepared each spring to create attractive displays.

Careful consideration should be given to selection of display tables for virtually all merchandise with the exception of large nursery stock. Customer convenience and good display of merchandise should dominate considerations rather than costs and ease of handling for employees.

Signs and posters play a major role in stimulating customers and answering common questions. You should avoid the traps of illegible hand-lettered signs, faded posters, and a clutter of sizes and shapes that confuse shoppers.

Overcrowding of plants ranks as one of the greatest sins of inexperienced and poorly operated firms. Plants are perishable and require room for inspection by customers. Geraniums left in shipping cartons will help conserve space required for the display, but this practice leads to broken stems and frustrated customers trying to dislodge plants from crowded quarters.

Outdoor displays require some protection from strong winds. Lath structures help protect many plants from the elements. Mass displays capture a great deal of attention. Color plays a vital role in stimulating impulse sales. Haphazard placement of material confuses shoppers and limits average sales per customer.

Customers must be protected from slippery walks, algae, and dirt on benches, slivers, and overhead wires. Wide aisles and peninsular benching systems provide for easy movement by customers and maximum traffic in a sales area. Greenhouse structures have a special appeal that attracts the attention of many gardeners. Customers normally can shop in pleasant surroundings out of strong winds, rain, and cold temperatures.

Carefully consider location of all major product lines. The necessity items may be displayed toward the rear of the store. Customers will then have to pass by numerous displays resulting in some impulse sales.

Good lighting is one of the key factors in proper display of plants and supply items. Unusually high light intensities help spotlight foliage plants and maintain indoor flowering plants. Consumers must have adequate light in reading labels on containers of pesticides.

Exciting displays sell merchandise and generate enthusiasm and repeat business. Slow periods of the year should be used effectively to create consumer oriented display tables and to plan traffic flow through the store.

1. Display units play an important role in stimulating sales of plant materials. Discuss several methods for displaying bedding and nursery material.

2. What guidelines should be considered when preparing and putting up signs?

3. What precautions can and should be taken to preserve plant material and enhance the shopping experience for customers?

4. Discuss the role of mass displays in capturing attention.

5. Why should retailers construct special displays? Give two examples.

6. What recommendations would you offer regarding aisle widths in a combination greenhouse-garden center operation?

7. What precautions should be taken near the close of the season?

8. What are the advantages of display gardens?

9. What publications, if any, might be given away free or sold? Why?

10. Why should a lighting engineer be employed to develop or review lighting facilities in a garden center? How much light is required for indoor plants?

11. How would you create an effective and attractive pesticide display?

12. What are the pros and cons of locating specific groups of products in different areas of the store?

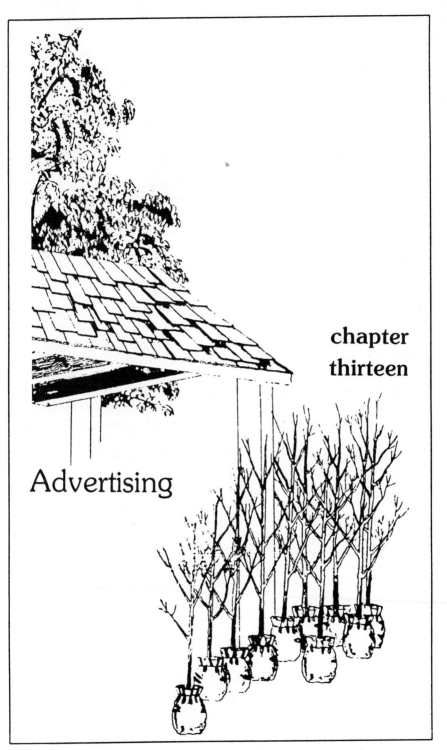

chapter
thirteen

Advertising

The advertising budget occupies an interesting and unique position in the eyes of many small business operators. It often becomes the first item sacrificed when economic screws have been tightened. Also, advertising is likely to be cut when business rolls along at a good pace. Why should you devote real dollars and a line in the profit and loss statement to advertising expenditures?

The aggressive, growth-minded operator recognizes the volatile nature of the market caused by frequent population changes in the area served by the firm. These individuals rely extensively on radio, television, newspapers, and direct mail to help reach sales targets. The advertising budget represents a vital and legitimate business expenditure. Conservative businessmen and women, often operating small businesses, strongly advocate "word of mouth" advertising as the primary means of developing and expanding a garden center. The fact that they often remain in the small category and experience modest growth may reflect the limitations of this concept.

It does take money to support an effective advertising program. The frustration of not being able to support a sustained program may account for some operators relying almost exclusively on word of mouth advertising. Advertising dollars have been wasted by many well intentioned people. Many dollars have disappeared through negligence and a naive approach to advertising.

It has been observed that only 50 percent of your advertising expenditures ever hit the intended target, the only problem being that one is never quite sure which 50 percent was wasted. Dollars often have been wasted by managers falling prey to aggressive salesmen and women. Relatively little time has been directed by management to creation of a specific plan. Rather, dollars have been committed to the first individual arriving with a good story.

Some individuals have counted dollars allocated for donations to worthy groups in their advertising account. A request for a page in a local church or graduation program also has fallen into the same category. These dollars should not be charged against your advertising program. They have been unplanned and contribute little toward long-run objectives of the firm. You would be much farther ahead by placing the expenditures in either a miscellaneous account or one set up for donations. Do not confuse donations with advertising.

ADVERTISING OBJECTIVES

What are you trying to accomplish with your advertising program? Do not spend a single dollar until advertising objectives have been placed on paper. The primary goal of advertising is to lure customers into your shop. Shoppers permit you to sell goods and services. Sales stimulate growth and enable one

264

A well-designed advertisement focuses attention on a specific holiday and selected items deemed suitable for that occasion. The layout and illustrations are bound to capture attention of shoppers.

to compete effectively with other firms. Too many small businessmen and women fail to recognize that advertising can be a powerful sales producing force. They fail to plan properly, study the market, and control expenditures. The practice of advertising only when timely opportunities present themselves limits potential benefits from advertising expenditures.

A major problem occurs when small operators try to spread their dollars over several media such as newspapers, direct mail, and radio. Diluting advertising dollars through support of several advertising media often hinders you in developing a strong message. Repetition improves impact and warrants placing most, if not all, eggs in a single basket. Switching from medium to medium every few months can be a dangerous practice for small operators. A change of pace is acceptable providing it doesn't come too often.

An effective advertising program must be built on the following:

1. Understanding and commitment to advertising as a legitimate and necessary business expenditure
2. Knowledge of market area and consumers
3. Realistic sales objectives
4. Advertising items wanted by consumers and when they want them
5. Careful selection of advertising media
6. Continued evaluation of progress and programs

Commitment

An advertising program shows vitality and imagination when long-term dollars have been committed for this important business activity. Stops and starts undercut all the energy put into a project. Bouncing around from medium to medium tends to destroy continuity and may confuse the intended audience. One garden center operator delayed creation of an advertising program for a year until new facilities were operating smoothly. The first step taken was to crystallize a specific goal for the firm. The owner established a sales target that exceeded the previous year by 25 percent. The next question was: What could advertising do and how much would have to be spent to reach this goal? Advertising was to play a prominent role in attracting people from a nearby metropolitan center and achieving the sales goal. Something a little different and unique was required to help entice people to drive 35 to 40 miles to and from the garden center.

The development of extensive gardens on the property featuring spring flowering bulbs and annual and perennial flowers has captured the fancy of many gardeners. A unique radio commercial providing daily garden tips also has proved successful in attracting shoppers to the rural garden center.

A decision was reached to allocate for advertising a sum of money equal to 10 percent of gross sales from the last fiscal year. This figure greatly exceeded the three percent often adopted by many operators.

Successful advertising programs reflect a commitment from management. Advertising and growth are linked arm in arm and will continue to be stressed for profit-oriented firms in the future.

Market

You must know something about your market. Who stands ready to buy your products and services? Are there enough potential customers to support your business? What is the composition of the market in terms of age, income, and sex? These questions must be answered and information available in planning an effective program.

Sales Objectives

Most operators do tend to think in terms of short-term goals. "I want to increase plant sales from 3500 units to 5000 for the coming holiday." A different approach focuses attention on overall sales for a quarter or the entire year. Know what you are trying to accomplish with your advertising dollars.

Timing

Products normally are advertised just prior to and during the season when used by consumers. A promotion to sell grass seed in January, even at a reduced price, would capture only modest attention, if any, from consumers. Crab grass control products should be advertised heavily just prior to the critical time for application of the chemicals.

Pre-season sales help bring customers into the store during otherwise slow periods of the year.

The season for some products such as poinsettias has been advanced from mid-December to late November and early December. This has permitted independent operators to market this particular product well before normal efforts by large discount firms and supermarkets. Pre-season sales may yield great dividends on selected lines of merchandise. Equipment such as lawn mowers can be promoted in late winter or early spring, with modest discounts offered to consumers. A close-out sale in September or October also can reduce inventory and generate income.

Media

The media selected should relate to the available dollars, the nature of the campaign, and the overall image desired for the organization. Television requires a large outlay of dollars over a period of time to have any substantial impact on an intended audience. It can be used effectively to portray a quality organization. Radio can be beamed to a rather specific audience. Proper selection of the radio station insures that one's message will reach gardeners. Direct mail, assuming a good mailing list, provides the most accurate means for reaching a select clientele. Combination programs may be developed when adequate funds are available for the total project.

Evaluation

Successful advertising programs, above all, must be based on the sale of a good product or service. This is a key assumption often overlooked by some business operators. Consumers shy away from faulty products and services. They have developed a keen sense for placing a value on the advertised item. The best advertising program is doomed from the start should you try to merchandise an inferior product or service.

Sales figures and plants remaining on hand after a holiday should aid you in evaluating the impact of an advertising program. Overall store sales may have increased substantially from the previous year. The item heavily advertised may have laid an egg. Dollars spent for advertising undoubtedly contributed to growth recorded for the holiday. The message or the product may have been at fault for lackluster sales of the item in question. A careful evaluation of the program will help guide future campaigns leading to success in reaching sales goals.

MESSAGE

The advertising message, except in general promotional programs, must promote items that will draw customers into your store. An advertisement featuring geraniums in the spring will undoubtedly capture more attention than one trying to sell peat moss. Analyze your assets and strike hard on the strongest factors including selection, service, convenience, and price. Choose a clear message designed to answer basic consumer questions. Every advertising message is comparable to a salesperson meeting face to face with a customer.

A good message contains four key elements:

1. An attention getter
2. Outline of a specific consumer need
3. Visualization of product or services
4. A bid for action

Another way of phrasing it would be to attract, inform, and convince customers to shop and buy at your place of business. Mass outlets focus attention on prices in newspaper, radio, and television advertisements. They often take a popular product and use it as a leader item. Price dominates the message and it comes through loud and clear.

What does an independent operator have to offer customers? Consider the following:

1. Quality
2. Service
3. A large product mix including unusual items
4. Newness

All of the above can and should provide potent ammunition in helping counter attractive prices featured by mass outlets. This is not the time to engage in a price war. You would be fighting the wrong battle on the wrong battlefield.

Price can be used selectively to attract attention of potential buyers. The offer must be attractive and in the same area as that offered by major competitors. An advertisement featuring price and quality can and should capture attention such as:

QUALITY GERANIUMS $1.59

(normally $1.79)

We invite your comparison on this excellent buy.

The $1.59 price tag was being featured in the same newspaper by a food chain. The suggestion to compare products reflects your confidence in the merchandise and expectations that it far exceeds that of the mass outlet. Carefully assess your own assets, especially those coming through loud and clear in comparison to competitors. The factors you identify should be enlisted and developed in your advertising programs.

This advertisement contains
an abundance of information.

Appearance

Some people believe that advertising is expensive and thus use every square inch of space in a newspaper ad. This philosophy has been adopted by many food stores featuring "500" items each week. Those operators featuring quality and service tend to maximize open spaces and minimize print. Advertisements with lots of open space are restful to the eyes and do capture attention. They have impact! The same philosophy applies to radio and television commercials.

The image of your firm should be reflected in the advertisements employed for all media. Don't confuse customers with loud, irritating messages when your shop provides a relaxing, enjoyable experience for shoppers.

Why People Buy

A good advertising program begins with a thorough knowledge of why people buy. Potential customers become actual customers when advertising messages zoom in on one or more buyer needs:

1. Personal adequacy
2. To obtain romance
3. Buy promise
4. Vitality

The list also includes enjoyment, comfort, cleanliness, health, praise, beautiful possessions, safety, making and saving money, savin time, avoiding effort, quality, curiosity, protecting family, being in style, escaping physical pain, being popular, attracting opposite sex, conserving possessions, satisfying appetite, imitating others, avoiding criticism, being an individual, protecting reputation, avoiding trouble, and taking advantage of opportunities.

You can probably identify other needs of gardeners that can be appealed to in an advertising message. The important point is to relate a message to specific needs in order to stimulate a desired action.

ADVERTISING BUDGETS

A well-planned budget can and should maximize dollars allocated for advertising programs. This process should be completed prior to the beginning of a new fiscal year. The budget helps assure management that a specific sum of dollars should be spent to support overall objectives of the merchandising program. All proposals advanced by representatives of advertising media and personnel within the firm will have to reflect and fall within budget allocations.

These are three approaches that can be utilized in allocating dollars throughout the year.

1. A percentage of past sales
2. A percentage of anticipated sales
3. Task or zero line method

The first option is a conservative approach in arriving at the dollar size of a budget. Last year's sales are on record and normally serve as a good indicator of what is in store for the coming year. Adoption of this practice tends to minimize risks in the event that sales do not meet anticipated goals.

A budget based on anticipated sales may prove to be an insurance policy in helping reach the new goal. This is especially true when one has planned for a substantial growth in sales for the coming fiscal year. More dollars would be available under this method than when a specified percentage is applied to last year's sales. Advertising expenditures based on planned sales may be highly speculative. The appearance of one or more new competitors could hinder a firm from reaching its objectives. One might not be able to afford the increased advertising dollars in this new competitive situation.

The task method begins with a zero budget. Each program must be justified by management. The most important programs receive top priority. Total expenditures might exceed industry averages but only on the basis that they were justified in helping achieve sales targets. Management might begin the process by concluding that it was essential to support a quarter-page advertisement in the Sunday newspaper every week of the year. This expenditure might come to $10,000 a year. The second priority, costing $5000, would support a one-minute radio program every day throughout the year. Two thousand dollars might be reserved for emergency or special promotion programs.

EMPLOYING PROFESSIONALS

The fear of wasting dollars has inhibited many small business operators from engaging in advertising programs. They simply don't know where to begin, who to contact, or what to say. Some retailers simply sign contracts with newspapers and virtually leave it up to the advertising representative to do the job. "Time is precious and I just can't be bothered to handle the chore on a busy day when the rep knows what you want to say."

Another involves employment of a pro to handle your advertising program. You may find someone working on the side and willing to handle the assignment for a modest fee. Your advertising dollars will go much further when you can employ a talented and sensitive party who understands and has a feel for your product. This is a tall order and one may have to do some searching to find the right individual.

Can you afford to work with an advertising agency on a regular basis? Professional help of this nature normally has been accessible only to larger firms grossing in excess of $1 million. An advertising executive in a community of 250,000 people recommended that a firm allocate a minimum of $30,000 for advertising before considering use of an agency. Twenty percent of this figure normally goes to the agency to cover its costs and 80 percent for media time and materials. Advertising agencies can be employed on an hourly

it's NOT too late!

It's still not too late to plant those vegetables for your garden. We have a great selection left for you, fresh in our greenhouses.

And don't forget about trees, shrubs, evergreens and potted or bedding plants to grace your lawn.
For the finishing touch on your garden and lawn, drive out to Schmidt Nursery today. Three miles from the West Beltline on Irish Lane at Fish Hatchery Road.

HOURS:
Monday—Saturday
9-5
Sunday 10-4
Phone 271-3230

SCHMIDT NURSERY

Three Miles South of West Beltline
On Fish Hatchery Road to Irish
Lane

What's not too late? This clever advertisement is bound to enjoy good readership and stimulate many new sales.

basis. This permits many medium-sized and even some smaller garden center operators to secure the services of professionals.

STRIKE WHILE IRON IS HOT

The time to advertise is, of course, during periods of greatest sales. For example, 60 percent or more of your advertising budget should be spent in May and June as these months account for 60 percent of gross sales. This philosophy captures attention because it tries to insure minimum wastage of dollars. It is a simple technique for allocating dollars based on percentage of sales occurring each month of the year. The program works exceptionally well when sales have few dramatic cycles throughout the year. The individual desiring to improve slow or humdrum periods must find some advertising dollars to help accomplish the desired objective. How can you attract people into a garden center store in November and February without an expenditure of advertising dollars?

The wise allocation of dollars must reflect:

1. Pattern of sales with emphasis on strong months
2. The extent to which a major effort will be made to improve weak months.

A growth-minded firm operating twelve months out of the year must remain in front of the public. Your advertising program must embrace the entire year rather than focusing all guns solely on the busy months.

SOMETHING SPECIAL

The extra touch in your advertising program will capture the attention of your audience. Consider the following thrust for an ad featuring geraniums:

"We are proud to offer Sincerity, one of the new, exciting geraniums designed to perform brilliantly all summer and well into the fall."

This has much more pizzazz than simply stating that red, pink, orange and white geraniums are ready for planting.

ATTACKING COMPETITORS

"Before you buy Bayer or Anacin, consider Bufferin." A television commercial sponsored by Bufferin names its competitors and tries to convince the viewer not to buy these products. The same approach has been used by manufacturers of many other products including cars and cigarettes. Can garden center operators benefit from this philosophy? Yes, if you have been promoting a quality product and you can identify something unique in comparison to competitors. It may not be necessary to directly mention competitors by name. You can allude to them by asking the reader or viewer to compare the following items:

1. *New introductions*—We always offer the latest introductions. Have you seen Sincerity or Carefree on the market?
2. *Quality*—We handle only premium quality geraniums that have three or more branches and several flower stalks. Inexpensive competitors often have just a single bloom on one elongated stem bearing few leaves.

3. *Guarantee*—You must be satisfied or we will happily provide you with a new plant. Some of our large friends open and close in just six weeks. We are open all year to insure your complete satisfaction.

4. *Information*—Have you had much luck receiving an answer to some very simple questions when shopping at a large discount firm? Chances are you might not find a clerk and if so they may not be able to tell the difference between a tomato and a petunia. Our staff has been carefully selected and trained to be of service to your needs.

This form of aggressive advertising requires that you have taken all steps to back up your pronouncements. A top quality operator should not hide his wares.

WORD OF MOUTH

The most common form of advertising employed by small businessmen appears to be word of mouth. Satisfied customers conveniently and enthusiastically relay the good word. Some small operators often give the impression that they have a monopoly on this advertising medium. All businessmen rely heavily on satisfied customers. This is a natural phenomenon that has existed since the earliest days and will continue as long as business is conducted in this world.

A satisfied customer has pride in making a good decision when purchasing a service or product. He or she likes to pass this information along to all who will stop and listen for a few minutes. The dissatisfied party may find his or her only recourse is to insure that friends and even strangers do not fall into the same trap.

Word of mouth messages cannot replace a well designed advertising program. The informal nature of the former has several significant limitations regarding your inability to control the message sender. You cannot control the accuracy of the message. The individual may emphasize some unimportant parts of the product or service and ignore important elements. The message may be overly brief. You cannot predetermine the degree of enthusiasm nor the context in which the message has been presented to the listener. There is also no way to control the frequency of the message being sent. It may occur once or a thousand times.

A negative message may occur and be based on false expectations. You could have been the victim of a freak situation happening once in a lifetime. Perhaps the message sender failed to report a deficiency that would have been corrected quickly by the seller. How often can something go wrong without it ever coming to your attention? What if someone waits until

November before reporting the source of a summer flowering basket? This provides no assistance during the season when baskets were on sale. You can only hope that listeners will remember the source next year.

NO COMPETITION

There are some areas where only one firm dominates a market. There is a temptation to avoid or minimize advertising expenditures. After all, everyone knows where to buy plants and supplies! This decision often starts a firm on the road down hill. Some operators have found a comfortable rocking chair and simply waited for business.

New people continue to move into our communities. An important reason to advertise is to insure that customers will not forget it's time to do something in the garden or indoors. Gardeners often need reminders that it's time to start spraying for crabgrass control. New gardeners soak up this information. Stay one step ahead of your customers rather than some day wondering why a new competitor gained a foothold in the market.

PUBLIC RELATIONS

Garden center operators occupy a unique position in terms of their ability to generate extensive publicity throughout the year. The attractiveness of the product as reflected by the public thirst for information has commanded attention of newspaper, radio, television, and magazine editors. Aggressive operators can provide a steady flow of information on gardening topics to be used at no cost and at the discretion of newspapers and radio and television stations. This asset remains in the potential category, however, for it requires some imagination and determination to make it become a reality.

This publicity is free only to the extent that one does not pay for newspaper space or radio time. You must budget out-of-pocket expenses to cover personal time and materials associated with these unique projects.

Television. Two television stations in a major metropolitan market have recognized that gardening information represents an important news item during many months of the year. The stations have provided almost daily time for one minute news spots on both the twelve and six o'clock programs. Film has been shot on location. All considerations relative to subject matter and location have been left to the discretion of the hosts.

One station offered the package to the local horticulture extension agent. The second program was hosted by a commercial operator who formerly held the horticulture extension position in the county. The commercial television stations specifically wanted individuals who would commit time to the project. Knowledgeable people were required and who felt at ease before cameras.

The garden center manager was able to identify his firm on each broadcast. This type of promotion could not have been purchased on a continuous basis due to the cost factor. The dollar value placed on this exposure to the gardening public far exceeded the impact of all dollars expended by the firm in support of its total advertising program.

What does it take for you to accomplish the same goal?

1. Management's recognition that time must be expended for the project, even during the busiest time of the year. This unfortunately occurs when the public's appetite reaches its highest point.

2. Identification of someone in the firm or employment of an individual who can deliver and feel free in front of television cameras.

3. An aggressive operator who can develop and then present a tempting package to television station managers.

An educational channel in a major metropolitan market has utilized the knowledge and abilities of a landscape–garden center operator in conducting a series of half hour garden programs each winter. This has been a major undertaking by the operator which fortunately occurs during the slack season of the year. The individual had only minor exposure to television cameras prior to the first series. He gained valuable experience by the end of the first year. The educational channel has attracted a reasonable audience in the market serviced by the operator. Sales have reached targeted goals partially reflecting rewards from his significant efforts in helping educate the public.

Radio. Gardeners have been noted for many things and especially their ability to ask questions and more questions. A number of radio station managers have capitalized on this thirst for information by scheduling regular question-and-answer or talk shows. One garden center operator has appeared weekly for a half hour fielding questions from the listening audience. His name and that of his firm have become familiar to most households in the market area. The garden center operator in question has found this to be one of the most profitable expenditures of time. Business has grown at an excellent rate and customers have come many miles to shop at the expert's garden center.

What does one do when it's not possible to answer a question? Simply write down the question, name of the party and their telephone number. Surprisingly, it has not taken a great deal of time to fulfill this service.

Newspapers and Magazines. Garden writers and newspaper editors like to focus on new and attention-getting stories. A tulip festival sponsored by a garden center operator has captured attention from one of the largest newspapers in the country. Color pictures tell the story each spring and help attract thousands and thousands of customers.

A garden writer was informed a decade ago that a new poinsettia cultivar was being introduced. It had the capability of retaining its leaves and bracts for a much longer period of time than existing selections. Some plants were being grown by a combination greenhouse–garden center firm. Members of the industry were surprised to see this firm featured in an article with a large color picture in early December. How did this character get all the publicity?

Newsworthy items keep garden writers in business. They rely on many sources for a fresh approach to their task each week. Imaginative and promotion-minded operators can play an important role in bringing new items to the attention of the public.

Good public relations does not come easy. You pay a price in terms of allocating valuable hours, often during the busiest time of the year. The impact often exceeds by far anything that can be realized by expenditures of advertising dollars. A growth-minded operator will find few other opportunities that can match the results of a well conceived program.

CHOOSING YOUR ADVERTISING MEDIA

Newspapers

Newspapers have been used extensively by small businessmen and women. Readership is high with a large percentage of people consulting advertisements before embarking on a shopping expedition. Newspaper rates in most areas are reasonable and in line with available dollars. Weekly newspapers in rural areas have high readership. People are interested in their communities and lives of their friends and neighbors.

Newspaper advertisers often feel that one must buy quarter, half or full pages to make a strong impact. Purchasing small spaces for insertion of several notices in a single issue and running them two or more times a week can command the attention of a large audience. Repetition captures attention and stimulates action. The keys to a successful program featuring small ads are:

1. Prepare a special creation for the available space and don't try to reduce a large advertisement.
2. Identify and focus on one concept.
3. Incorporate only essential features.
4. Use eye catchers, headlines, and art.
5. Make the headline brief and legible.

6. Incorporate a dominant and clever illustration.

7. Clearly describe the product.

8. Try for originality.

A series of smaller advertisements in major metropolitan newspapers would appear to have more impact than one measuring even a sixth of a page. There is the risk that your single message will become lost in the maze of larger advertisements. Something unique and distinct must be developed to attract readers in our larger newspapers.

The gardening public buys an exceptionally large percentage of its supplies on weekends. Newspaper advertisements should appear toward the end of the week. Unfortunately, many other advertisers find themselves in a similar situation. Newspaper advertisements provide great flexibility from day to day. They call for prompt action on the part of the readers. Most importantly, readers do not have to be at a particular location or time to receive the message. You can purchase an entire page or a fraction of it to bring it in line with the budgets of all retailers.

Shopper Newspapers

Many cities feature weekly or biweekly shopper newspapers. The circulation list may cover an entire community or be directed to specific areas. This publication often reaches the primary audience of a particular firm. An advertiser can buy more space than that commonly available in a local newspaper. Shopper newspapers have high readership worthy of your attention and consideration.

Outdoor Ads

Outdoor advertising or billboards have appeal to some operators in that their messages appear as large as those of national companies. They can be highly effective as reminders to customers and for selling long-range concepts. The audience normally passes by billboards in three seconds. The message must be clever, brief, colorful, and eye catching. Vivid colors and bold letters help attract attention.

Billboard advertising normally should be maintained for a period of months rather than shorter periods. The themes employed should be linked to that of other advertising projects. Bedding Plants Incorporated (B.P.I.) has developed a poster featuring spring bedding plants.

Television

This advertising medium has been employed by larger operators. Time, especially prime time, normally has been priced out of sight for most small and medium sized businessmen and women. Preparation of the message represents an important expenditure. One aggressive operator sought to overcome this barrier by use of a series of illustrations. The message was coordinated with each image. Spot announcements may have appeal due to modest costs. They could be employed much more extensively than lengthier commercials and those sponsoring 30/60-minute programs.

Radio

Radio has made an excellent comeback in recent years. Advertising rates compete effectively with those for shoppers and daily newspapers. You must create a visual image with words on radio and an emotional response. Your task is to plant a visual picture in the minds of the audience such as a luscious tomato or a colorful display of geraniums. The radio message does quickly fade from memory. Ten second, thirty second, and one minute spots must have a strong impact on the audience. A weak message becomes just another opportunity for listeners to focus attention on other matters.

A particular message promoting yogurt has stayed with me for several years. Some brands feature fruit which must be stirred into the yogurt since it settles at the bottom of the container. This message says "Be sure to stir since our tasty peaches nestle to the bottom of the container." This clever choice of words helped overcome a potential problem of having to stir the product.

Local radio news programs during the noon hour can be expected to capture a large listening audience. Interest is high in local names and happenings. The premium price for spots at this time should be more than compensated for by audience size. Some radio stations feature one minute gardening tips prepared by university personnel. You may wish to buy a spot just before or after this timely tip on the care of garden and indoor plants.

Direct Mail

Direct mail provides opportunities for reaching a specific prospect with a personal message in contrast to newspaper, radio, and television commercials. A well prepared communication can be forwarded at critical times designed to reach potential buyers at the most opportune moment. The message remains confidential and unknown for a period of time to competitors. One can measure results quite effectively when a coupon on specific action has been requested of the reader.

There are some problems associated with direct mail. The following items, with the exception of the first, have to be phrased in a positive manner. Poorly designed direct mail pieces often violate one or more of the remaining five items.

1. Costs have been steadily rising for postage.
2. Mailing list must be continuously updated.
3. You must suggest a specific course of action.
4. The message must tell them what they want to hear and specific benefits must be pointed out to the audience.
5. The enclosure must reflect the image of the store.
6. The message must be personal.

A good mailing list can be maintained by collecting names and addresses from customers. All credit sales including bank credit cards provide opportunities for identification of customers.

Some firms annually sponsor open houses in the spring. A good mailing list can be obtained by offering door prizes. Each person must register providing name and address. Garden center operators have used direct mail for:

1. Distribution of catalogues in early spring
2. Periodic offers just prior to a specific garden activity
    a. crabgrass control
    b. planting spring flowering bulbs
3. Special winter promotions

Direct mail offers some distinct advantages over other forms of advertising. You can mail samples. There is really no limit on size, shape, and color of materials. Your message reaches a specified audience and one tuned into gardening. The audience, when carefully selected, reads and remembers the message.

Bumper Stickers

Bumper stickers have become a colorful and popular fad in recent years. One operator has prepared several slogans tied into other facets of his advertising campaign. The cost is modest for someone interested in capturing attention through a unique medium.

Catalogues

Catalogues were once used quite extensively by garden center operators. The cost of postage, paper, and printing has risen significantly in more recent years, contributing to a decline in popularity of this form of advertising.

A catalogue provides an opportunity to acquaint potential customers with a full line of products. You are not cramped for space in comparison to newspaper advertisements. You can do a more effective job in describing the product and relating it to customers' needs. Many gardeners annually look forward to the newest catalogue arriving just prior to the planting season. Most catalogues are sent through the mails to potential customers. It is essential that one have an up-to-date mailing list to avoid wasting dollars.

Transit

Garden centers located in urban areas featuring an extensive transit system may consider advertising messages inside and outside of buses, trolleys, and in subways. One can anticipate high circulation and readership at a minimum cost. Interior advertisements can contain up to 100 words since readers spend an adequate amount of time on the vehicle. Outdoor messages must be brief and colorful.

"Yellow Pages"

The "Yellow Pages" carries a free listing for each commercial firm. A number of operators have chosen to purchase space for insertion of an illustration and a brief message. Bold type commonly has been used to feature the firm name. A "Yellow Pages" usage study conducted many years ago showed almost three-fourths of all adults used the directory.

Point of Purchase

Window displays capture a great deal of attention from shoppers on foot as well as from passing vehicles. They must be well lit, attractive, eye catching, and current. You should focus on a specific theme reflecting the season of the year. In-store displays trigger impulse sales. Material often becomes available from manufacturers and has a tie-in with national advertising programs. Strive to make your displays imaginative, appealing, and attractive.

COOPERATIVE ADS

Small and medium sized operators can pool their limited resources for purchase of space on a cooperative basis. The total size of the advertisement often equals that of major operators in a market and especially of large discount and food chains.

One advertisement appearing in a major newspaper and measuring one quarter of a page cost each of fifteen participants approximately $20. The name of each retailer appeared in bold print. The middleman must work in advance of the publication date to coordinate products with the garden season. He must assure that stock is in the hands of cooperating retailers.

This cooperative advertisement features the names of local hardware dealers operating under the banner of a national organization. Each firm has been allocated a reasonable amount of space for proper identification.

Manufacturers also contribute to the cost of such cooperative advertisements.

Individual retailers become trapped during the normal and hectic activities of the garden center season. Time has not been available for development of creative programs. Suppliers have played an important coordinating role in promoting cooperative advertisements and handling time consuming chores.

One potential drawback relates to the fact that consumers can choose between a number of independent outlets to acquire a product featured in the advertisement. Some operators fear that they will be lost in the shuffle. They would prefer to advertise only as an independent operator and not in concert with competitors. This argument has been partially countered by the logic that real competitors have been discount and food chains. Cooperative advertising provides the means to counter their massive programs capturing attention of customers.

The responsibility for conducting cooperative advertising programs often rotates from member to member. The volunteer must work with newspaper and radio and television personnel well betore the start of each season in preparing plans and layouts.

ASSISTANCE AND AIDS

The advertising departments of most newspapers and radio and television stations can supply marketing data for your area along with some assistance in formulating a program. Contact their representatives to determine the nature of assistance they can offer your firm.

Suppliers often provide copy mats, layouts, and photographs in addition to suggestions for advertising specific products. They may offer radio scripts and visuals for television programs.

The advertising rates in local media are more attractive for area firms than national or regional organizations. Suppliers may be interested in cooperative advertisements in which costs are shared fifty-fifty. The amount or percentage of matching dollars may be related to purchases of advertised products.

MEASURING EFFECTIVENESS

The most difficult task in advertising occurs when attempting to measure results. Part of the problem often related to management's failure to identify specific goals. The task is complicated by the fact that many marketing forces continue to operate every day. Results of a specific program can and will be influenced by the product, price, displays, personnel, competition, weather and the economic climate. Some advertisements trigger action well after the message captured attention of a customer. This is one of the factors complicating the task.

Coupons represent an important vehicle by which one can measure the impact of an advertisement. One simply has to count the number of coupons returned for merchandise. Some retailers have instructed sales personnel to engage customers in brief discussions regarding particular advertisements. Did the customer see the ad? How did one respond to the message? What do you remember?

A check on store traffic prior to, during, and after the advertisement may help provide information on the impact of the program. Sales of nonadvertised items might increase substantially from increased store traffic. Sales figures can be compared from year to year for a specific period of time. The analysis is vulnerable to many variables including weather and whether other products were advertised last year.

ADVERTISING THRUST

Garden center operators are in a unique position of having a wealth of information desired by their customers. This information can be used most successfully in satisfying needs and at the same time attracting customers into your store.

1. One operator has contracted for one minute garden tips in late afternoon on a major radio station and running Monday through Friday. The announcer often adds some informal comments providing additional input to the messages. Each program consists of a single tip such as the proper time to prune lilacs or plant seeds in the garden. The selling message has been rather brief with the main emphasis on the garden tip.

2. A telephone line has been rented by another firm permitting gardeners to dial a number for a daily tip. The message has been recorded every morning and gardeners can dial twenty-four hours a day for timely information. Rental of the unit, installation costs, and telephone lines come to much less than $500 a year. This excellent service has produced many sales from gardeners appreciative of the service.

3. A series of newspaper advertisements in the spring carried a number of timely garden tips. Naturally, the tips included products available from the sponsor.

LIMITED RESOURCES

Many small operators and especially those just entering the business have limited resources for support of advertising programs. These situations require that the operator carefully control all expenditures to maximize impact of each and every advertising dollar.

An ambitious and aggressive operator with limited funds might choose to devote initial resources toward a public relations program. This involves a willingness to speak to garden and service clubs and participation in radio and television talk shows. The operator may spend time feeding ideas and stories to local newspaper editors. These projects have been designed to place the name of the firm in front of the public with a modest expenditure of funds.

The public has a great thirst for information. A small advertising budget might be devoted almost exclusively to helping satisfy this thirst. The telephone garden tip service could attract considerable attention in many communities featuring a population in excess of 10,000 people.

Advertising rates on local radio stations and newspapers in small communities should be within reach of most small operators. You should avoid the temptation of spreading dollars to remain in the good graces of all advertising people. Weekly shoppers in larger communities provide excellent opportunities for reaching a targeted audience at a minimum of cost. One normally can purchase much more space in these publications than in daily newspapers.

A series of small advertisements in local newspapers may provide much more impact than single notices. Repetition, even though advertisements are small in size, does capture attention.

The advertiser with a small budget often has to work harder than one with extensive resources. You must select the medium providing greatest impact to insure that your dollars will not go down the drain. The task is not impossible. It requires determination and hard work. Capitalize on your knowledge and the public's thirst for information.

SUMMARY

Advertising dollars can be flushed down the drain in a matter of seconds. This legitimate business expenditure requires as much thought and concern as that applied to all other items in the profit and loss statement. Good results can be anticipated when one puts some effort into creation of a viable program.

What are you trying to accomplish by buying space in a newspaper, on radio or television? Some operators give the impression that their primary concern has been to keep the name of the organization in front of customers. This is a legitimate goal although quite narrow in scope. You could spend a fortune just to boost your ego.

A firm may be engaged in a highly competitive market and fighting to stay afloat. They may be in battle against a mass outlet. Advertising can help to differentiate products and services from the giant competitor.

The operator unwilling to create a specific advertising program runs the risk of wasting more than half of his expenditures. The simplistic approach has about as much chance for success as dropping dollars in a wishing well.

A successful advertising program requires:

1. Management's understanding and commitment to advertising as a legitimate and necessary business expenditure.
2. The creation of growth targets for the firm.
3. A well thought out plan for wise use of advertising dollars.
4. An imaginative program.
5. Methods for reviewing programs.

Some managers bounce around like jack rabbits financing a series of newspaper advertisements and then trying radio. They seem to respond to the latest sales pitch. A successful advertising program is planned, not haphazardly thrown together.

The public's thirst for gardening information should be capitalized upon by aggressive and growth-minded garden center operators. Advertising programs, whether utilizing radio, newspaper, or direct mail, can attract attention through timely information designed to aid gardeners in producing quality plants.

Advertising programs must be designed to bring customers into your place of business. Store traffic represents the first element in generating sales. Sales lead to profits and in turn to growth.

1. Identify and discuss four reasons why managers often fail to develop effective advertising programs.

2. Select three products commonly marketed in garden centers and pinpoint most appropriate times to advertise them to consumers.

3. Identify and discuss four key elements in a good advertising message.

4. Discuss two approaches toward developing an advertising budget.

5. Discuss pros and cons of attacking directly or indirectly your competitors in an advertising message.

6. Why do many small operators rely on "word of mouth advertising?" How effective is it?

7. What are the advantages of public relations programs? Provide examples. To what extent can and should garden center managers take advantage of this method?

8. Compare shopper newspapers with daily newspapers.

9. What considerations must be given weight by someone wishing to advertise on radio?

10. How can you measure the effectiveness of an advertising program?

11. How can managers capitalize on the consumers' thirst for information? Discuss.

chapter
fourteen

Quality

Specifications for perishable plants are much more flexible and subjective than those associated with most supply and hard good items. One can pick up a telephone and easily order a gross of hand tools, fertilizers, and insecticides and have full confidence of receiving exactly the item pictured and described in a catalogue. A great deal more sophistication must be employed to purchase nursery stock, annual and perennial flowers, sod, indoor plants, and peat products.

Three rather general rules can help guide the inexperienced as well as experienced buyer trying to determine quality of perishable and some non-perishable products.

1. Always buy from a reputable dealer.

2. Price serves as an excellent indicator of quality.

3. An inspection of the production site helps evaluate the crop condition.

REPUTATION

The first rule applies to all suppliers. Deal with a firm that has a reputation for supplying the quality of product ordered by buyers. One supplier attracted new buyers by delivering superior quality merchandise for a number of months. A second grade product was slowly blended in with the top quality material. The intent was to further dilute each shipment until only average quality plants comprised each delivery. The superior material was then used to bait new buyers. One must seriously question this scheme and the extent to which buyers failed to distinguish the changing composition of each shipment.

One of the major problems with some producers has been their failure to deliver the specified number of plants. This can become extremely critical with deliveries scheduled just before a major holiday. The seller may have unknowingly accepted orders far in excess of available supplies. This practice may be fairly routine with growers not wishing to lose accounts by admitting their inability to provide the desired number of plants.

Plant material has been purchased by some growers from competitors to fill orders. The buyer often receives a mix of questionable plants along with the specified crop. Occasionally, the supplier may acquire merchandise superior to that from his own greenhouse.

A breakdown in communications often leads to buyer disenchantment with suppliers. The language covering quality specifications has never been very precise. "Tall" Easter lilies may range in height from 18 to 36 inches. "Large" poinsettia bracts could include those 10 inches in diameter to over 15 inches.

A major supplier of supermarket chains has developed specific language regarding the quality of the product to be shipped to the buyer. This action was instituted as a means of reducing if not eliminating difficulties encountered at time of shipment. Differences of opinion over original discussions regarding the quality of the final product have threatened cancellation of some orders. The buyer now receives written specifications for the crop, and they guarantee that the passage of time will not result in significant alterations in language and ultimate quality of the product.

An order for geranium plants in flower might include a significant percentage of those showing only tight buds. The shipper may rationalize that something is better than nothing. Most retailers prefer one or more open on a plant. A major problem pertains to the shipment of poorly rooted foliage plants. Quick turnover of plants leads to shipment of material resembling rooted cuttings. Packages of peat moss often vary from shipment to shipment. Some bags may contain a large percentage of foreign matter such as branches or sticks, others an unusually large quantity of small particles.

A supplier with a good and consistent reputation helps overcome many language problems and questions regarding grades and standards. Good, dependable growers can be identified with the assistance of other buyers, sales personnel from noncompeting organizations, and periodic visits to the production site.

PRICE

Price is an important factor in helping determine product quality. Quantity discounts do affect price but not nearly as much as overall quality of a product. Someone has said, "You know the value of your own product and thus I can't quibble with your price." Top quality merchandise almost always commands a premium price in a particular market.

In 1982 good quality geraniums in one market commanded a wholesale price of $1.10. Retailers sold this product anywhere from $1.50 up to $1.79. Poor or average quality geraniums in the same market could have been procured for 80 cents to 85 cents, and were commonly sold for $1.10 to $1.25. The buyer must determine, first, which geranium meets the needs and pocketbook of his or her clientele, and, second, which product can produce the highest profit for the garden center.

You can generally find a price and level of quality to suit your market needs. There are few truly good bargains unless one buys in large volume or happens to find a grower in trouble. Most producers have learned to play the game with buyers interested only in price. They have the potential of providing a product in almost any price range. A cheap product will be provided minimum space while expensive items command more room on the production site. A second tool relates to time allocated for production. An inexpensive geranium often will be produced in less than two months. The

Price captures attention
in this advertisement,
especially when most
geraniums have been
retailed at $1.00 and
above in the same market.
The higher priced items
have been planted in
4-1/2-inch containers
while this plant may have
been in the 3-1/2-inch
category.

final product may contain one flower on a single stemmed plant. Quality geraniums can be produced in a period of six weeks. These plants have been grown at warm temperatures, fed regularly, and provided room for proper development.

INSPECTION

A visit to the production site can be most revealing for buyers. You can tell a great deal about the crop by looking at the uniformity of the plants. When viewing poinsettias from the best quality growers in a market, you will see that their plants are extremely uniform. All plants on the bench are saleable to the extent that 90 percent would fall into top grade, were grades and standards available for this crop. Poor quality growers have plants that remind one of a roller coaster.

How much space has been allocated to each plant? Poor and average quality growers often shave a little space in hopes of putting a few more plants on the bench.

A visit to a greenhouse during the early stages of a crop can prove misleading in evaluating space and quality. Small or young plants do not require nearly as much space as mature plants.

Good quality geraniums in 4 to 4½-inch pots require a ¼ square foot area, or a space 6 by 6 inches. Branched poinsettias with one plant in a 6-inch diameter container need approximately 1¼ square feet. You just can't cut corners and still produce a premium sized product.

Some growers inadvertently allow plants to decline in quality toward the end of the crop. A certain geranium grower provided only a minimum amount of space for his crop. Botrytis, a fungus disease, attacked because of the tightly packed plants and high moisture conditions. Try to visit local suppliers just before the first shipment to double check on your plants.

Grades and Standards.   Market grades and standards have not been established for floricultural crops. A language has been developed over the years that provides some guidelines, but always subject to interpretation by buyer and seller. Experience and a critical eye become extremely important for buyers shopping for specific merchandise.

The American Association of Nurserymen (AAN) early in its history developed a standardized system of sizing and describing plants to facilitate trade in trees and shrubs. The AAN decided in 1948 to adhere to the procedures of the American Standards Association in making their standards recognized at the national level. The adoption of standards remains purely voluntary on the part of sellers as well as buyers and middlemen.

Two-spotted spider mites attack a wide range of indoor plants. Small yellowish spots, the size of a pinhead signal attack by this sucking pest. The leaves take on a light yellowish cast following large populations feeding on the plant.

Pests. Quality plants should be free from noticeable injury and presence of insect and disease organisms. Questionable quality merchandise cannot be handled by organizations developing an image for top products. Some producers may do a poor job in controlling pests on a regular basis. Your plants may arrive looking clean, but warm weather may stimulate rapid increases in insect populations and seriously reduce the vigor and appearance of plants. Careful inspection of plants immediately upon arrival and at periodic intervals is a must to protect your reputation.

Labels. Quality producers normally have taken special pains to properly label all material. The cultivar name and where possible cultural recommendations should be attached to each specimen or pack of plants.

Appearances. The general appearance of an operation often tells a great deal about the organization. A quality organization normally maintains its buildings and grounds in top shape. The office looks like it operates efficiently and in a businesslike manner. People at all levels appear friendly and cooperative. The best recommendation often comes from competitors who respect the firm and its performance over the years.

GERANIUMS

The product available for sale in any size pot varies according to the source of cuttings, the length of time on the production bench, space allocation, the ability of the grower, and the cultivar.

Source. Long and sometimes hard cuttings have been shipped from western sources to producers throughout the country. These cuttings have been noted for their branching characteristics, which result in few breaks and then only breaks far above the soil line. However, the lower four inches often have been bare of leaves and new shoots. Shorter and softer cuttings have appeared on the scene from some western sources in more recent years. This product, when properly handled, has resulted in the ultimate sale of quality plants.

One of the common diseases of stock grown outdoors in certain parts of the country works internally to inhibit water uptake to leaves and flowers. Symptoms may not appear until customers have the product and plants exposed to very hot conditions. This type of stress increases the need for water. Leaves may quickly turn yellow and entire plants deteriorate in a matter of days due to the disease being present in noncultured cuttings.

Cultured cuttings essentially free from most diseases and soon to be free from virus organisms have greatly altered the geranium crop. A fairly uniform, vigorous, well-branched, many-blossomed, high-quality crop has become a reality and all to the benefit of the final consumer. The capability is now present for growers to acquire and then produce top quality plants every year.

Production Period. New cultural practices utilizing well-rooted cultured cuttings have resulted in the production of flowering plants in about six weeks after potting. This requires a top quality rooted cutting, good soil mix, warm temperature and an adequate fertilization program.

Spacing. Growers continually need additional space in the spring, and thus it has not been uncommon to crowd plants. Failure to allocate adequate room results in the production of tall, leggy, spindly plants, often minus many lower leaves. Inadequate light and botrytis annually take their toll in terms of poor quality foliage.

The Grower. The grower naturally makes an important contribution to the quality of the final product. In addition to selection of the source of cuttings, he or she determines planting time, spacing, soil mix, temperature, watering, and fertilization practices. There is an art and a science in the production of quality plants. Some growers have the touch, some don't, and some continually try to cut corners.

Cultivars. Some popular cultivars have been grown primarily for their showy appearance at time of sale. The fact that the cultivar may have problems in some outdoor situations has not altered popularity of the selection from the grower's point of view. They have been sold as red, white, and pink geraniums. Consumers have not had the best opportunity to express preferences when buying unnamed cultivars from large retail or discount stores.

Hybrid seed geraniums have started to capture a growing segment of the market. Most produce single flowers which have a tendency to shatter when handled roughly. These plants normally are very symmetrical and feature a large number of breaks and leaves. Growers have sold this item in the green stage and with one flower cluster open.

Quality. The primary criterion influencing saleability, in simple terms, has been the presence of a single bloom regardless of plant size, shape, or condition of foliage. This marketing practice tends to penalize the quality grower by making it difficult for him to obtain a fair price for the product.

What constitutes a good quality geranium?

1. *Well branched.* The presence of three or more branches arising near the soil line gives excellent prospects for a strong plant blooming continuously throughout the summer.

2. *Good root system.* The root system is frequently ignored when evaluating quality. A good, extensive, whitish root system is a prerequisite for a strong plant.

The seed or hybrid geranium features a large number of basal breaks, symmetrical growth pattern, and ultimately a large number of single flowers.

3. *Compact.* A tall, leggy plant did not receive adequate room on the greenhouse bench. A good plant in a 4½-inch container will range from 6 to 8 inches above the rim, excluding flowers.

4. *Symmetrical.* A quality plant should be round with the diameter in the vicinity of 6 inches. This permits 4 pots to be placed in a square foot with leaves just overlapping.

5. *Dark, green leaves.* Yellowing and light green new leaves often suggest that the plant has not received an adequate supply of nutrients. Small leaves may suggest that water and nutrients were withheld from plants, often as a means of limiting excessive stretching.

6. *Flowers.* A truly good quality plant really does not have to have open flowers. This is important, however, in terms of attracting attention of consumers. A well-branched plant may have two or three clusters in partial or full color and some flower heads just starting to develop.

7. *Identification.* The name of the cultivar should appear on a label attached to each plant.

An overhead view of the geranium emphasizes the type of symmetry deemed important when looking for quality plants. In the bottom photograph you can see the many shoots appearing close to the soil line. This plant has the capability of producing a large number of geranium flowers throughout the growing season.

A visit to your supplier and an inspection of facilities can provide much information regarding ultimate quality of the product. Try to determine source of cuttings, potting time and space allocation. Knock out a plant from the container and inspect the root system. There is no need to guess or buy purely on reputation once you have had an opportunity to see the crop in midspring.

BEDDING PLANTS

Producers of bedding plants often schedule two crops for sale in early, mid, or late season. This insures that customers will receive plants in peak condition for transplanting into the garden, window boxes, planters, and hanging baskets. Some producers focus their attention on the sale of crops that have spent only a minimum of time in the greenhouse after transplanting. The foliage barely covers the soil surface. It generally takes several more weeks for these plants to come into flower.

Poor cultural conditions, a delayed outdoor planting season, and growers making only a single sowing can contribute to the sale of leggy and over mature crops. The petunia crop, for example, may stand eight or more in-

A large concentration of roots around the soil ball reflects a healthy plant. Whitish or light brown roots will help support extensive growth above the soil line.

ches above the soil line and be in full flower. These plants should be cut back by the conscientious and knowledgeable gardener.

Tall, leggy plants may indicate that the producer failed to use a growth regulator. These chemicals retard growth and in the process insure that plants will not become unsightly.

Some producers tend to harden plants by limiting the supply of water and nutrients. This technique can leave the plants with an off or light yellow color. It may take several weeks before they produce new and vigorous growth once transplanted to the border.

A late frost can severely injure soft plants. Good growers condition bedding plants by exposing them gradually to cool night temperatures common in late spring.

Bedding plant containers should be free of weeds. They compete for moisture and nutrients with desired plants and impair the appearance of a display. Good quality growers will sterilize soil with heat or chemicals to control weeds.

Look for the following characteristics reflecting quality bedding stock:

1. Good green colored leaves
2. Well-branched and compact plants
3. Extensive, white root system
4. A few flowers in full color
5. Leaves that are moderately large and typical for the cultivar
6. Plants conditioned for the outdoors
7. Identification tags

TOMATOES

Tomatoes grow rapidly in the greenhouse. Some producers seemingly have been in a hurry to start seed in midspring. An early sowing generally results in the production of tall, leggy plants with light foliage. It is true that tomatoes can be buried deeply to encourage rooting from the stem. The practice also counters leggy growth since only lush foliage is exposed after planting. The preferred technique would insure the sale of small- to medium-sized plants. Registration of B-9, a growth retardant, now enables growers to tailor height according to market needs.

There has been a growing tendency for many urban gardeners to buy mature potted plants with the expectation of harvesting a large and early crop. This product does capture the attention of neighbors. An early and heavy crop rarely is realized because large plants have difficulty adjusting to a new location. Cool night temperatures may stall plants. Young, vigorous plants often catch up by midsummer to those plants already in flower and showing some fruit at sale time.

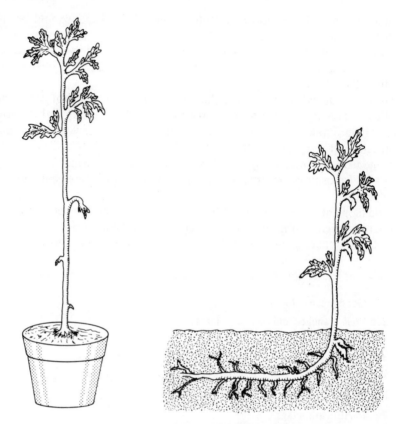

Tomatoes are one of the few plants that can be buried deeply, with roots originating along the stem. Tall, leggy plants can be laid horizontally in a trench, 5 to 7 inches deep, with the tip bent upwards, permitting the green leaves to remain above the soil line. When staked, plants require a 2 x 2 x 4 foot spacing. From 10 to 15 square feet are required for unsupported plants. While all plants should be mulched, it is especially important to do so with unstaked plants to keep the fruit off the ground.

Tall and leggy tomatoes can be salvaged by planting deeply as shown in this illustration. Roots will appear along the stem and help support strong, vigorous growth.

Some tomatoes have been produced in peat pots or similar material. The root system of mature plants will appear on the outside walls. There is a danger that these roots may dry out and break off with inadequate moisture and rough handling. The consumer would then receive a "hardened" plant that might stall and produce little growth after being transferred to the garden. Tallish plants in very small sized containers require frequent waterings and feedings to remain in lush condition. Customers tend to shy away from tall, ungainly, and light green plants.

Greenhouses unfortunately have been the source of many white flies that have plagued gardeners. These uninvited pests come from the greenhouses and often return indoors on neighboring plants such as the coleus in the fall.

A selection of early, mid, and late-season cultivars should be offered to gardeners. Early season fruiting selections are especially important to gardeners facing short growing seasons. The cultivars should be identified and plants labeled with signs bearing information on how long it will take to produce an average crop. University extension recommendations should be followed in selecting cultivars for your area of the country.

A quality tomato plant has the following attributes:

1. Good, green color
2. White, extensive root system
3. Medium in height and stocky
4. Freedom from white flies

HANGING BASKETS

The market for hanging baskets developed rapidly in the mid-1970s. Growers used all available space in the production of seemingly every item whether suited or not for baskets.

There are two forms of fuchsia used by gardeners for hanging baskets.

Cascading growth appearing around the entire basket, luxurious foliage, and large numbers of flowers signal a quality flowering basket.

The upright form, used occasionally by some producers, should not be used in baskets. The trailing form works exceptionally well, cascading down over the basket. A similar situation applies to tuberous rooted begonias. Some excellent trailing cultivars can be procured for baskets.

Ivy geraniums work exceptionally well in 8- and 10-inch baskets. The standard, upright geraniums should not be featured in this container.

Many petunia cultivars grow upward rather than trailing down and masking the basket. They also can become leggy when started too early.

Look for the following when selecting quality baskets:

1. Symmetrical growth indicating adequate space provided for proper development

2. Good, dark color in foliage

3. Well-pinched and branched plants

4. Absence of leggy growth

5. Cultivars suitable and recommended for baskets

6. Growth already starting to cascade down over sides of basket.

ROSE BUSHES

You can procure hybrid tea rose bushes on the basis of a fairly uniform and rigid grading system. The standards apply to field-grown, two-year roses when sold bare root or individually wrapped and packaged in cartons. All grades must have a well-developed root system. The specifications outlined for length apply before pruning in preparation for sale. The number of heavy or strong canes reflects the quality of the plant. The system currently employed provides for the following:

Grade	Specifications
No. 1	3 or more strong canes, 2 of which are to be 18 inches and up, with the exception of a few of the light-growing sorts*, which are to have three or more canes, two of which are to be 16 inches and up, branched not higher than 3 inches above the bud union.
No. 1½	2 or more strong canes, to be 15 inches and up with the exception of a few of the light-growing sorts, which are to have 2 strong canes 13 inches and up, branched not higher than 3 inches above the bud union.
No. 2	2 or more strong canes 12 inches and up, with the exception of a few light-growing sorts, which are to have 2 or more canes, 10 inches and up, branched not higher than 3 inches above the bud union.

*Many varieties of hybrid tea roses express varying growth characteristics in different parts of the country. Some varieties may be generally known to be less vigorous in some regions than in others. The term used above, "light-growing sorts" cannot therefore be used in a universal or rigid sense. Examples of varieties generally considered to be "light growing" are President Hoover, Etoile de Holland, The Doctor, and Mojave. Other examples that are often considered in some areas as "light-growing varieties" are New Yorker, Charlotte Armstrong, and Helen Traubel.

Similar specifications have been prepared for floribunda roses, polyantha, dwarf and light-growing floribunda roses, climbing roses, and container-grown roses.

The price you pay reflects grade, size, and age of newness of cultivar. Patented cultivars and those just introduced bear the highest price tags. Old-time favorites whose patent rights no longer exist now sell at modest prices.

Bare root roses have been packaged in an attractive wrapper. The above ground portion of the plant has been coated with a layer of wax. Inexperienced personnel often have displayed this product in full sunlight. Warm temperatures force bud development to occur. The root system cannot supply moisture and customers occasionally receive plants that have been drained of all vitality.

Several producers sell preplanted roses. Top grade merchandise has been used for this product.

Plants in full flower can be purchased from some producers. Normally, plants with several good canes have been forced into early flower. Tall, leggy plants have been crowded in the greenhouse. The growth tends to be rather weak. Greenhouse-grown roses may have contracted a common disease known as powdery mildew. Inspect foliage for the presence of powdery, gray areas that ultimately turn leaves brown and defoliate plants.

Good, dark green leaves are indicators of a strong plant. Leaf size should be typical for the cultivar. Be suspicious of unusually small leaves suggesting the presence of a poorly developed root system.

BULB STOCK

Bulb stocks such as tulips and gladiolus corms seem to resemble hard good items in that they don't appear highly perishable. The diameter or circumference of bulbs and corms often reflects the vigor and potential for development of large flowers and plants. While cultivars vary in terms of average bulb size, you will find that prices often reflect overall size and diameter along with newness.

Gladiolus corms often carry virus particles or organisms responsible for white break, mosaic, or other plant distortions. The source of the product should be checked to insure that you do not buy questionable merchandise. Discolorations of surface plant tissue may indicate the presence of some potential disease problems. Slicing gladiolus corms horizontally and in half, on a sample basis, can help pinpoint the presence of a fusarium organism. The base of the corm also may have broken down and look exceptionally dry. All suspected shipments should be sampled before being displayed for sale. Small sized corms and bulbs may be acquired at attractive prices.

This gladiolus corm shows signs of basal rot. Roots normally develop from this area. The diseased corm is not capable of producing healthy growth.

However, your customers may become discouraged having to wait two growing seasons before seeing mature plants.

Spring flowering bulbs normally have been shipped in temperature controlled compartments. Storage at warm temperatures prior to arrival at your store can lead to breakdown of tissue and spread of disease organisms. Sample each shipment for presence of soft bulbs and corms.

Dahlia roots often break down in storage. Quality material frequently has been coated with wax to protect them from decay. These roots should be checked periodically to protect against decaying material and unnecessary drying and shriveling.

New introductions, especially gladiolus cultivars, have been packed in a see-through net material. Special packaging identifying All-American winners requires that a premium price be paid for and charged for the product. Newness and special care call for the premium in comparison to normal packaging techniques.

Standards for bulbs, corms, and tubers may be found in *American Standard for Nursery Stock,* produced by AAN.[1] The standard is revised approxi-

American Association of Nurserymen, *American Standard for Nursery Stock* (Washington, D.C.: the Association, 1973), pp. 25–26.

mately every five years. Bulbs and corms generally have been sold under grade names such as forcing-size, top-size, and large. Double-nose bulbs indicate a split bulb probably containing two flower buds. The number of buds or eyes on the tuber can be designated for peonies, cannas and bleeding heart. Small bulbs or corms that cannot be expected to bloom should not be offered for sale to consumers. Here are examples of standards[2] for gladiolus and amaryllis:

GLADIOLI	
Jumbo	over 2″ in diameter
Large	
No. 1	1½″-2″ diameter
No. 2	1¼″-1½″ diameter
Medium	
No. 3	1″-1¼″ diameter
No. 4	¾″-1″ diameter
Small	
No. 5	½″-¾″ diameter
No. 6	⅜″-½″ diameter
No grade name	
No. 7	under ⅜″ diameter
AMARYLLIS	
Fancy	over 3½″ in diameter
Top-size	3¼″-3½″ up in diameter
Large	3″-3¼″ up in diameter
Medium	2¾″-3″ up in diameter
Small	2¼″-2¾″ up in diameter
Under 2¼″—not acceptable	

POTTING SOIL

The rapidly developing green plant boom has stimulated the demand for accessory products such as potting soils. There are a number of soil mixes sold locally, regionally, and nationally. Relatively few, if any rules govern what can and cannot be done in the sale of soil mixes for indoor plants. Many mixes reportedly have been sterilized by the manufacturer. The presence of an exceptionally large number of common symphilids in one large batch by a national firm suggests that the sterilization process failed to accomplish the intended goals.

What should go into a mix? Black or dark brown seems to be the magic

[2]*Ibid.*

color. The source of the desired color may or may not contribute to the development of a strong root system. Customers appear willing to pay an unusually high price for the convenience of procuring a small volume of soil. A garden center operator must remember, however, that the customer will be around for months and years. Will the sale of a poor soil mix at $1.29 drive a good customer away to another competitor?

A home mix consisting of small quantities of sand blended in with a heavy clay soil can lead to disaster. The heavy weight of the product becomes a liability to you in handling and to the customer. The mix may turn out to be a form of concrete with just enough sand to fill the pore spaces. A conscientious operator should test the soil mix before sale to the public. This applies whether you handle a nationally advertised product or prepare your own mix. How do plants perform in the material? You can see some results in two or three months. Knock out the soil ball and look at the root system. It should be near white and beginning to cover the soil ball. Water should penetrate and disappear from the soil surface in less than thirty seconds after each watering. If not, it suggests that the soil is compacting and restricting root development. Top growth also is a measure of quality of the soil mix. A reasonable amount of new growth should be evident providing the plant has adequate light and receives water and nutrients on a regular basis.

A small bag of soil can yield excellent profits. Select only those mixes that can benefit your customers. An ounce of protection is worth avoiding all the grief coming from a customer who lost a prized plant because of your soil.

FLOWERING PLANTS

A growing number of garden center operators have increased their product mix and now handle flowering plants at holidays and slack periods of the year. This commodity carries with it some risks that are magnified by inexperienced buyers. Price often dominates the discussion between buyer and seller. Most markets of any size provide opportunities for procurement of plants at inexpensive, average, and above average prices.

Many flowering plants have been marketed in a simplistic fashion. Pot size, as with the geranium, commands a great deal of attention. You can procure flowering or potted chrysanthemums in 4½-, 5½-, 6-, 6½-, 7-, and 8-inch pots. There may be a few other sizes common to some markets. Pot size tells you almost everything you want to know about the container. It provides but few clues regarding quality, display, and plant size.

Some crops have been marketed on the basis of flower count. This applies especially to the Easter lily and poinsettia crops. Lily flowers are fairly uniform in size although plant height can vary from those 12 inches above the rim to 3 feet in height. An ideal plant ranges from 16 to 20 inches including the pot. The flowers or bracts of a poinsettia vary extensively from just a few inches up to 15 or more inches in diameter. Bract size reflects cultural conditions including spacing, light, watering, and fertilizing practices.

Upright or single-stemmed poinsettia plants generally produce larger bracts than those found on branched plants. The latter category has captured a great deal of attention from producers since the introduction of free-branching cultivars. The switch from upright plants also was motivated by buyers from large chains seeking modestly priced plants. A typical producer could shave from 50 cents to $1 a unit for popular sizes by growing only a branched crop. Top quality growers can produce branched specimens that compare favorably or exceed overall quality and appearance of upright merchandise.

One anticipates large poinsettia bracts or blooms on plants that have been grown with one main stem. This is in contrast to smaller sized bracts produced on plants featuring many branches.

A quality garden center must determine whether to feature merchandise comparable to that offered by chains or to display upright or single-stemmed plants. The image of the firm might well be enhanced by procuring some branched material along with a supply of premium, single-stemmed plants.

Some producers start planting or panning rooted cuttings in late July and others in August and September. Earlier plantings have been scheduled for large, specimen plants. The last batch of cuttings in September produces smaller plants of average quality. Wholesale prices for upright plants should be much higher than comparable branched material. Four single-stemmed plants producing four large bracts can appear, on the surface, equal to one branched plant also featuring a comparable number of "flowers." The producer invested somewhere in the vicinity of 25 cents in each plant. The branched unit required an initial investment of 25 cents compared to $1 for the four upright plants. The wholesale price should reflect this cost factor and also the fact that bracts on single-stemmed plants normally are larger than those on branched plants.

A visit to a greenhouse can yield much information with respect to growing conditions on the bench. A good quality plant has many, if not all, of the following attributes:

1. Good, dark green, dense foliage with leaf size at least average for the cultivar
2. Strong stems with a plant proportional to the container. Most often, plant should stand straight without support
3. Symmetrical growth
4. Foliage free from insect and disease injury
5. Flowers generally just reaching peak of maturity
6. Extensive, white root ststem

Critical points have been outlined for twelve major flowering plant crops.

1. Azaleas
   a. Flowers and buds should be distributed evenly over the plant and potential color equal to that of leaf area. One third to one half of the flowers should be open and the rest in bud stage.
   b. Plants should be free from new vegetative growth (light colored) around the flowers and from abnormally long or wild shoots.
   c. The pot may contain one or two plants. Top quality plants have branches at or near the soil surfaces.
2. African violets
   a. Single-crown plants have generally been preferred by the trade and consumer. This plant has one growing point and the leaves lay flat like an inverted plate. Leaves should overlap to the extent of avoiding noticeable gaps in the appearance of the plant.
   b. There should be a reasonable number of flowers standing well above the foliage and generally clustered near the center of the plant.
3. Calceolaria
   a. Flowers should be borne on stiff, upright stems. An overripe plant generally can be detected by missing florets in the influorescence or

The flowering plant shown above features dense, dark green foliage, strong stems, and a nice spread of berries over the entire surface of the plant. The Jerusalem cherry plant below contains only a few berries and has produced overly tall and awkward growth.

Azaleas are available to consumers throughout the year. Flowers develop over a period of time, providing the soil is maintained on the moist side. This plant features wide open flowers and few tight buds. It will last only a few days in an average home.

       display. A good quality plant features several clusters of flowers displayed just above the foliage.

  b. A single plant generally will be grown in a 5- or 6-inch pot.

4. Chrysanthemums

  a. The number of plants and ultimate color display associated with a particular container may vary from grower to grower. Some operators will place four plants in a 6-inch unit while others insert five. Normally, display area has been related to the number of plants in the pot.

  b. Foliage should be lush and compact to the point where it is difficult to see through the plant. Small leaves and leggy growth permit a great deal of light to show when viewing the plant from a horizontal perspective.

  c. The top of the plant should be slightly mounded to nearly flat.

  d. All flowers should be approximately uniform in their development. Well-grown plants will feature a large number of flowers virtually covering the entire upper surface of the plant.

  e. Disbudding techniques vary according to the cultivar and individual grower. Some plants feature one flower on each stem while others have not been or are partially disbudded. The latter will produce a multitude of smaller flowers.

Free-flowering violets are available in a wide variety of colors. One can anticipate flowering most of the year, providing plants are exposed to rather bright light.

5. Cineraria

    a. This cool-temperature crop normally has grown with one plant in a 5- or 6-inch pot. Be on the lookout for aphids.

    b. Composite flowers in the center of the spray open first and those on the perimeter at a later date. A good spray will be compact and free from foliage sticking through the flowers. Faded blooms and off-colored or dry pollen suggest an overripe plant. From one third to one half of the flowers should be open at the time of sale.

6. Cyclamen

    a. A cool crop, cyclamen is capable of producing one flower for every leaf on the plant. Spread the leaves and look into the center of the plant. A cluster of buds assures that there will be color for several weeks.

    b. Foliage should be crisp so that you could turn it upside down, in the absence of flowers, and it would be capable of supporting itself.

7. Easter lilies

    a. Wide basal leaves provide an overall better display and profile than narrow, short leaves. Plants that have been crowded often feature a narrow profile or small diameter in comparison to well-grown lilies. Browning of lower leaves often signifies crowding, some root loss or lack of nitrogen. Tip burn or browning of the tips impairs quality and over-all appearance of the plant.

The cyclamen desires cool temperatures, bright light, and a moist soil. It normally appears on the market in mid to late fall and on through late winter.

    b.   A good lily has five or more buds. One third to one half should be in full bloom. Flowers should be spaced uniformly and face all directions. The anthers should be removed as soon as possible to avoid staining petals, furniture, and clothing.

8. Gloxinia

    a.   One fourth of the flowers should be open with the remaining buds in various stages of development. Bright light, a humid atmosphere, and moist soil are all necessary to insure buds opening and not turning brown. Flowers should be borne well above the foliage.

    b.   The foliage is unusually large and often cracks from rough handling. Foliage should spread out in horizontal fashion and extend slightly down below the rim of the pot.

9. Hydrangea

    a.   This plant requires large quantities of water to avoid leaf and blossom wilting. Approximately 90 percent of the florets in the panicle or display should be open and in full color.

    b.   Stems should be strong enough to hold the plant upright without support from stakes.

    c.   Muddy or off-colored blooms fail to capture the attention of customers. A good, branched plant in a 5- or 6-inch pot should feature three blooms.

Gloxinias are available throughout the year. This plant can be reflowered a second year.

10. Kalanchoe

    a. This warm temperature crop consists of a multitude of flowers covering the plant. One third to one half of the buds should be wide open.

    b. Foliage is an important consideration with this plant. Leaves can be broken easily with rough handling.

11. Poinsettia

    a. New introductions (red, white, pink, and bicolors) retain leaves and bracts for long periods of time. Branched plants have replaced single-stem or upright plants in many sections of the country.

    b. Weak stems indicate crowding, poor light, and excessive shoots allowed to develop on the plant. Strong stems, large bracts, and plant in proportion to container reflect good cultural practices.

    c. The loss of flowers in the center of the bract suggests that the plant matured too early in the greenhouse.

    d. Faded or light colors reflect warm growing conditions and poor light intensity.

12. Rieger begonia

    a. One plant normally has been placed in a pot. It will be slightly wider than its height.

    b. The stems should be strong enough to support the floral display. A good quality plant will have five or more major shoots.

The poinsettia can be marketed immediately after Thanksgiving. New cultivars will last many weeks, if not months, under average conditions in the home.

The browning and ultimate disappearance of flowers in the center of the bract signal a plant that has been salable many weeks and probably exposed to warm conditions.

This quality Rieger begonia basket features cascading growth and an abundance of flowers.

    c.   One third to one half of the flowers should be open and displayed over the entire surface of the plant.

FOLIAGE PLANTS

Foliage plants commonly have been marketed on the basis of pot size. The larger items start in 5-inch pots and specimens in 8, 10, and 12-inch containers. Smaller pots, representing the bulk of unit sales, range from 2¼ to 3½ and 4 inches in diameter.

The condition of plants in the smaller units has to be checked carefully. Some plants, in reality, should be classified as well-rooted cuttings. The soil crumbles upon inspection with the shallow and modest root system unable to hold the ball intact. These plants are subject to a high fatality rate because of excess watering by overanxious "parents."

The root ball of plants in larger containers can and should be inspected to determine condition of that part of the plant residing below the soil line. The size and extent of the root system is a good indicator of overall plant quality.

Most foliage plants tend to grow in a symmetrical pattern except those attached to a supporting post located in the center or toward the rear of the

Compact growth often
signals a high-quality
plant. Relatively large
leaves, free from all
forms of damage, also
suggest a strong, healthy
root system.

pot. A one-sided or poorly formed plant suggests that crowded conditions
prevailed on the growing bench.

Prominent characteristics of a quality plant include:

1. Luxurious and relatively dark green foliage
2. Compact growth in contrast to long internodes
3. Large leaves for the cultivar
4. Freedom from insects, disease, and mechanical injury
5. Symmetrical plant well proportioned in terms of height and diameter to overall size of container
6. Extensive, white root system.

Hanging foliage baskets can be evaluated in much the same fashion as outdoor flowering baskets. The diameter of the basket has been used as a major
factor in determining price of a unit.

Some producers have adopted rather strict house grades governing the minimum size of a plant offered for sale. A ball-shaped plant with a generous amount of foliage cascading over the rim of the container signals a quality basket. Relatively thick growth contrasted to spindly or only a modest number of shoots also signals a quality plant. Price cutters often have sold rather immature baskets with the product occupying greenhouse space for a minimum amount of time.

FRESH FLOWERS

A growing number of garden centers have diversified into the business normally associated with retail florists. Specifically, this has involved the sale of fresh flowers in the loose or arranged form. Fresh flowers may be procured from wholesale florists. These operations have been located in major metropolitan areas. The decline of rail and bus transportation has led to truck transportation supplied by many wholesale operations.

Some wholesalers ship only merchandise that has been preordered by the retailer. A few truckers carry preordered merchandise along with stock that can be purchased along the route. Fresh flowers may be ordered direct from major supply areas such as Florida, California, and Colorado. Some medium and large retailers in markets serviced by air transportation have purchased direct from suppliers. Producers have sold merchandise direct to retailers and bypassed local wholesale firms. The merchandise may be delivered by growers establishing truck routes or picked up at the greenhouse by retailers.

Fresh flowers commonly have been bunched in units of 10, 12, and 25. The nature of the crop, in terms of overall length and flower display, has had an influence on bunching practices. National grades and standards have been adopted by the Society of American Florists for carnations and chrysanthemums. The standards have not been widely adopted by producers. Each bunch of flowers should exhibit the following characteristics:

1. Uniform or near uniform stem length
2. Flowers at the same stage of development
3. Good, green foliage free from mechanical, insect, and disease injury
4. Strong stems capable of holding flowers in an upright position
5. Uniform-sized flowers
6. Flowers free from bruising and injury from insects and diseases

The insertion of some weak stems, undersized flowers, or overmature flowers in a bunch seriously impairs overall quality. This practice is frowned upon by industry leaders and often leads to a reduction in price paid for the commodity.

Standard chrysanthemums have been shipped from California by the box. The flowers are packed singly with a specific count depending upon diameter of the bloom. Local producers often bunch this crop by the dozen. Spray chrysanthemums have been sold by the bunch. Stem count varies from five to a dozen units. A plastic or paper wrap sleeve has often been placed around the upper portions of each bunch. The size of this wrap largely governs the number of stems or flowers placed in the bunch. The wrap must remain secure and thus provides a fairly standard display area from bunch to bunch.

Stem composition varies in spray chrysanthemum bunches. They may contain one or two extra-strong stems, a comparable number of weak stems, and the remainder in the average category. Retail florists generally have preferred to work with medium weight or caliber stems. Individual flowers and their short stems have been removed from heavy stems for use in bowl arrangements.

The primary problem facing buyers has been avoiding old or relatively mature stock. Blooms that are fairly wide open signify age and should be avoided by discriminating buyers. Growers rarely ship green merchandise since returns suffer because of small diameter and size of blooms. Flowers can be stored under refrigeration for a number of days to more than a week. Low humidity and improper temperatures in storage seriously impair the quality of fresh flowers.

QUALITY SOD

Sod has been marketed by the yard with some rolls measuring 18 and others 24 inches in width. The weight of a single roll varies according to moisture content and type of soil. Sod grown on upland soil may weigh from 45 to 50 pounds a yard in contrast to 20 to 25 pounds for that produced on peat. Good quality sod has the following characteristics:

1. Weed free
2. Good green color
3. High density
4. Free from disease
5. Square corners
6. Uniform thickness
7. Approximately one-half inch thick
8. Recommended cultivars

A roll of quality sod can be picked up at the corners and hung like a blanket. High density of plants and a well-knit piece of sod permit you to

This roll of sod is well-knit, cut uniformly at corners, and less than 3/4 inch thick.

handle the product in this fashion without its disintegrating into several pieces. Immature sod will break apart into several pieces since the root system has not had an opportunity to spread out and interlock.

Old sod can be detected by a build-up of thatch. This is the accumulation of partially decayed grass clippings at or near the soil line. New or quality sod will be virtually free of this material.

Good quality producers have adopted recommendations of extension specialists regarding cultivars and blends of different grasses. It is important for both the grower and the consumer to work with cultivars that are disease resistant.

It can be difficult to detect the presence of undesirable perennials such as quack grass. An examination of the underside of sod will reveal the presence of thick, white rhizomes associated with this highly undesirable perennial.

Grasses grown on muck soils normally do not do well on athletic fields or when laid on fill soil near the foundation of homes. The heavy wear and tear arising from pounding require a grass grown on an upland or loam soil. An upland soil also compares more favorably than a peat soil in adapting to fill soil.

Cutting sod more than one-half inch thick greatly increases weight of the product. It is relatively easy to handle and work with thin sod that has square corners and has been cut uniformly.

NURSERY STOCK

Trees and shrubs often have been procured from distant suppliers. Relatively few opportunities may exist for actual inspection of stock and condition of the nursery. Local suppliers should be visited on a regular basis. This provides an opportunity for inspection of merchandise and cementing relationships with buyers. The latter has been especially important in recent years with shortages occurring on many items. Poor relationships with suppliers can result in receipt of notices informing of delays and possible cancellation of orders.

An inspection of a nursery should be conducted along the same lines as that for a greenhouse. Uniformity of plant material on a particular block suggests that a quality grower has handled the product. Weed-free plantings are another sign of a good operation. Sloppy maintenance should warn buyers of questionable merchandise.

Water stress and inadequate fertilization will affect both color and growth of plant material. A dull color and limited new growth may suggest that plants have not been irrigated properly. Container-grown stock must be under irrigation at all times. Facilities must be present to irrigate field-grown materials during dry periods. Modest growth and foliage rather light in color also may suggest inadequate fertilization programs. Carefully examine plants for signs of chemical damage. Overfertilization may injure roots limiting uptake of water and nutrients. The tips of young shoots may show severe signs of water stress such as browning or curled and twisted leaves.

Herbicide injury has become more and more prevalent with increased use of these compounds. Poor application techniques including overdosage at wrong time of year plus seepage from neighboring areas may stunt growth, discolor foliage, and produce unusual and distorted leaf characteristics.

Container Stock

Container-grown stock includes plant material grown initially in the field and transplanted to the pot. Some roses have been handled in this fashion. Plants may be started in containers at a very early stage of development.

Containers are a convenient method for growing and transplanting nursery stock. Care must be taken to insure adequate watering and supply of nutrients.

Most nursery stock has been grown for a long period of time in containers to allow ease of handling and shipment. Containers generally are much lighter in weight than balled and burlapped material.

Balled and Burlapped (B and B)

Balled and burlapped material features a large volume of soil surrounding and protecting the root system which is then enclosed in burlap. This product must be mulched and protected from hot surfaces while at the garden center. The soil ball needs to be in proper proportion to the top growth. A small ball cannot adequately support large top growth because of the loss of many roots in the digging and balling process.

Mechanical injury often occurs during cultivation and digging of field-grown plants. Root injury will be hard to detect, especially that occurring during the B and B process. Poorly shaped and broken root balls might indicate serious root injury. That broken branches occur frequently surely suggests poor field practices. The overall appearance of the nursery should command attention of the buyer. Poor blocks intermingled among top material should cause you to look extra carefully before committing a firm to the purchase of material.

Balled and burlapped trees and shrubs must be handled carefully to minimize root damage.

Here are some excerpts taken from *American Standard for Nursery Stock*[3] that apply to coniferous evergreen:

3.1.1 QUALITY DEFINITIONS

The quality of evergreens offered is assumed to be normal for the species of variety unless otherwise designated as:

Specimen (Spec.)   This designation may be used to indicate exceptionally heavy, well shaped plants and is usually applied to the larger commercial sizes and plants which have been cut back or trimmed to form a perfectly symmetrical, tightly knit plant. The letters "X," "XX" or "XXX" may be used to designate the degree of heavy grades in place of using the word "specimen" (spec.).

Collected (Coll.)   Natural seedling plants dug from native stands or forest plantings must be so designated.

3.1.2.4 Type 4. Cone Type (Pyramidal)

Measurement designates height.
Use 3 inch intervals up to 18 inches

[3]*Ibid.*

Use 6 inch intervals from 18 inches to 3 feet
Use 1 foot intervals from 3 feet to 10 feet
Use 2 foot intervals from 10 feet up
    The ratio of height to spread of properly grown material should not be less than 5 to 3.

Height	*Spread*
12 to 15 inch	8 to 12 inches
15 to 18 inch	9 to 15 inches
18 to 24 inch	12 to 18 inches
2 to 2½ feet	15 to 21 inches
2½ to 3 feet	18 to 24 inches
3 to 4 feet	21 to 30 inches
4 to 5 feet	2½ to 3 feet
5 to 6 feet	3 to 4 feet

Examples

Abies
Cedrus deodara
Chamaecyparis pisifera and varieties (except dwarf types)
Picea abies (conical types)
Pinus (except dwarf type)
Pseudotsuga menzeisi
Taxus cuspidata capitata
Thuja occidentalis, orientalis (conical types)
Tsuga canadensis, caroliniana

3.3   CONTAINER GROWN SPECIFICATIONS

All container grown conifers shall be healthy, vigorous, well-rooted and established in the container in which they are sold. They shall have tops which are of good quality and are in a healthy growing condition.
    An established container grown conifer shall be a conifer transplanted into a container and grown in that container sufficiently long for the new fibrous roots to have developed so that the root mass will retain its shape and hold together when removed from the container.
    The container shall be sufficiently rigid to hold the ball shape protecting the root mass during shipping.
    Dwarf and light growing varieties may be 1 or 2 sizes smaller than standard for a given size container.
    The following table gives conifer sizes and acceptable container sizes:

3.3.1   TYPES 1, 2 AND 3

Spread (Type 1, Spreading and Type 2, Semi-Spreading Conifers)
Height (Type 3, Globe or Dwarf Conifers)

Container Size

6 to 9 in.	1 gal. (trade designation) Minimum of 5½
9 to 12 in.	inches across top and height of 6 inches
12 to 15 in.	or equivalent volume
12 to 15 in.	2 gal. (trade designation) Minimum of 7
15 to 18 in.	inches across top and height of 7½ inches
	or equivalent volume
18 to 24 in.	5 gal. egg can or square can (trade designation)
2 to 2½ ft.	Minimum of 9 inches across top and height of 10
2½ to 3 ft.	inches
	or equivalent volume

The specifications provide for clean foliage free from mechanical injury, insects, and disease organisms. Plants and trees should be symmetrical and the main trunk should be straight. Foliage should be dark green and appropriate for the cultivar. The handbook from AAN should be purchased for all buyers as well as wholesale producers and middlemen. A common language minimizes misunderstandings and facilitates buying by telephone and catalogues.

Tree and Small Fruits

The AAN handbook on standards for nursery stock also includes two sections on tree and small fruits. Dwarf fruit trees have increased in popularity at a rapid rate because of their compatibility with small backyards. Small fruits such as strawberries, raspberries, and asparagus plants provide gardeners with an opportunity to realize fresh produce with a minimum of effort and space.

The minimum grade specifications for strawberries state that there should be ten main roots, not less than 3 inches long and a minimum crown diameter of five-sixteenths of an inch measured at the base. The crown can be thought of as the junction between roots and leaf petioles. A number one grade, two year grape should have 12 inches or more of live topgrowth. A number one and grade one year requires 6 inches or more of live top. A grade two year, number two has the same specifications as a grade one year, number one.

A one year, number one asparagus weighs not less than 60 pounds per thousand with 50 percent of the root system exceeding 5 inches in length. A two year, number one weighs not less than 120 pounds and 50 percent of the root system shall exceed 7 inches in length. A two year, number two shall weigh not less than 60 pounds with 50 percent of the root system exceeding 5 inches. A three and four year, number one (super size, bearing age) weighs not less than 200 pounds per thousand, and 50 percent of the root system shall exceed 10 inches in length.

PEATS

A variety of peat products has been used for conditioning soils for both outdoor and indoor plants. Terminology has been loosely employed in terms of defining too many brown or blackish products simply as "peat." There are specific types of peat. They vary in terms of usefulness in potting soil mixes, seed germination, golf green mixes, and surface mulches.

An excellent resource publication of peat was prepared by the Cooperative Extension Service, Michigan State University.[4] The following excerpts taken from this publication help define the various types of peats and discuss their use in the outdoor garden and for indoor plants.

TYPES OF PEAT

Peat can be defined as the organic remains of plants which have accumulated in places where decay has been retarded by excessively wet conditions. It takes 100 to 500 years to produce a one-foot layer of the residue. The rate depends upon type of plant cover and environmental conditions.

Peats used for soil improvement are generally classified into three types: moss peat, reed-sedge, and peat humus. Peat deposits of any of the three types may contain a considerable amount of woody material.

Most peats produced in the United States are either the reed-sedge or humus type. In recent years, however, production of sphagnum moss peat has started in Minnesota, Michigan, Maine, and Washington. Practically all peat imported from Canada or Europe is derived from sphagnum moss.

Moss Peat.   Moss peat is that type which has been formed principally from sphagnum, hypnum, and other mosses. Moss peat, often called "peat moss" is derived mostly from sphagnum moss and is the least decomposed of the various peat types. It is light tan to brown in color, light weight, porous, high in moisture-holding capacity, high in acidity, and low in nitrogen. Hypnum moss peat is a darker brown color, has low acidity, and possesses physical characteristics similar to reed-sedge peat. Moss peats having high acidity are slowly decomposed. On the

[4]Robert E. Lucas, Paul E. Riecke, and Rouse S. Farnham, "Peats for Soil Improvement and Soil Mixes" (Michigan State University, Extension Bulletin 516, Farm Science Series).

other hand, after liming, exposure to air, and incorporation in soil, they decompose at moderate rates because of the high cellulose content.

Sphagnum moss is the young residue or live portion of the plant often called "top moss" and should not be confused with moss peat which has aged and partially decomposed. Sphagnum moss (top moss) is marketed for shipping tender plants and for starting root cuttings, seedlings and also for mulching.

Reed-Sedge Peat. This type is formed principally from reeds, sedges, marsh grasses, cattails and other associated swamp plants. The peats of this type found on the market differ considerably in the degree of decomposition and acidity. Fibrous, partially decomposed peats are brown to reddish brown in color. More decomposed peats are darker in color. The moisture-retention capacity and the nitrogen content are of medium range.

Peat Humus. Peat that is of an advanced stage of decomposition and in which the original plant remains are not identifiable is called "peat humus." It is usually derived from reed-sedge or hypnum moss peat. Peat humus is dark brown to black in color, has low moisture-retention capacity, and a medium to high nitrogen content. This type has a high amount of lignin material which is more resistant to decomposition than the moss and reed-sedge peats.

SOILS HIGH IN ORGANIC MATTER

In addition to the three major types of peat, there may be other organic soils offered for sale. Some of these types are called sedimentary peat, top soil, "black dirt," muck soil, or black humus. They are often low in quality. Such materials can be recommended for soil improvement only if they are inexpensive and have acceptable mineral content and acidity readings. Such information can only be obtained by having the soil tested.

Sedimentary peats are found in the bottom of lakes and ponds and in the lower levels of most peat deposits. They are derived from algae, plankton, pond weeds, and similar plant species. Such peats often contain considerable marl and mineral soil impurities. For most purposes, sedimentary peats are too finely divided, and shrink and swell greatly with varying moisture content. Some that are found near the bottom of a peat deposit have a sheet-like structure which turns hard upon drying.

Much soil is highly weathered peat that has been modified greatly by soil microorganisms and is usually granular in structure. It has low moisture retention and is seldom advised for soil improvements.

TABLE 1. RECOMMENDED USES AND APPLICATION RATES FOR DIFFERENT TYPES OF PEAT.

Peat use	Normal application*	Sphagnum moss peat	Hypnum moss peat	Reed-sedge peat	Peat humus (decomposed)
Soil conditioning	2" layer worked into soil	Fair	Good	Good	Good
Top-dressing lawns, golf courses	1/8-1/4" layer worked into soil	Fair	Good	Good	Good
Surface mulch	2" layer	Excellent	Fair	Fair	Poor
Potting soil mix	50% peat 50% vermiculite or soil	Excellent	Good	Good	Fair
Golf green soil mix	80% sand† 10% clay loam 10% peat	Poor	Good	Good	Excellent
Rooting cuttings	50% peat 50% vermiculite	Excellent	Good	Fair	Poor
Seed flat germination	Pure milled peat	Excellent	Good	Fair	Poor
For acid-loving plants	25% mixture in soil	Excellent	Not recommended	Good if below pH 4.8	Not recommended
For acid-intolerant plants	25% mixture in soil	Recommended only if limed	Good	Good if above pH 4.8	Good
Shipping tender plants	Wrap roots (wet)	Excellent	Fair	Fair	Poor
Adding stable organic matter	2" layer worked into soil	Poor	Fair	Good	Excellent
Liquid absorbent (litter)	2" layer on floor	Excellent	Fair	Fair	Poor
Nitrogen source	Soil mixes top-dressing	Poor	Good	Fair	Good

*By volume. †General Formula—U.S. Golf Association.
Often needs modification for specific situations.

SOURCE: Robert E. Lucas, Paul E. Riecke, and Rouse S. Farnham, "Peats for Soil Improvement and Soil Mixes," Extension Bulletin 516 (Michigan State University, Farm Science Series).

Quality at Arrival Point

An inspection of production facilities represents an important step in acquiring the desired quality product for a firm. Buyers representing large chain organizations often visit in midseason and again just prior to shipment. A great deal can happen to a product in transit and thus it is very important to evaluate products immediately after receipt at your operation.

Nursery Stock. Nursery stock should be shipped in an enclosed truck. Air conditioning equipment is necessary during warmer periods of the year to prevent stock from overheating. Check the material in the truck for the following:

1. Potted material should be placed in neat, orderly rows rather than in a haphazard pattern and be in an upright position.
2. B and B material should not be crushed or the balls showing signs of having broken while in transit or during loading operations.
3. B and B should be stacked so that the lighter balls have been placed at the upper levels. Crushed, lower balls suggest that material was stacked too high in the truck.
4. The shipment should be packed in the truck in an orderly fashion. All material comparable in terms of type and size should be located in one area to ease the inventory operation.
5. Bare root stock must be packaged with appropriate material such as sphagnum moss to maintain an adequate moisture supply around the roots.
6. The material should appear green and have a fresh aroma.
7. The water content should be on the high side within containers and B and B merchandise. This can be determined when unloading merchandise.
8. The trucker should have adequate information relative to which material goes to which buyer.
9. Receiving time should be coordinated with availability of personnel to unload the truck.

Hanging Baskets. Hanging baskets are one of the most vulnerable groupings of plant materials in terms of injury sustained during transit. Foliage and blooms often cascade below the container and are forced to rest on the floor or shelves in a truck. Some parts of the plant may be crushed as containers accidentally or carelessly have been allowed to rest on portions of the plant. A shipment of fuchsia baskets was partially ruined while traveling only 100 miles. Baskets were set on the floor and tender flowers and buds were discolored and damaged.

One enterprising operator has placed foliage baskets in a plastic sleeve. Long stems normally draping over the container have been carefully raised in the process of sleeving and rest above the rim of the container. A great deal more work has been involved in sleeving baskets. Customers have received a product far superior to that from other competitors. Protected baskets have been loaded and unloaded quickly, cutting down time of all personnel.

Flowering Plants.   Poinsettias and other winter flowering plants must be protected against freezing temperatures. Plants have been wrapped or placed in plastic or brown paper sleeves. The product must be shipped in heated vehicles. Poinsettia leaves and bracts often have a tendency to droop a little for a few days after being unwrapped. More serious and prolonged drooping suggests that plants were exposed to cold temperatures around roots, or ethylene gas or a similar product of incomplete combustion in delivery trucks.

There have been occasions when chemicals present in brown wrapping paper have vaporized, causing bracts and leaves to hang limp. This occurred in one situation when plants had been wrapped for at least a day prior to shipment in an overly warm truck.

The top of sleeves or plant wrap generally has been stapled to protect plants from brief exposures to cold temperatures. Those wrapping plants must take care to avoid stapling through the top of bracts. Plants should be carefully unwrapped and plants examined for frost injury. Injured leaves often are discolored, watery, and soon curl or hang limp.

Chrysanthemum plants can be stored at near freezing temperatures for a week or longer. There have been occasions when plants have been sleeved, boxed and stored well in advance of shipping. Plants handled in this fashion and at warmer than recommended temperatures may become unsaleable because of severe yellowing of lower leaves. The condition looks very similar to that of chrysanthemum plants crowded together on display tables and in poor light.

Chrysanthemums represent the major potted plant crop grown throughout the year. Attractive prices in the short run may reflect slightly overmature plants. Old flowers show pollen and opening or spreading out of petals to reveal the center of the flower.

Bedding Plants.   Flats of bedding plants should be examined upon arrival for presence of partially filled packs. The presence of these packs will adversely affect appearance of the total flat. Poor quality packs will have to be put on special sale and in the process cut overall profits.

Geraniums that have been boxed or stored for several days will begin to show yellowing of lower leaves. Blasted buds reflect inadequate watering of pots before shipment. Broken flower stalks occur because of rough handling in packing, unpacking, and occasionally during transit.

Fresh Flowers.   Exposure to subfreezing temperatures represents a major concern when shipping fresh flowers in winter months. This applies largely to the northern states. Flowers lose their turgidity and petals and leaves appear watery and discolored. Warm temperatures are a major problem for shippers in southern states during summer months. An overheated box results in rapid decline in quality from loss of moisture. You may notice a musty odor coming from decaying plant parts.

Sleepy blooms have been one of the major problems facing the carnation shipper. The condition may be noticeable upon arrival or within 24 hours after unboxing. This problem has been associated with the presence of ethylene gas arising from decaying tissue and nearby presence of fruits and vegetables.

Roses stored for a week or longer will go downhill rapidly when exposed to normal room temperatures. You can anticipate this problem by inspecting the flowers at the time of unpacking shipments. Petals already unfurling and discoloration of the outer ones suggest that the product has been in storage for more than the desired number of days.

A number of flowers including spray and standard chrysanthemums and carnations have been shipped in the dry stage. A minimum amount of injury seems to occur when leaves and petals have been transported in a limp or less than turgid condition. The lower inch or two of the stem must be removed and stems immediately placed in warm water containing a preservative. Standard chrysanthemums and carnations have been shipped in fairly tight condition. Ideally, the flowers can be cut in the bud stage with only a modest amount of color showing in the petals. These flowers ship easily and transportation costs can be greatly reduced because of the size of the unit compared to an open flower. The practice has not been generally adopted because of special handling required by the receiver of this product. Flowers must be placed in warm water containing a preservative after removing the lower inch from each stem. It will take a day or longer for flowers to begin to swell and reach a saleable condition.

SUMMARY

The manager-owner or garden center buyer must become familiar with terminology employed by nurserymen, florists, sod, and peat producers. The language often tends to be somewhat loose and flexible and subject to different interpretations at different times of the year. Part of this reflects the role of Mother Nature in changing environmental conditions and in the process influencing size and quality of plants.

A basic rule calls for dealers to conduct business only with reputable suppliers. This is a good rule to follow and generally will insure the delivery of quality merchandise. Reputable suppliers also deliver at the appointed time and the quantity and quality specified in the order.

The price you pay for a commodity truly reflects quality. Beware of unusually low prices unless growers have been faced with slow or sloppy markets. Producers often can tailor a crop to meet your price requirements. There are few bargains as growers have become quite astute in countering pressures from buyers for low, low prices.

The best policy has been and will continue to be to visit production sites. This provides an opportunity to inspect premises for cleanliness. You will have an opportunity to see plants during the production period. Take time to observe spacing practices, uniformity of crop and general vigor of plants.

The following factors can and should be analyzed when evaluating quality of plant materials:

1. Recommended cultivar
2. Color of foliage
3. Condition and extent of root system
4. Size and number of flowers
5. Freedom from mechanical injury, insects, and disease organisms
6. Size and uniformity of crop
7. Height (not being too short or too tall)
8. Maturity—production period
9. Symmetry and compactness of plant
10. Plants well proportioned to size of root ball or container
11. Weed free

Purchase of questionable merchandise ultimately will be reflected in the bottom line on a profit and loss or income statement. The overall image of the firm and profits will be enhanced when good merchandise has been procured to service the needs of customers.

1. Identify and discuss three general rules for selecting a supplier of perishable and nonperishable products.

2. Identify and discuss four factors influencing quality of geraniums.

3. A good quality geranium can be identified as having which key characteristics?

4. How would you describe quality bedding plants?

5. Poor quality hanging baskets generally lack one or more factors associated with quality. Identify five factors.

6. Discuss problems relating to quality of potting soil.

7. What should one look for in purchasing quality poinsettia plants?

8. Identify six keys to selecting good quality sod.

9. How can you be assured of procuring quality nursery stock?

10. What are the primary differences between moss peat or peat moss and peat humus?

11. Identify and describe five things to look for during unloading of nursery stock.

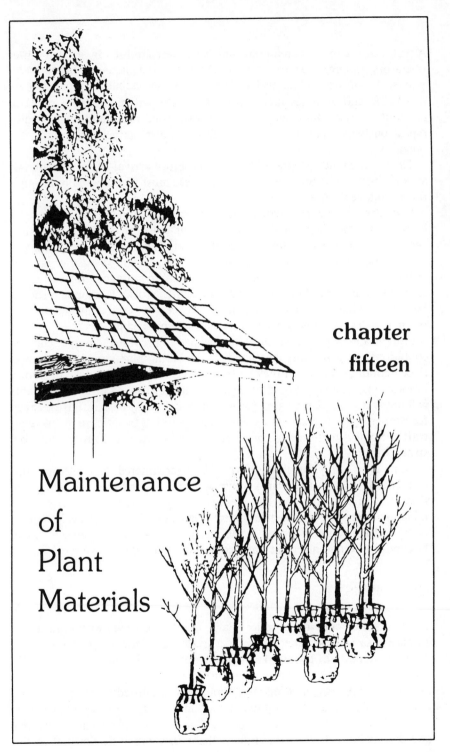

Maintenance
of
Plant
Materials

A wide variety of plant materials has been merchandised by garden center operators, ranging from trees and shrubs to bedding plants and indoor green plants. All of these materials have a common denominator in that they are perishable and at times highly perishable. Proper maintenance of plant materials reduces dumpage and sale of distressed merchandise. It insures repeat business from satisfied customers and attracts new buyers to your operation.

The maintenance program begins even before arrival of plant materials at your front door. Storage and display areas must be prepared in advance for perishable products.

Plants require light to avoid leggy growth and shipping containers must be opened immediately upon arrival at your place of business. Personnel should be instructed to check orders for count and quality specifications.

A damage report including presence of insects and disease organisms should be prepared prior to transfer of material to storage or display areas. Infested plants should not be placed with healthy stock. The supplier should be notified regarding any discrepancies between material delivered and the original order, and any damaged or unsaleable merchandise.

Storage and display areas must be designed to provide the proper climatic conditions for perishable merchandise. Flowering plants cannot remain in closed containers nor can they be transferred to warm and dark or poorly lit locations. The soil should be checked for moisture to insure that plants will not wilt. The display area for nursery stock must be carefully designed for proper light, drainage of excess water, watering facilities, and customer traffic. Some attention must be given to weed control and protection from strong winds.

Some trees and shrubs may have to be overwintered. Special care must be exercised in protecting plants grown in containers or balled and burlapped. Flowering and green plants and fresh flowers must be handled carefully to minimize losses and to attract customers. Plants should be thoroughly watered if the soil is dry upon arrival at the receiving room. Fresh flowers should be conditioned and placed in water containing a floral preservative.

GERANIUMS

Most geranium cultivars produce a large number of leaves with some above average in size. These varieties require a great deal of display space to properly capture attention of buyers. Tight spacing on the sales bench leads to rapid decline of older leaves. They often turn a pale, sickly yellow, destroying sales appeal. A gray mold disease, commonly identified as botrytis blight, can spread from plant to plant under cool, humid conditions and tight spacing. It affects leaves, stems and flowers. This popular plant must be stored and displayed in bright light. Full sunlight may prove detrimental to the

This poor-quality geranium has two main shoots which are quite long and leggy. The plant is already beginning to become top heavy.

flowers of some selections, especially when plants were not properly hardened before shipment from the producer.

Crowded plants are difficult to water and customers cannot easily inspect them. High plant losses can be anticipated, with consumers avoiding wilted plants and breaking stems and leaves as they reach for the best specimen. Inexperienced help may not thoroughly water the entire soil ball. The area between the soil line and the rim of the pot holds only a small volume of water. Water stress occasionally leads to flower stalk injury in some cultivars. The "neck" or stem bends and many buds turn brown.

A poor root system cannot support large plants during bright, hot, and windy periods. Check the root system when plants continue to wilt, even though the soil contains an adequate supply of water. The root system should be extensive and white.

Relatively few insects can be expected to attack geraniums at the garden center. The two-spotted spider mite occasionally causes some trouble, especially to the foliage. A simple hand lens will help you spot them feeding and moving about on the undersides of leaves.

A yellowing and subsequent decline of older, larger leaves may be caused by a physiological condition known as oedema. This problem generally appears in early spring. The plant seems to absorb and contain more water than it can utilize. High moisture conditions in the greenhouse associated

The underside of geranium leaves, especially the ivy types, often have large numbers of watery spots. This signals a problem with oedema.

with cloudy weather and close spacing of plants contribute to the decline of many leaves.

Oedema can be spotted by examining the undersides of leaves, especially those that are large and luxurious. You will notice a series of small water spots or blisters. Older lesions will tend to cork over and appear whitish to brownish. A hand lens should be used to insure that damage has not been inflicted by spider mites.

There is relatively little one can do in a garden center other than to remove the poorest leaves to improve appearance of some plants. A good grower will avoid marketing questionable quality geraniums.

Most geraniums normally occupy space in a garden center for only a few days. Rapid turnover minimizes problems, especially the need for fertilization. Frequently watered plants in a small volume of soil will require periodic feedings, if remaining on the premises a week or longer. Nitrogen deficiency often evidenced by a yellowing of lower leaves can ruin saleability of geraniums. Quick turnover of the geranium crop encourages operators to display plants in shipping cartons. Growers use every available square inch of space to minimize stem breakage during transit. A good operator removes geraniums from shipping containers and provides adequate room for best display of the product. Some operators have displayed geraniums on blacktop and concrete in full sun. The heat coming from the ground, along with reflected light from nearby structures, virtually cooks plants.

BEDDING PLANTS

Sun-loving bedding plants should be displayed outdoors or in lightly shaded greenhouses. Shading compounds on glass help keep temperatures cooler for plants and customers. A bright location must be provided to prevent stretching and leggy growth.

Shade-loving plants such as impatiens may be displayed under a lath structure or in shaded greenhouses. These plants cannot tolerate full sun except in early morning and late afternoon.

Some operators have stored and displayed bedding plants on shelving with four to seven levels. The plants on the upper shelf and those on the perimeter of each level often receive sufficient light, but you must rotate flats to insure that adequate light reaches each unit.

Packs or containers of bedding plants should not be displayed on blacktop and concrete. The small volume of soil in a typical pack contains only a modest reservoir of water to support stem, leaves and flowers. It is essential that staff be prepared to water plants one or more times a day.

Lath structures help protect shade-loving plants. Care must be taken to insure that plants requiring full sun are rotated to avoid excess growth. Petunias near the base of the stand are just beginning to show signs of stretching.

Some operators display flats on the ground in cold frames. The sides protect plants from strong winds. A layer of shredded bark or similar material placed under flats helps maintain a good moisture supply and increases humidity in the area. Sometimes, slugs can multiply in moist, protected areas and eat holes in leaves at night. Recommended materials such as slug bait should be used at first signs of the problem.

Sprinkler systems cannot be used during business hours, but they should be turned on before or after business hours to thoroughly moisten containers. Protection from wind also helps reduce water loss from plants.

Hoses may be employed to touch up plants during the day. They should be removed from the selling area when not in use to avoid tripping and injury to consumers.

Insects can become a problem on bedding plants and tomatoes when material remains on the premises for a week or longer. White flies can be found on tomatoes, fuchsia, and lantana in great numbers. Spider mites feast on many plants including marigolds. Aphids can infest almost any crop. Periodically look at the undersides of leaves for evidence of white flies and spider mites. Aphids can be found sucking juices from new growth.

Placement of flatted material on white stone can lead to wilting of many plants due to reflected light and rapid drying out of the soil.

Cold frames permit growers to harden-off plants. This process helps reduce shock when plants ultimately are moved into the garden.

Do not leave hoses lying around as they present hazards to customers.

Aphids cluster on new growth.

Diseases have not represented a real problem to garden center operators handling plants for a short period of time. Crowded conditions associated with poor ventilation and excessive growth, however, can lead to a breakdown of foliage and spread of some disease organisms.

Apple scab plagues gardeners, making it extremely difficult to produce quality fruit.

Plants marketed at the prime stage can be displayed pack against pack. Overgrown plants require more space. Failure to do so often leads to further stretching of growth and breakdown of lower leaves. Potted plants in 2½-inch to 4-inch containers may be tightly spaced on display tables. The spacing problems discussed for the geranium crop can plague small potted plants such as petunias, impatiens, begonias, and tomatoes. Small pots will dry out rapidly.

Excessive growth can occur after plants arrive on the premises, as well as at the production site. Leggy plants will be hard to sell. Pinching back growth will require that they be grown for a number of weeks before becoming saleable again. Only an operator having a greenhouse can consider this option. Most operators will try to sell them at a normal price or place selected packs on special sale.

The supply of nutrients available to bedding plants quickly becomes depleted because of the small volume of soil and frequent waterings. Rapid turnover of stock generally occurs before deficiency symptoms become noticeable to buyers. Underfertilized plants arriving from a greenhouse can quickly show signs of nutritional problems. Consumers often pass by these lightly colored plants. A siphoning unit can be attached to the watering system for injection of soluble fertilizers.

Some new soil mixes contain large quantities of peat moss and shredded bark. The nutrient reserve may be quite small, leading to problems once plants have been transplanted to the garden. Consumers should be encouraged to feed the young plants at planting time to assure their rapid takeoff.

Outdoor displays require that you be prepared to protect plants when temperatures go down into the thirties and below freezing. One operator constructed mini-quonset frames spaced periodically along display tables. Poly material or cheese cloth could be pulled over displays in just a few minutes with minimum damage to plants.

HANGING BASKETS

Hanging baskets have become increasingly important in more recent years. A wide variety of plants has been used in construction of flowering and green plant baskets. Plants designed for the outdoors such as fuchsia and petunias have been displayed under lath, in greenhouses, and outdoors. The particular likes and dislikes of each plant dictate the proper location.

A discount outlet displayed fuchsia baskets indoors under fluorescent lights. Quality declined noticeably after a few days with buds dropping because of insufficient light. Ceiling lights provided the only illumination for plants. Fuchsias often have been taken indoors by consumers before displaying them on a patio. This practice has been prompted by the threat of late killing frosts. Buds often fall off because of the low light intensities, warm temperatures, and low humidity.

Green plants normally featured indoors often have been exhibited in poorly lit areas. The growth quickly becomes leggy and new leaves never seem to reach their potential size. Do not display green baskets in full sunlight. They generally do best in bright areas free from direct rays of the sun from midmorning through late afternoon.

Hanging baskets require a great deal of water. This is a major problem for both operators and consumers. Frequent waterings also lead to nutritional problems. The use of a slow-release fertilizer can prove helpful to the operator and aid the consumer in developing an attractive plant.

Protection from strong winds is important to minimize frequency of waterings and to maintain plants in good condition. Weather-beaten plants attract very little attention and often end up on the special sales table. Crowding baskets can lead to development of nonsymmetrical plants. Consumers have shown a decided preference for round or well-balanced growth.

Insects are attracted to a number of flowering plants commonly grown in baskets. Carefully inspect them upon arrival and periodically check before they leave in the hands of a customer. The problems described for bedding plants are applicable to baskets.

This basket is lopsided and does not exhibit good trailing habits deemed desirable for petunias.

GARDEN ROSES

Potted roses in full flower attract a great deal of attention each spring. Many gardeners like to be a step ahead of neighbors and friends and appear willing to pay a premium price for this merchandise.

Large plants are susceptible to mildew and black spot. Stored in a greenhouse, they can become highly susceptible to these major disease problems. They need lots of air circulation to remain clean. Close spacing in the display and storage areas can lead to some real headaches.

Two-spotted spider mites working on the undersides of leaves, and aphids attacking new growth can plague operations handling mature plants. A control program will be required in those instances where roses will remain on the premises for several weeks. Flowering plants require a fair amount of water. Protection from strong winds helps reduce frequency of waterings.

Potted roses can be displayed in full sunlight or lightly shaded areas. Poor light leads to weak and unattractive growth. Plants must be fed regularly to maintain luxurious foliage. A slow-release fertilizer can minimize problems and time in feeding this crop.

A large number of roses have been sold in pots but with little or no growth evident other than developing buds. This provides consumers with a well-rooted and top-grade plant. These plants have been quite superior to bare rooted material. Young potted plants can be displayed in full sunlight. Watering has not been a major problem since few if any leaves have appeared on the plant.

Packaged roses should be placed in an upright position. Do not display them in direct sunlight. Heat and bright light stimulates bud development. This places a heavy burden on bare rooted roses. Plants soon exhaust their supply of moisture and begin to deteriorate.

Packaged roses can be stored temporarily at temperatures just above 33 °F. A portion of the shipment may be placed in cold storage to avoid injury to buds from high temperatures. The waxy material, usually paraffin, placed on bare root or packaged roses helps extend shelf life in a store. You can provide the consumer with a top quality rose through proper display and care of this item.

PERENNIAL FLOWER PLANTS

Packaged perennials often have been brought out of winter storage just prior to shipment to retailers. Crowding, excessive moisture, and high humidity in storage can result in the spread of disease organisms. Open boxes immediately upon arrival and display in a bright location. These plants are quite sensitive to even light frost. Be prepared to protect them outdoors or temporarily transport them to an indoor location. Locally produced perennials normally can tolerate temperatures much lower than packaged stock.

Potted perennials require regular waterings with the same frequency as geraniums. Water stress can lead to a decline in quality and a hardening of the plant. This hardened material may not transplant easily into the garden soil. Poor light leads to stretching of sun-loving plants. You should display this material in full sunlight or under very light shade. Insects should not become a major problem with young perennial plants. A periodic examination of foliage will reveal presence of two-spotted spider mites and aphids.

HARDY BULB STOCK

Lily bulbs for spring and fall plantings are packaged in wood shavings or a similar material. Bulbs will rot when the packaging material becomes excessively moist. Packaged bulbs in polyethylene film can rot when exposed to high temperatures. Warm temperatures also stimulate bulb sprouting. The tips can easily break in transit to the gardener's home unless some shavings have been placed in the retail package.

All shipments of bulb stock should be inspected immediately or soon

Dahlia roots often shrivel when exposed to warm and dry conditions in storage. Roots may be covered with a thin layer of wax or stored in a slightly moistened material such as peat moss.

after arrival at your place of business. Damaged and rotting stock should be removed to avoid contamination of healthy material.

Consumers often have a tendency to lift bulbs, roots, and corms from one bin and place them in an adjacent unit. Sales personnel should inspect display bins periodically to maintain them in proper condition.

Hot and dry conditions can prove detrimental to bulbs being planted in the fall. Store containers or part of the shipment at cool temperatures (33° plus) prior to being placed on display.

Spring materials such as dahlias can dry out in a couple of weeks. Roots protected with a wax covering hold up for a reasonable period of time.

FLOWERING PLANTS

Flowering plants have become an increasingly important item for many garden center operators. This is especially true for firms seeking additional business in winter and early spring months. Most flowering plants require high light intensity. Normal store illumination will prove adequate for only a short period of time, perhaps a week.

Crowded displays limit light intensity reaching lower leaves. This foliage turns yellow rapidly and soon ruins the appearance of plants. Stem, flower, and foliage injury also occur as consumers inspect plants. This problem becomes acute during holidays when clerks try to display twice the number of plants that can normally occupy a given area.

Wilted plants have no sales appeal. In fact, they can destroy or impair saleability of all plants in the display. It takes lots and lots of watering to maintain flowering plants in proper condition. Overly mature plants should be removed from displays.

Most flowering plants have been well fed and few, if any, problems can be anticipated from insects and disease organisms. Light yellow leaves rather than more typical green foliage can signal that plants were not properly grown and have been starved. An inspection of the foliage, especially the undersides of leaves, will reveal whether growers were careless in controlling one or more pests. Infested plants should be immediately returned to suppliers.

FRESH FLOWERS

The sale of fresh flowers generally has been associated with those garden center operators featuring typical retail florist products and services. Perishability along with limited demand have restricted sales of fresh, unarranged flowers in garden centers. The operator wishing to develop this business must focus attention on ways of maintaining the product in top condition. Losses can be minimized and flower life extended by:

1. Adding a fresh flower preservative to the water.
2. Using clean buckets. Containers should be cleaned with a good detergent or bleach every week.
3. Warm water enhances uptake of moisture to the foliage and blooms.
4. Strip lower leaves, especially those below the water line, to reduce problems with water contamination.
5. Refrigerate at or just below 40 °F for most crops and with relatively high humidity levels.
6. Do not crowd displays leading to breakage and decline in foliage quality.
7. Display in a well-lit area.
8. Use deionized water.

FOLIAGE PLANTS

Foliage plants often have been thought of as tolerating low light conditions. This is true when comparing them with flowering plants such as the chrysanthemum and poinsettia. Excessive losses have been incurred, however, from crowded conditions and poorly lit displays.

Green plants should not be stacked like cans of peas and corn. They must have adequate room for light to penetrate to lower leaves. Close spacing leads to breakage of stems and leaves. This is especially true for brittle plants like *Zebrina*.

Foliage materials often occupy space for several weeks. Clerks should be instructed to inspect plants for insects. Schefflera is a most attractive plant to two-spotted spider mites. Leaves tend to curl downward and the foliage takes on a sickly green-yellow coloring because the juices are being removed by mites. Care and identification tags can be accidentally removed by browsing customers. A regular clean-up program insures proper labeling.

Wilted plants ruin a display. Some operators have become so conscious of this matter that inexperienced clerks have been instructed to water almost daily. This practice may prove acceptable in those instances when plants have been grown in a highly sandy soil. Some soil mixes retain water for a number of days. Excessive watering and tight spacing can lead to breakdown of the root system as well as stem and foliage. Poorly rooted plants cannot tolerate unusually wet or dry soil conditions. This problem can be acute when suppliers try to turn over crops too quickly.

Poor light conditions and inadequate moisture quickly lead to a breakdown of older leaves. Mature *Zebrina* leaves of the reddish types often rot and turn black. Most plants will not need an application of fertilizer for a month or longer. This is especially true of Florida-grown plants that have been heavily fertilized. Excessive fertilization leads to a decline of the root system and burning of the margins of tender leaves.

Good displays are well lit and provide adequate room for all plants. Some contrast in color, size, and texture of foliage adds to the attractiveness and saleability of plants. Drip pans often become unsightly because of the accumulation of soil and old leaves. They should be cleaned each week.

NURSERY STOCK

Sloppy maintenance practices lead to high losses and unsatisfied customers. Precautionary measures should be instituted to protect your reputation and image. The following general rules apply to most plant materials handled by a typical garden center.

1. Immediately open and inspect merchandise.
2. Store nursery stock in a cool location such as a damp basement until ready for transfer to display areas.
3. Do not stack cartons in storage facilities in a manner prohibiting good air circulation.
4. Rotate merchandise on the basis of first in and first out.
5. Do not place nursery stock or bedding plants on blacktop or concrete.
6. Mulch balled and burlapped material and containers of shrubs and trees.
7. Protect all plant materials from strong winds.
8. Provide good drainage for excess water to avoid root injury and subsequent problems for consumers.
9. Do not place rose bushes and similar packaged material in hot, sunny windows.
10. Do not transport nursery stock by holding plants at the "neck."
11. Do not handle or move frozen stock.
12. See that all plants are properly labeled.

Display areas should be planned to protect consumers and to stimulate sales. Plants should be properly labeled to minimize time required for servicing each gardener. Excess water should drain properly from the display area to avoid slippage and discouraging customers from browsing. Aisles should be sufficiently wide to permit easy flow of people and shopping carts.

INSPECTING STOCK

Each shipment should be carefully inspected immediately upon arrival at your store. The products should be checked against quality listed in the original order. Shortages often lead to a change in sizes of material. Mechanical damage may have occurred in transit. Insects may appear, especially with the onset of warm weather. All claims should be processed immediately rather than waiting until the end of the busy season. A good quality producer ships only healthy stock and meets specifications of the order. This applies both to the root ball and top growth. Colorful labels should be attached to the product identifying each plant and specifying cultural recommendations. This service should be requested of all suppliers.

The retailer must bear responsibility for quick unpacking of stock and watering both B and B and container-grown materials. Failure to maintain an adequate moisture supply leads to rapid deterioration of stock.

Weeds

Weeds quickly destroy the appearance of display areas. They provide an attractive home to many insects that ultimately migrate to nursery stock, perennials, and annual flowers. Weeds also rob moisture and nutrients from plants. Hand weeding often controls the major problems. Chemicals can be used in problem areas. Contact your local extension office for recommended materials.

Freeze Damage

Late killing frosts can be injurious to fruit trees and some shrubs. This is especially true of materials just brought out of storage and not acclimated to outdoor conditions.

New, tender growth also is most susceptible to subfreezing temperatures. The tips may turn brown. Sprinkler systems turned on at night and in early morning hours can minimize injury. Water releases heat in the process of freezing, providing a measure of protection when temperatures dip just below freezing. Do not try to handle frozen stock. Frost injury may not appear for several days or weeks after plants have been exposed to exceptionally cold temperatures. This often occurs with container-grown stock.

Feeding

The extent to which you feed nursery stock will be dependent upon your practices and the length of time material will be on hand. Quick turnover minimizes need for feeding, while stock remaining for a good part of the season often will have to be fed on a weekly or regular basis.

Some growers have incorporated slow-release fertilizers into the potting soil. These products often last three to four months during good growing weather. Grower directions regarding care and maintenance should include information on past and recommended feeding programs. The nature of the soil mix also influences fertilizer programs. Light-weight soil mixes featuring peat moss and bark products often require more nutrients due to heavy watering in late spring and summer.

Garden center operators may top dress some stock with slow-release fertilizer products according to directions of the producer. This is to insure that too much fertilizer will not be applied and in the process destroy roots.

Plants entering a period of rapid growth require an abundant supply of nutrients. The fertilizer program should be based on growth as well as the specific likes and dislikes of each plant. Some operators have injected water-soluble fertilizers into the irrigation lines once a week or with every watering. A 15-15-15 fertilizer can be added in dilute form to insure that a steady supply of nutrients becomes available to plants. Injectors have been commonly used by greenhouse and nursery operators to facilitate application of fertilizers.

Space

Many operators suffer from inadequate display and storage space. The short selling period each spring requires that a large volume of merchandise be

During the busy season large supplies of stock often necessitate crowding. This situation should be relieved as soon as possible to prevent development of weak growth and potential spread of disease organisms.

acquired to assure maximum sales and service to consumers. Reordering stock can become a problem when long distances separate you from suppliers and when crops are in short supply.

Tight spacing of plants often occurs because of large amounts of stock on hand at some times. Customers have a hard time inspecting plants in crowded conditions. Employees find it difficult to water and may miss some plants. Close spacing with branches touching may lead to some injury of foliage. Poor growth may result with plants literally fighting for some light. Water may accumulate around the base of plants and damage root systems. Inadequate space can be tolerated for a very brief period of time, but for more extended periods, you should seek additional storage facilities.

Watering

Water dehydration can severely injure plants with some not being able to recuperate. Evergreens will be severely damaged with needles turning brown in late winter and early spring from winter dehydration. Limited moisture supplies can destroy portions of the root system. Failure to water stock immediately upon arrival can result in injury to buds and new growth.

Container-grown plants often must be watered daily during the spring and summer. The small volume of light-weight soil can require watering several times on hot days.

There are some signals that can be watched for in trying to know when it is time to water. The color of the soil often changes and becomes lighter when the supply of moisture declines in the soil mix. The container becomes lighter in weight with a reduction in moisture supply. Some plants show moisture stress through wilting of leaves. One also can feel several inches down in the soil to gauge the moisture supply.

All containers do not dry uniformly. This compounds the problem of knowing when to water. Some operators will use a hose to spot water dry plants and especially those on the perimeter of a display. The entire soil ball should be moistened with each watering. Light waterings stimulate root development near the top of the soil ball. These plants are susceptible to dry conditions because of inadequate root development.

A hose or sprinkler system can be used on hot dry days to cool plants. The system can be turned on briefly at intervals during the day to lightly cover the foliage with a film of moisture.

Overwintering

Close-out sales help reduce inventory and avoid special care in overwintering stock. Winter storage normally cannot be avoided for the operator handling a large product mix and a large quantity of plants. Nursery material can be stored in quonset or small plastic covered structures. A single layer of four or six mil white or opaque polyethylene material helps reduce excessive light and heat. Clear polyethylene can be painted with a cheap white latex paint mixed one part paint to one part water. Barns and storage buildings can be used when light conditions are fairly good. Poorly lit areas lead to a decline in quality during winter and early spring months. Good air circulation becomes very important when temperatures begin to warm up in late winter and early spring.

Balled and burlapped plants can be heeled in sawdust, wood chips, shredded bark, and similar mulch materials. The root system must be protected against excessively cold temperatures. Antidessicants can be used in December and again in February on tender plants requiring protection from sun and wind. The use of a wind barrier such as a snow fence also helps bring plants through the winter in good condition.

Potted or container-grown materials have a limited volume of soil surrounding roots. This means that containers also have a modest reserve of water. A major problem can occur during unusually warm spells with top growth conceivably sending out signals for moisture which is only available in small quantities.

Rodent injury can become a serious problem leading to excessive loss of plants. Repellents help to control some rodents.

Storage areas outdoors or indoors should be selected for good drainage. Water draining into an area with poor drainage conditions leads to the loss of many plants in winter and early spring. An accumulation of water injures and ultimately destroys the root system.

SOD

Sod has been stocked by some firms largely as a service to customers requiring small quantities for patch-up or replacement areas in home lawns. The garden center operator also has something to handle and display during a sales presentation for large jobs. This product has a very short life and only small quantities can and should be procured at any one time. The shelf life of sod during the hot days of August may be only one or two days. This contrasts with five days during cooler spring days. Heat rapidly builds up in rolled up sod resulting in a yellowing of grass and loss of roots.

Yellowing of grass will occur soon after sod has been cut, rolled and delivered to a retailer. You must distinguish between dead sod or that which has remained too long on the premises and fresh or saleable material which has just started to turn yellow. The product still has life when you can hold sod in a vertical position. Healthy roots prevent the roll of sod from disintegrating into several pieces.

Sod should be stored on pallets to minimize damage from moisture present in the soil (or at soil surface).

Stacking sod over 3-½ feet high will crush and destroy the lower layers, making them unsaleable.

Sod can be displayed on pallets or similar supports just above the ground. This keeps the lowest rolls out of contact with a moist surface and possible standing water. The roll may break apart with modest handling because of moisture content and a buildup of heat on warm days.

The short shelf life suggests that rolled sod be displayed in a cool, shady location. Avoid watering since it will become difficult to separate muddy rolls. A layer of plastic may be placed over the top during rainy periods on a temporary basis.

Sod should not be stacked more than $3\frac{1}{2}$ feet high. The weight will crush material on the lowest layer. Sod displays look best when not surrounded by patches of weeds. Customers may become unduly suspicious that the product has become contaminated with weed seeds.

Some operators lay sod on a piece of plastic. This practice helps extend the shelf life of the product. Gardeners also have an opportunity to see the product and occasionally compare different cultivars and blends or mixes of recommended grasses. Sod that has been placed on plastic may knit together if rolls are allowed to make contact with each other. This is acceptable only if you do not wish to sell the product. The grass must be cut when it starts to produce new growth. Periodic waterings become necessary to sustain the product. Water will be captured on the plastic and minimize the amount required during each application.

A policy of first-in and first-out should be applied to sod as well as other perishable products. Old sod should be inspected, however, to determine if it is still in saleable condition. Local producers normally can supply sod for delivery each week. The perishable nature of the product requires that you purchase small quantities, and only the amount needed for a weekend or up to four days.

SUMMARY

The ability to maintain and enhance your image and to achieve sales hinges to a large degree on proper maintenance of plant materials. Customers shy away from those operations noted for poor handling techniques leading to bruised and injured plants that fail to last a reasonable period of time. The rush and bustle of a busy spring or holiday cannot justify incompetence of personnel and management. Plants are perishable and they must be handled with kid gloves. A good maintenance program features:

1. Well-trained personnel knowledgeable in the art and science of providing proper care to garden and indoor plants.
2. Purchase of quality merchandise from reputable firms.

3. Immediate inspection of all stock.

4. Written report on condition of damaged material or return to supplier of all unsaleable plants.

5. Proper conditioning of plants immediately after arrival including watering and storage.

6. Preparation of facilities in advance of shipment.

7. Proper facilities for storage and display including light, watering, fertilizing, weed control, and wind protection.

8. Proper labeling of all plants.

9. Removal of injured or old stock.

10. Cultural programs to maintain stock in condition.

Perishable plants are a real challenge to garden center operators. The ability to maintain plants in saleable condition separates the real professional from those seeking to reap profits with a minimum of effort.

Gardeners are becoming more sophisticated and demanding of retailers in procurement of good merchandise. You can develop a good image and identity based on selling high quality products properly cared for while on the premises of your garden center.

1. Geranium leaves and blossoms decline rapidly after arrival at a garden center. What should be done to properly handle this plant?

2. What are the major do's and don'ts in handling bedding plants?

3. Identify and discuss two major problems of maintaining bedding plants in good condition.

4. What precautions should be taken with bulb stock?

5. Flowering and green plants often decline prematurely in retail stores. Identify and discuss three main problems.

6. What steps should be taken in maintaining fresh flowers?

7. Identify and discuss briefly five or more measures for maintaining nursery stock.

8. What can be done to minimize losses of sod?

9. What factors should be considered in overwintering nursery stock?

10. Nursery material on display will require special care to attract attention of consumers. Identify and discuss three special needs.

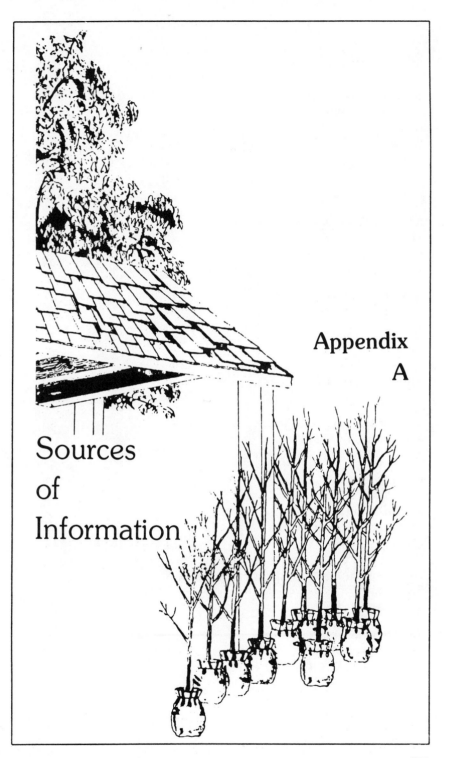

Appendix
A

Sources
of
Information

Associations:

Garden Centers of America
230 Southern Building
15th & H Streets, N.W.
Washington, D.C. 20005

Bedding Plants Incorporated
P.O. Box 286
Okemos, MI 48864

American Association of Nurserymen, Inc.
230 Southern Building
15th & H Streets, N.W.
Washington, D.C. 20005

American Horticulture Society, Inc.
Mount Vernon, VA 22121

Better Lawn and Turf Institute
Route 4
Kimberdale
Maryville, OH 43040

Society of American Florists
901 North Washington Street
Alexandria, VA 22314

Publications:

Florists' Review
310 South Michigan Avenue
Chicago, IL 60604

American Nurseryman
310 South Michigan Avenue
Chicago, IL 60604

Southern Florist & Nurseryman
120 St. Luke Avenue
Fort Worth, TX 76101

Grounds Maintenance
9221 Quivera Road
P.O. Box 12901
Overland Park, KS 66212

Lawn & Garden Marketing
9221 Quivera Road
P.O. Box 12901
Overland Park, KS 66212

Pacific Coast Nurseryman and Garden Supply Dealer
832 South Baldwin Avenue
Arcadia, CA 91006

Nursery Business
P.O. Drawer 77
Elm Grove, WI 53122

Landscape Industry
P.O. Drawer 77
Elm Grove, WI 53122

Home & Garden Supply Merchandiser
2501 Wayzata Blvd.
Minneapolis, MN 55440

Extension Circulars, Bulletins, Fact
Sheets and Leaflets are available
from local county extension offices
and from bulletin offices at the
land grant institutions (College of
Agriculture) in your state.

Resources:

The Small Business Reporter
Bank of America
Department 3120
P.O. Box 37000
San Francisco, CA 94137
  a. Business Profiles
  b. Business Operations

Ball Red Book
George Ball Company
West Chicago, IL 60185
Production of Bedding Plants

Small Business Administration Publications
  Management Aids
  Technical Aids
  Small Marketers' Aids
Regional offices located in major cities

Wyman's Gardening Encyclopedia
Donald Wyman
The Macmillan Company
New York, NY 10022

Environmental Plant Production and Marketing
Tokuji Furuta
Cox Publishing Company
832 S. Baldwin Avenue
Arcadia, CA 91006

Directory of American Horticulture
The American Horticulture Society
Mount Vernon, VA 22121

Care and Handling of Flowers and Plants
Society of American Florists
901 N. Washington Street
Alexandria, VA 22314

Gardening Illustrated—150 Concepts
Miriam and Lou Berninger
NASCO, Fort Atkinson, WI 53538
Training new personnel

Greenhouse Operation and Management
Paul V. Nelson
Reston Publishing Company, Inc.
11480 Sunset Hills Road
Reston, VA 22090

Correspondence Courses:

Independent Study
University of Wisconsin-Extension
432 N. Lake Street
Madison, WI 53706

Correspondence Courses in Agriculture
202 Agriculture Education Building
The Pennsylvania State University
University Park, PA 16802

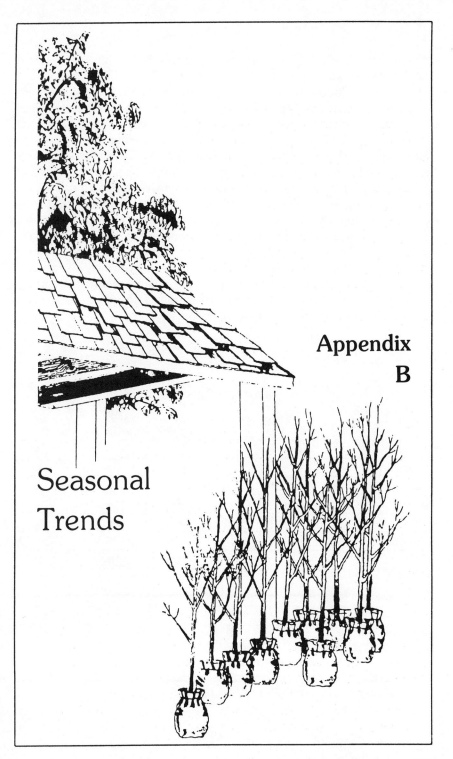

Appendix
B

Seasonal
Trends

A study conducted many years ago by the Vaughn Seed Company[1] reported on the breakdown of sales for a twelve-month period of a typical garden center in the Chicago area. The information can serve as a guide to new operators trying to plan purchases to coincide with the selling season. The percentage figures for each category undoubtedly have changed since the late 1960s. Monthly percentages can help in the development of forecasts for the major categories. Seed sales are heaviest in April and May for flowers and vegetables. Grass seed captures a great deal of attention in April and September with some 50% of total sales occurring in these two months.

Nursery sales have changed with increased availability of canned merchandise for summer sales. Gardeners still plant heavily in early spring.

Geraniums are an important part of the total product mix. You can expect 5-10% of sales in the Chicago area occurring in the last half of April. An additional 15% will move at the beginning of May. Thirty-five percent of the crop will move during the middle of the month and a similar amount around Decoration Day. Sales slump off in June with only 5-10% of the crop moving after the normal planting season.

SEASONAL TRENDS[2]

Months	Nursery	Bulbs	Grass Seed	Flower & Veg. Seed	Fert. & Supplies	Plant Dept. & Greenhouse	Total Store Sales
January					1%		1%
February		1%			1%		2%
March	2%	1%	2%	1%	3%		9%
April	10%	2%	4%	2%	5%	2%	25%
May	4%	1%	2%	2%	6%	6%	21%
June	1%		1%	1%	3%	2%	8%
July					2%	1%	3%
August			3%		2%		5%
September	1%	2%	5%		3%		11%
October	2%	3%	1%		2%		8%
November	2%	2%			1%		5%
December	1%					1%	2%
Totals[2]	23%	12%	18%	6%	29%	12%	100%

[2] *Home and Garden Supply Magazine* (March 1967), p. 11.

[1] Vaughn Seed Company

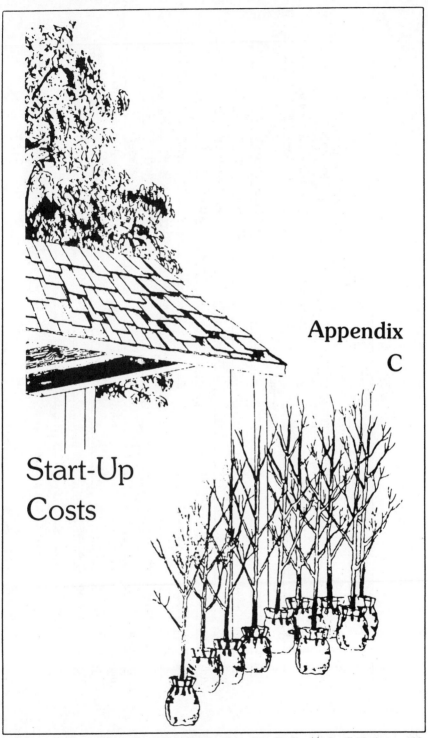

Appendix
C

Start-Up
Costs

¹Small Business Administration, "Checklist for Going Into Business," Small Marketers Aid No. 71 (Washington, D.C.: the Administration, 1975), pp. 6–7, 12.

WORKSHEET 2

ESTIMATED MONTHLY EXPENSES

Item	Your estimate of monthly expenses based on sales of $_____ per year Column 1	Your estimate of how much cash you need to start your business (See column 3.) Column 2	What to put in column 2 (These figures are typical for one kind of business. You will have to decide how many months to allow for in your business.) Column 3
Salary of owner-manager	$	$	2 times column 1
All other salaries and wages			3 times column 1
Rent			3 times column 1
Advertising			3 times column 1
Delivery expense			3 times column 1
Supplies			3 times column 1
Telephone and telegraph			3 times column 1
Other utilities			3 times column 1
Insurance			Payment required by insurance company
Taxes, including Social Security			4 times column 1
Interest			3 times column 1
Maintenance			3 times column 1

Item		Instructions
Legal and other professional fees		3 times column 1
Miscellaneous		3 times column 1
STARTING COSTS YOU ONLY HAVE TO PAY ONCE		Leave column 2 blank
Fixtures and equipment		Fill in worksheet 3 on the following page and put the total here
Decorating and remodeling		Talk it over with a contractor
Installation of fixtures and equipment		Talk to suppliers from whom you buy these
Starting inventory		Suppliers will probably help you estimate this
Deposits with public utilities		Find out from utilities companies
Legal and other professional fees		Lawyer, accountant, others
Licenses and permits		Find out from city offices what you have to have
Advertising and promotion for opening		Estimate what you'll use
Accounts receivable		What you need to buy more stock until credit customers pay
Cash		For unexpected expenses or losses, special purchases, etc.
Other		Make a separate list and enter total
TOTAL ESTIMATED CASH YOU NEED TO START WITH	$	Add up all the numbers in column 2

WORKSHEET 3

LIST OF FURNITURE, FIXTURES, AND EQUIPMENT

Leave out or add items to suit your business. Use separate sheets to list exactly what you need for each of the items below.	If you plan to pay cash in full, enter the full amount below and in the last column.	If you are going to pay by installments, fill out the columns below. Enter in the last column your downpayment plus at least one installment.			Estimate of the cash you need for furniture, fixtures, and equipment.
		Price	Down payment	Amount of each installment	
Greenhouse–Lath	$	$	$	$	$
Counters					
Storage shelves, cabinets					
Display stands, shelves, tables					
Cash register					
Safe					
Window display fixtures					
Special lighting					
Outside sign					
Delivery equipment if needed					
TOTAL FURNITURE, FIXTURES, AND EQUIPMENT (Enter this figure also in worksheet 2 under "Starting Costs You Only Have To Pay Once.")					$

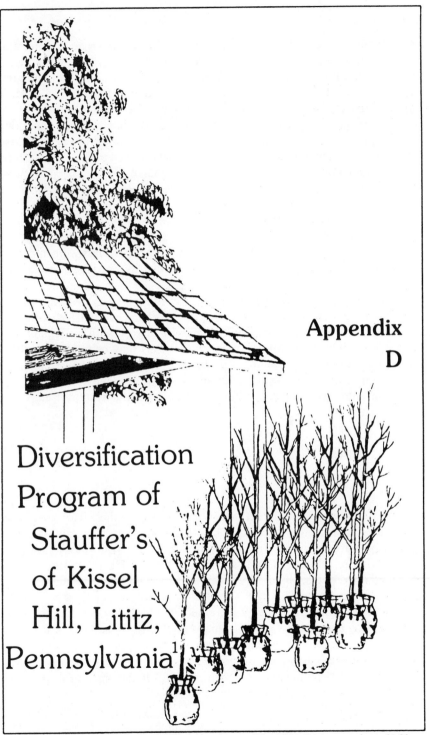

Appendix
D

Diversification
Program of
Stauffer's
of Kissel
Hill, Lititz,
Pennsylvania[1]

[1]Ninth International Bedding Plant Conference, 1976, Bedding Plants Incorporated, pp. 31-33.

A thriving, increasingly successful business, today known as Stauffer's of Kissel Hill, had its origin in humble beginnings. On a very small scale, it was organized in the year 1933 by its founder, Roy M. Stauffer, who grew up on the Stauffer fruit farm. His father, Tilman Stauffer, peddled produce in Lititz together with supplying local stores with fresh produce.

The strength and stability of the business in the hands of hard working owners and a forward looking corporation made it possible to open a second store in 1964 featuring the same line of products offered at the original store. This is located on Route 222, one mile north of Lancaster. Business prospered with the years so that a third store was opened south of Rohrerstown in 1970.

The greatly expanded business now includes the following retail divisions, namely produce, meat, garden department, nursery and landscaping. In addition to these are trim shops, a floral design shop, a classroom and work shop, a wholesale produce center, warehouse distribution center and central business office.

After forty years of operation the number of employees has expanded to involve more than two hundred persons. The policy of Stauffer's of Kissel Hill is to select employees who indicate a desire to grow with the organization and whose interest will involve them so that they may be promoted within the organization. Sales training is provided as a means for the development of the employee. We consider each employee as an important member of the team and strive for cooperation and good will in employer-employee relationships.

PRODUCE DEPARTMENT

Our goal in the produce department is to have the freshest fruits and vegetables available to our customers. This we maintain by using a lot of home-grown produce. We are bringing shipped products from the Philadelphia and Baltimore produce terminals. We specialize in Florida citrus, at least one load a week, trucking it direct. We also specialize in large amounts and many varieties of apples.

Seasonal highlights of each year: Halloween . . . apples and pumpkins, Thanksgiving and Easter . . . fruits and vegetables, Christmas . . . fruit and our fancy packed fruit baskets. Our goal for 12,000 fancy packed fruit baskets should be easily met.

The produce department and garden department combination works really well to stabilize movement of traffic.

NURSERY DEPARTMENT

Each of our retail facilities has a nursery retail department, which is staffed with a manager, assistant manager and employees. We specialize in quality plants, trees, shrubs, fencing, flagstones, concrete products and planting materials at promotional prices.

We spend approximately 3 percent of gross volume on advertising which largely consists of three-day newspaper specials.

LANDSCAPE CENTER

Our three landscape designers have assigned foremen and workmen who have separate tool compartments and assigned color coded tools. We work with two man crews, a working job foreman and one helper.

Residential landscape is 85 percent of jobs contracted and 15 percent is small commercial jobs, of which 90 percent are within a 30-mile radius. Our average landscape planting job is $500. We do very little bid work, mostly our own design and specification. Two crews specialize in seeding and two crews on construction of brick patios, walks, railroad tie walls, etc., with additional crews specializing in planting and pruning.

CRAFT AND FLORAL DESIGN DEPARTMENTS

Our craft departments are the newest field of endeavor for Stauffer's of Kissel Hill. Formed out of the original Floral Trims Department, they now encompass almost the full spectrum of craft supplies . . . Paint to Macrame, Quilling to Chenille.

Two special features from our crafty folk are the Fall Craft and Flower Festival in our Lititz workshops, where thousands of people come in early September to see and make the new season Craft Mini-Classes, which are held in each store's craft department. Here any number from one to six people may be seated around our special demonstration tables and make a quick, easy craft project to take home.

The Craft and Floral Design departments have grown much over the years, but there has always been a strong feeling for continuity with the rest of the store's operations. We make it a point to see what our customers ask for, to meet their needs, and to realize the separate needs of the clientele in each of our stores.

GARDEN DEPARTMENT

The Garden Department is a combination of merchandising lines and ideas that are constantly growing and changing.

The Garden Department progresses through four seasonal changes. Because these are overlapped and not separated from each other, the changes are sometimes subtle but always effective. Spring and Easter are the most fragrant of our seasons. In preparation, the entire department is re-aligned for spring gardening supplies and continued fertilizer sales. For Easter major portions of our greenhouses and porches are opened for thousands of Easter flowers. As a highlight, a grower surplus sale is held the day before Easter. Flowers purchased for the sale are constantly reduced in price by the manager until all of the flowers are sold.

Bedding plants have already started to move. With the clearance of Easter flowers, double-tiered plant tables and additional displays are built. Each store may have at any one time a maximum stock peak of over 1000 flats including vegetables and flowers which continue through July.

Starting in April, managers have received shipments of wrought iron and redwood furniture, picnic tables, picnic supplies, barbecue grills and ornamental concrete. Spring and summer fertilizers are joined by preventative sprays and dusts as well as lawn and garden problem solvers. Advertising continues to make people aware that the "Lawn Pros" at Stauffer's welcome the opportunity to answer questions about insect damage, fungus and disease control or to solve your lawn and garden problems.

As our bedding plant sales taper off, the greenhouses are restocked with large selections of foliage plants and tropicals. House plant sales continue to be an attraction within our stores as fall approaches. Managers see the increased need at this time for greater stock levels in pots and potting soils as Fall sales are initiated.

The area's largest selection of imported bulbs receives prime attention. As for the bulbs, the manager's slogan is "A handful brings a spring full." Our big clearance sales will end the inventory by mid-November.

Fall fertilizer, tools and gardening supplies are still recognized as a need, however, the displays must be moved to accommodate Christmas. These areas are rebuilt with partial partitions and items that are now out of season are packed and removed.

A Christmas Wonderland is created. Shimmering canopies of tinsel cover displays of decorated and undecorated trees. There are aisles of candles, candle rings, lights and trims. Every shopper should find something to his liking as dozens of novelties and decorating ideas are displayed nearby.

While the entire garden department reflects our Christmas theme, we have not forgotten fire logs, bird seed and feeders, snow tools, and house plant needs. Even now, as throughout the year, weekly deliveries of mums add color to our store.

As we finish our after Christmas clearance, sales managers are already planning and preparing for the spring season.

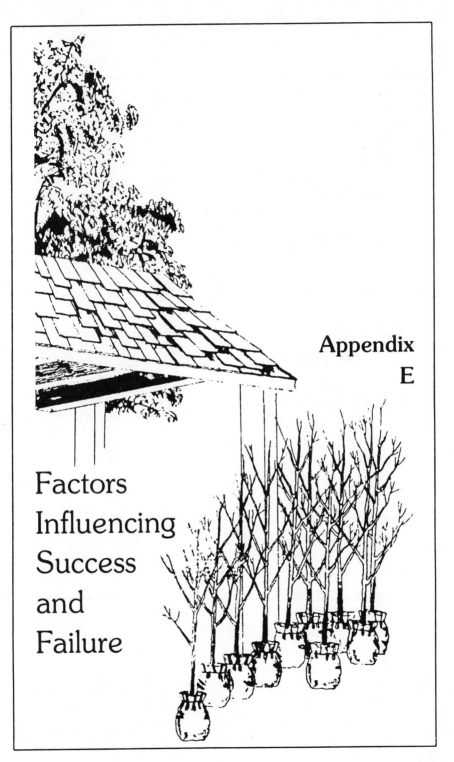

Appendix
E

Factors
Influencing
Success
and
Failure

A strong character is fundamental to survival in the business world. This can be thought of partially in terms of the performance of people under stress. Moral fibre and a willingness to fight harder when the going gets rough are elements of a strong character. The ability to manage wisely reflects management's overall capacity. Does the individual have good judgement and wisdom to guide a budding or growing enterprise?

Factors contributing to success include:

1. Technical knowledge of business;
2. Willingness to work long hours;
3. Background in field;
4. Can work effectively with people;
5. Good knowledge of product and services;
6. Reputation for dependable service and quality;
7. Ability to recover quickly in face of setbacks;
8. Competitive and aggressive in attitude and actions;
9. Willingness to take minimal profit to establish strong financial picture.

Problem areas include:

1. Poor accounting and inventory procedures;
2. Lack of experience;
3. Lack of money;
4. Investing excessively in fixed assets;
5. Too many family members on payroll;
6. Poor location;
7. Poor credit policies;
8. Unplanned expansion;
9. High salary for self;
10. No organized sales plan;
11. Limited business knowledge and experience;
12. Failure to diversify;
13. Poor attitude and capacity to work;
14. Inability to plan and manage time.

Successful and unsuccessful business people differ both in their personal attitudes as well as their application of good business principles. The two listings help distinguish good from questionable or poor traits. A potential entrepreneur should carefully assess his or her own assets and liabilities before making the plunge into a new business.

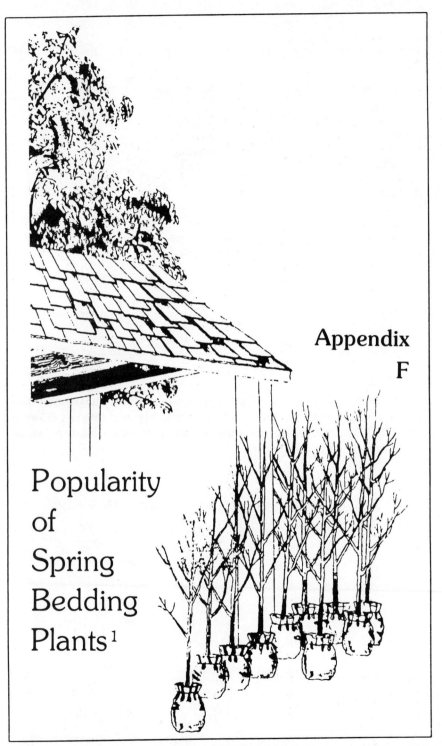

Appendix
F

Popularity
of
Spring
Bedding
Plants[1]

[1]Ninth International Bedding Plant Conference, 1976, Bedding Plants Incorporated, p. 186.

PERCENTAGE EACH ANNUAL IS OF TOTAL, 1975 (FROM DECEMBER, 1975, BPI NEWS)

Kind of Annual	"Mostly"	Kind of Annual	"Mostly"
Ageratum	1–3 %	Phlox	1 %
Alyssum	1–3	Portulaca	1–2
Asters	1	Salvia	2
Begonia	5	Snapdragon	1–2
Browallia	1	Verbena	1
Celosia	1	Vinca	1
Dahlias	1	Zinnia	1–2
Geraniums (seed)	2	Cabbage	1–3
Geraniums (cuttings)	10	Peppers	5–10
Garden Mums	1–2	Tomatoes	10
Lobelia	1	(Others)	5
Marigolds	5–10		
Pansies	2–5		
Petunias (as a group)	20		
Multiflora	1–5	TOTAL	About 105%
Grandiflora	10		
Doubles	1–2		

From our experience, we would suggest a higher percentage of petunias (25%), marigolds (14%), impatiens (12%), and begonias (6%) as shown on the next table, but we do not include asters, geranium cuttings, garden mums or cabbage in our figuring.

BALL RECOMMENDED PERCENTAGE BASED ON 1976 SEASON

Class	%	%†	Class	%	%†
Ageratum	2	1	Petunia		
				25*	20
Alyssum	2	1	Phlox	1	1
Begonia	6	8	Portulaca	1	
					− 1
Browallia	1	− 1	Salvia	2	2
Celosia	1	1	Snapdragon	1	1
Coleus	2	3	Verbena	1	1
Dahlias	1	− 1	Vinca	1	
					− 1
Geranium	3	10	Zinnia	2	3
Impatiens	12	10	Pepper	3	3
Lobelia	1	− 1	Tomato	10	10
Marigold	14	12	Others	4	6
Pansy	4	4	Total	100	100

*Single Multiflora, 1%; Single Grandiflora, 20%; Doubles, 4%.
†Author's estimate of 1982 season.

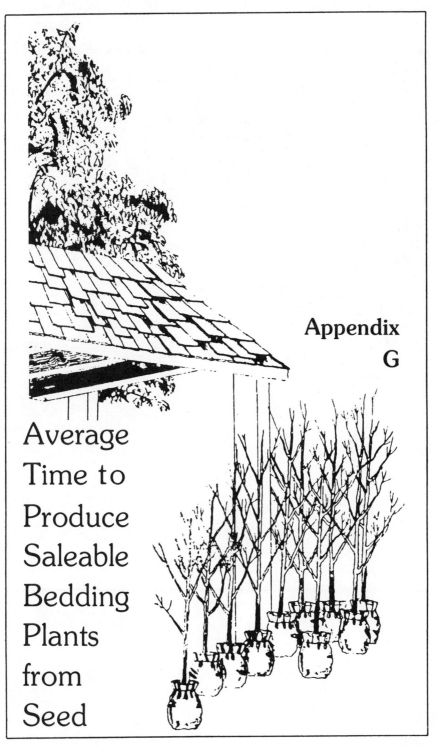

Appendix
G

Average
Time to
Produce
Saleable
Bedding
Plants
from
Seed

Average Time to Saleable Plant for Major Bedding Plant Varieties

4 Weeks	5 Weeks	6 Weeks	7 Weeks
Kochia	Tomato	Pepper	Eggplant
	Cabbage	Asters	Alyssum
	Tall Marigold	Balsam	Canendula
	(Not to flower)		Coleus
	Tall Zinnia		Dahlias
	(Not to flower)		Impatiens

8 Weeks	9 Weeks	10 Weeks	11 Weeks
Celosia	Onion	Double Petunia	Carnations
Single Petunia	Ageratum		Dusty Miller
Salvia	Dianthus		Larkspur
Tall Snapdragon	Lobelia		Dwarf Snapdragon
(Not to flower)	Dwarf Marigold		
Dwarf Zinnia	Stock		
	Verbena		

12 Weeks	13 Weeks	14 Weeks	15 Weeks
Portulaca	Pansy	Begonia	Geranium
Vinca Rosea		Browallia	
		Nierembergia	

SOURCE: Ninth International Bedding Plant Conference, 1976, Bedding Plants Incorporated, p. 191.

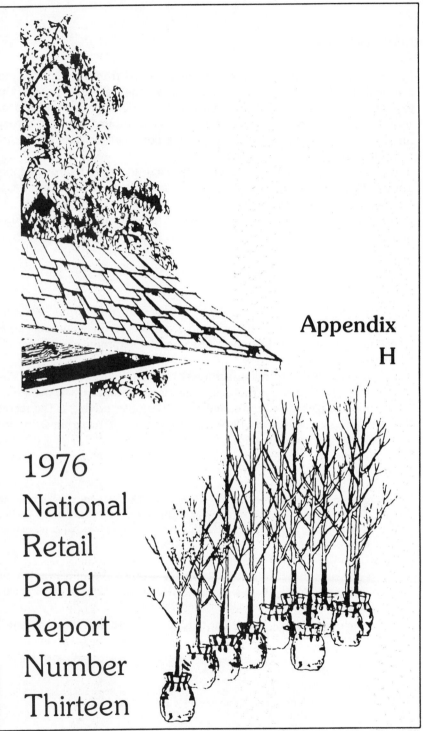

Appendix
H

1976
National
Retail
Panel
Report
Number
Thirteen

INTRODUCTION

Information in this thirteenth report was obtained from members of our National Retail Panel. The panel conforms to known characteristics of the total retail garden and lawn supply market on a national basis. It reflects, as accurately as possible, the current activities, changes, and trends in garden supplies retailing. The panel operates on a continuing basis; reports are published periodically.

The National Retail Panel is currently made up of 500 garden supply dealers. Data in this report is based on returns from 362 panel members, representing 72.4% of the panel.

This report can be projected for the total market for estimate purposes only.

OBJECTIVES AND SUMMARY

Among the purposes of this study were the determination of (a) 1976 sales volume of our readers' garden stores and departments, (b) the product areas contributing to sales, and (c) the "fastest growth" product lines over the past five years.

Our readers' ratings of manufacturers on such points as advertising support, consumer information, packaging, etc., is reported, as is sale of flexible line trimmers, long-handled tools, and numerous other products. The report also contains our readers' outlook for 1977 sales of terrariums, indoor plants, crafts, and associated lines.

In summary, the survey says this about readers of *Home and Garden Supply Merchandiser*:

> Average sales volume per outlet for 1976 was $299,526, down slightly from $307,200 in 1975, accountable largely by the dip in fertilizer prices and a decline in power equipment units. Total market for our readers is projected at more than $10.7 billion.
>
> Of the eight points asking for ratings from poor to good, manufacturers get their largest number of "good" grades in Packaging, where 47.5% of our readers say a good job is being done. Worst area for a "good" rating (7.2%) is for Missionary Salesmen, although 42.5% rated that category as "average."
>
> In the capital goods area, almost one-third (32.3%) plan new display and store fixtures in 1977. Indoor plants, power equipment, and nursery stock are among the leaders in "fastest growth" over the last five years.

[Home and Garden Supply Merchandiser,](#) National Retail Panel Report Number 13 (Minneapolis, Minn.: The Miller Publishing Company, copyright 1977). pp. 1-5, 8-15.

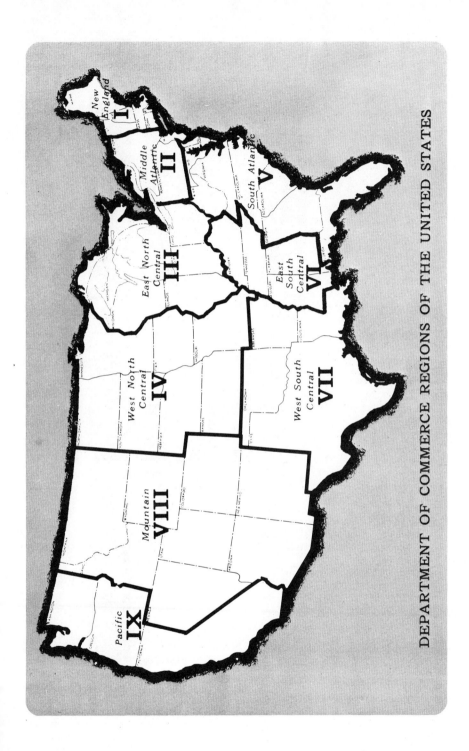

NEW ENGLAND
(Region 1)

CONNECTICUT
MAINE
MASSACHUSETTS
NEW HAMPSHIRE
RHODE ISLAND
VERMONT

WEST NORTH CENTRAL
(Region 4)

IOWA
KANSAS
MINNESOTA
MISSOURI
NEBRASKA
NORTH DAKOTA
SOUTH DAKOTA

WEST SOUTH CENTRAL
(Region 7)

ARKANSAS
LOUISIANA
OKLAHOMA
TEXAS

MIDDLE ATLANTIC
(Region 2)

NEW JERSEY
NEW YORK
PENNSYLVANIA

SOUTH ATLANTIC
(Region 5)

DELAWARE
DISTRICT OF COLUMBIA
FLORIDA
GEORGIA
MARYLAND
NORTH CAROLINA
SOUTH CAROLINA
VIRGINIA
WEST VIRGINIA

MOUNTAIN
(Region 8)

ARIZONA
COLORADO
IDAHO
MONTANA
NEVADA
NEW MEXICO
UTAH
WYOMING

EAST NORTH CENTRAL
(Region 3)

ILLINOIS
INDIANA
MICHIGAN
OHIO
WISCONSIN

EAST SOUTH CENTRAL
(Region 6)

ALABAMA
KENTUCKY
MISSISSIPPI
TENNESSEE

PACIFIC
(Region 9)

CALIFORNIA
OREGON
WASHINGTON

Main Business		Region									
	I	II	III	IV	V	VI	VII	VIII	IX	Total
Lawn & garden	12.5%	17.5%	20.7%	11.5%	14.5%	20.0%	4.8%	22.2%	3.6%	14.9%
Lawn mowers, power equipment	34.4%	23.8%	28.7%	25.0%	23.6%	13.3%	23.8%	11.1%	35.7%	26.2%
Building supply & home improvement center	–	3.2%	2.3%	–	1.8%	–	–	11.1%	7.1%	2.2%
Hardware	15.6%	20.6%	14.9%	17.3%	18.2%	6.7%	4.8%	11.1%	14.3%	15.7%
Nursery/garden supplies	28.1%	20.6%	18.4%	26.9%	32.7%	33.3%	57.1%	33.3%	32.1%	27.3%
Farm store	3.1%	3.2%	9.2%	9.6%	5.5%	20.0%	–	–	–	6.1%
Department & discount stores, variety/chain stores	3.1%	1.6%	–	5.8%	–	–	4.8%	–	3.6%	1.9%
Other	3.1%	9.5%	5.7%	3.8%	3.6%	6.7%	4.8%	11.1%	3.6%	5.5%

Main Business	Under $100,000	$100,000-$199,999	Dollar Volume $200,000-$399,999	$400,000-$799,999	$800,000 and Over
Lawn & garden	12.2%	11.6%	10.8%	23.1%	28.6%
Lawn mowers, power equipment	30.9%	29.0%	26.2%	15.4%	19.0%
Building supply & home improvement center	1.6%	1.4%	3.1%	2.6%	—
Hardware	18.7%	8.7%	6.2%	25.6%	9.5%
Nursery/garden supplies	21.1%	30.4%	46.2%	30.8%	9.5%
Farm store	6.5%	8.7%	6.2%	2.6%	14.3%
Department & discount stores, variety/ chain stores	2.4%	—	—	—	14.3%
Other	6.5%	10.1%	1.5%	—	4.8%

Region

Sales Volume	I	II	III	IV	V	VI	VII	VIII	IX	Total
1. Percent of stores obtaining revenue from the following product lines:										
Nursery stock & accessories	53.1%	50.8%	42.5%	51.9%	65.5%	66.7%	61.9%	55.6%	42.9%	52.2%
Indoor plants & accessories	40.6%	41.3%	31.0%	42.3%	50.9%	53.3%	57.1%	33.3%	32.1%	40.9%
Chemicals, fertilizer, soil cond.	62.5%	74.6%	59.8%	65.4%	72.7%	73.3%	57.1%	88.9%	67.9%	67.1%
Hose, reels & sprinklers	50.0%	60.3%	47.1%	48.1%	61.8%	40.0%	52.4%	77.8%	64.3%	54.1%
Power equipment	65.6%	66.7%	62.1%	63.5%	65.5%	53.3%	47.6%	55.6%	89.3%	64.6%
Hand tools (electric & cordless)	46.9%	71.4%	54.0%	53.8%	63.6%	46.7%	42.9%	66.7%	82.1%	59.4%
Outdoor furniture, patio products	9.4%	15.9%	13.8%	19.2%	18.2%	6.7%	9.5%	11.1%	10.7%	14.4%
Giftware & holiday goods	31.3%	33.3%	31.0%	32.7%	34.5%	26.7%	28.6%	11.1%	28.6%	31.2%
Landscaping services	12.5%	25.4%	18.4%	25.0%	27.3%	40.0%	33.3%	11.1%	14.3%	22.7%
Rental services	25.0%	30.2%	25.3%	25.0%	23.6%	13.3%	4.8%	–	21.4%	23.2%
Repair services	50.0%	52.4%	49.4%	48.1%	49.1%	40.0%	33.3%	22.2%	46.4%	47.5%
Other	34.4%	22.2%	21.8%	34.6%	25.5%	60.0%	23.8%	22.2%	17.9%	26.8%

383

2. Average sales volume for those carrying 1976:

Average percent of sales by category (if carried):

	$403,379	$273,243	$289,613	$187,372	$238,777	$293,452	$145,722	$107,055	$506,270	$299,526
Nursery stock & accessories	35.9%	28.6%	34.5%	33.0%	27.8%	27.2%	28.3%	32.2%	22.9%	30.5%
Indoor plants & accessories	13.3%	9.6%	9.0%	11.2%	13.0%	15.5%	13.9%	10.0%	11.7%	11.5%
Chemicals, fertilizers, soil cond.	14.9%	19.3%	16.0%	19.0%	18.4%	21.4%	17.8%	23.1%	24.9%	18.7%
Hose, reels & sprinklers	3.0%	5.4%	5.6%	5.1%	4.4%	2.8%	6.1%	5.5%	8.5%	5.2%
Power equipment	45.8%	32.2%	46.7%	41.8%	32.5%	40.0%	30.0%	30.4%	27.2%	37.7%
Hand tools (electric & cordless)	3.8%	6.4%	6.6%	7.7%	8.3%	5.5%	4.7%	4.6%	6.9%	6.7%
Outdoor furniture, patio products	14.3%	6.2%	5.3%	6.0%	18.0%	20.0%	8.5%	—	5.7%	9.3%
Giftware & holiday goods	7.7%	7.9%	9.5%	7.9%	7.1%	10.0%	7.4%	10.0%	6.8%	8.1%
Landscaping services	23.0%	37.8%	24.9%	20.8%	21.4%	21.8%	26.9%	47.0%	26.3%	26.3%
Rental services	2.6%	3.7%	4.3%	2.9%	4.6%	1.5%	2.0%	—	9.2%	4.1%
Repair services	30.2%	22.8%	22.7%	18.4%	18.8%	10.3%	35.0%	27.5%	28.8%	22.7%
Other	25.7%	19.0%	32.1%	19.3%	22.1%	19.6%	22.0%	42.5%	17.5%	23.5%

Sales Volume	Under $100,000	$100,000-$199,999	Dollar Volume $200,000-$399,999	$400,000-$799,999	$800,000 and Over
1. Percent of stores obtaining revenue from the following product lines:					
Nursery stock & accessories	47.2%	56.5%	66.2%	59.0%	57.1%
Indoor plants & accessories	33.3%	43.5%	53.8%	53.8%	57.1%
Chemicals, fertilizers, soil cond.	61.0%	69.6%	75.4%	84.6%	81.0%
Hose, reels & sprinklers	41.5%	56.5%	64.6%	79.5%	76.2%
Power equipment	64.2%	66.7%	64.6%	71.8%	81.0%
Hand tools (electric & cordless)					
Outdoor furniture, patio products	47.2%	59.4%	72.3%	87.2%	81.0%
	9.8%	10.1%	15.4%	28.2%	33.3%
Giftware & holiday goods	22.0%	26.1%	47.7%	51.3%	38.1%
Landscaping services	21.1%	26.1%	36.9%	12.8%	14.3%
Rental services	22.0%	20.3%	29.2%	23.1%	38.1%
Repair services	49.6%	49.3%	50.8%	43.6%	57.1%
Other	20.3%	24.6%	44.6%	25.6%	42.9%

385

2. Average sales volume for those carrying 1976:

	$39,453	$131,375	$265,954	$557,975	$1,697,333
Average percent of sales by category (if carried):					
Nursery stock & accessories	38.5%	32.6%	25.8%	21.2%	15.3%
Indoor plants & accessories	11.1%	13.8%	9.3%	13.3%	11.8%
Chemicals, fertilizers, soil cond.	18.9%	17.7%	18.8%	16.2%	21.1%
Hose, reels & sprinklers	7.4%	5.0%	4.3%	3.3%	5.2%
Power equipment	39.5%	36.8%	34.5%	36.2%	31.4%
Hand tools (electric & cordless)	9.5%	5.4%	4.8%	5.6%	5.4%
Outdoor furniture, patio products	5.2%	8.5%	8.0%	5.0%	9.8%
Giftware & holiday goods	10.3%	6.1%	7.2%	10.1%	6.6%
Landscaping services	22.2%	34.0%	24.0%	21.0%	10.0%
Rental services	6.2%	3.7%	3.1%	1.5%	3.5%
Repair services	31.6%	22.9%	15.4%	10.7%	4.4%
Other	18.8%	26.1%	19.6%	35.3%	26.9%

1. Percent Selling

Tools		I	II	III	IV	V	VI	VII	VIII	IX	Total
							Region				
Long-Handled Tools		56.3%	76.2%	62.1%	67.3%	78.2%	60.0%	66.7%	88.9%	78.6%	69.3%
If Selling:											
Rakes		94.3%	83.3%	92.6%	85.7%	97.7%	100.0%	78.6%	100.0%	90.8%	90.5%
Avg. Annual $ Volume		$302.00	$701.85	$319.58	$267.27	$658.62	$525.00	$224.29	$400.00	$386.92	$470.00
Shovels		88.8%	85.4%	92.6%	88.6%	97.7%	100.0%	78.6%	87.5%	90.8%	90.5%
Avg. Annual $ Volume		$290.00	$835.00	$514.00	$396.82	$709.31	$510.00	$424.29	$112.50	$858.87	$611.29
Hoes		88.8%	75.0%	88.9%	82.9%	95.3%	100.0%	78.6%	100.0%	90.8%	86.9%
Avg. Annual $ Volume		$302.50	$389.59	$211.30	$204.76	$481.43	$515.00	$290.00	$380.00	$780.00	$387.42
Spades		88.8%	81.2%	87.0%	79.9%	83.8%	100.0%	64.4%	62.5%	81.8%	82.5%
Avg. Annual $ Volume		$262.50	$377.04	$139.52	$175.00	$313.48	$254.00	$540.00	$550.00	$163.33	$270.42
Scythes		38.9%	50.0%	37.0%	34.3%	41.8%	44.5%	21.5%	25.0%	59.0%	41.1%
Avg. Annual $ Volume		$200.00	$189.33	$152.86	$ 64.44	$148.33	$600.02	$165.00	–	$126.25	$162.40
Brooms		50.0%	73.0%	50.0%	45.8%	58.2%	77.8%	35.7%	25.0%	81.8%	57.4%
Avg. Annual $ Volume		$300.00	$507.92	$305.45	$179.23	$355.00	$306.00	$ 76.67	–	$219.17	$331.23
Other		27.7%	14.6%	22.2%	14.3%	25.6%	22.2%	7.2%	12.5%	18.2%	19.2%

Of those selling major brands of long-handled tools, number of respondents handling the following brands:

True Temper	125	Seymour, Smith & Sons	3
Ames	124	McGuire, George W. & Co.	2
Union Fork &		Disston	4
Hoe	39	Other	37
Douglass	3		

387

2. Percent Selling

Edgers/Trimmers/Shears	71.9%	82.5%	65.5%	67.3%	78.2%	40.0%	76.2%	88.9%	100.0%	74.0%
If Selling:										
Edgers	65.2%	69.2%	73.7%	71.5%	88.4%	66.8%	56.3%	50.0%	96.4%	74.6%
Avg. Annual $ Volume	$350.00	$636.67	$775.00	$212.35	$1624.58	$2216.67	$1790.00	$350.00	$1118.42	$934.14
Trimmers	78.3%	77.0%	86.0%	82.9%	88.4%	66.8%	50.0%	75.0%	89.3%	80.9%
Avg. Annual $ Volume	$777.78	$878.00	$1022.73	$244.50	$1398.18	$1100.00	$1602.50	$905.00	$1280.00	$963.85
Shears	73.9%	71.2%	82.4%	77.1%	86.1%	100.0%	56.3%	87.5%	78.6%	78.0%
Avg. Annual $ Volume	$200.00	$668.57	$258.42	$218.89	$473.48	$362.50	$474.00	$184.00	$772.86	$448.55
Loppers	65.2%	65.5%	73.7%	71.5%	74.4%	83.3%	50.0%	75.0%	78.6%	70.5%
Avg. Annual $ Volume	$171.43	$245.93	$150.59	$131.18	$251.05	$330.00	$540.00	$132.50	$480.00	$249.47

Of those selling major brands of edgers, trimmers or shears, number of respondents handling the following brands:

Black & Decker	.99	Seymour, Smith & Sons	14
Ames	40	Wiss, J. & Sons	24
Corona Clipper	26	Rockwell	16
Disston	73	True Temper	46
Weed Eater	22	John Deere	5
Little Wonder	14	Sunbeam	2
Village Blacksmith	4	Other	67
Stanley	10		

3. Percent Selling Flexible Line (fishline)

Tools	Region									Total
	I	II	III	IV	V	VI	VII	VIII	IX	
Trimmers	56.3%	63.5%	44.8%	50.0%	69.1%	40.0%	66.7%	44.4%	67.9%	56.4%
Gasoline Powered	38.9%	27.6%	46.2%	38.4%	42.1%	83.3%	42.9%	50.0%	42.1%	40.6%
Avg. Units Sold	4.4	7.5	13.8	10.8	11.9	4.0	28.5	15.0	19.4	12.5
Electric	72.1%	75.0%	74.3%	80.8%	73.7%	100.0%	92.9%	100.0%	94.7%	79.4%
Avg. Units Sold	13.0	41.2	92.8	20.3	23.2	45.2	79.3	25.0	77.9	53.2

Of those selling major brands of flexible line trimmers, number of respondents handling the following brands:

Weed Eater	128	Toro	5
Black & Decker	45	K & S	5
Spin Trim (Garden Pro)	20	John Deere	3
HMC, Inc.	6	Other	20

| | | Dollar Volume | | |
Tools	Under $100,000	$100,000-$199,999	$200,000-$399,999	$400,000-$799,999	$800,000 and Over
1. Percent Selling Long-Handled Tools	53.7%	65.2%	83.1%	92.3%	90.5%
If Selling:					
Rakes	93.9%	91.1%	90.7%	91.7%	89.5%
Avg. Annual $ Volume	$268.42	$383.57	$484.59	$619.09	$1163.33
Shovels	92.4%	93.4%	90.7%	91.7%	89.5%
Avg. Annual $ Volume	$278.72	$524.44	$651.89	$801.36	$1577.00
Hoes	87.9%	89.0%	87.0%	91.7%	84.2%
Avg. Annual $ Volume	$200.28	$329.23	$366.57	$287.73	$1667.78
Spades	83.2%	82.2%	83.3%	91.7%	78.9%
Avg. Annual $ Volume	$133.82	$311.82	$292.12	$356.82	$478.57
Scythes	41.0%	26.7%	40.7%	47.2%	47.4%
Avg. Annual $ Volume	$110.00	$78.00	$158.33	$220.00	$305.00
Brooms	59.0%	44.5%	51.9%	72.3%	52.6%
Avg. Annual $ Volume	$204.35	$472.00	$260.45	$334.12	$780.00
Other	16.6%	11.0%	25.9%	19.4%	26.3%

Of those selling major brands of long-handled tools, number of respondents handling the following brands:

True Temper	125	Seymour, Smith & Sons	3
Ames	124	McGuire, George W. & Co.	2
Union Fork & Hoe	39	Disston	4
Douglas	2	Other	37

Tools	Under $100,000	$100,000-$199,000	Dollar Volume $200,000-$399,000	$400,000-$799,999	$800,000 and Over
2. Percent Selling					
Edgers/Trimmers/ Shears	60.2%	76.8%	83.1%	89.7%	85.7%
If Selling:					
Edgers	66.1%	71.7%	83.3%	88.6%	77.8%
Avg. Annual $ Volume	$480.83	$1247.60	$623.64	$1081.36	$2000.00
Trimmers	78.4%	79.3%	85.2%	91.5%	83.3%
Avg. Annual $ Volume	$395.15	$1046.80	$901.21	$1944.55	$892.86
Shears	74.3%	68.0%	88.8%	85.7%	88.9%
Avg. Annual $ Volume	$217.14	$270.00	$514.41	$719.50	$991.11
Loppers	67.6%	64.2%	75.9%	77.1%	83.3%
Avg. Annual $ Volume	$113.13	$240.48	$235.17	$298.33	$287.50

Of those selling major brands of edgers, trimmers or shears, number of respondents handling the following brands:

Black & Decker	99	Seymour, Smith & Sons	14
Ames	40	Wiss, J. & Sons	24
Corona Clipper	26	Rockwell	16
Disston	73	True Temper	46
Weed Eater	22	John Deere	5
Little Wonder	14	Sunbeam	2
Village Blacksmith	4	Other	67
Stanley	10		

3. Percent Selling
   Flexible Line
   (fishline)

Trimmers	44.7%	53.6%	60.0%	76.9%	81.0%
Gasoline	21.9%	45.9%	53.8%	63.3%	41.1%
Avg. Units Sold	8.1	14.6	8.9	16.2	18.0
Electric	72.7%	75.7%	92.3%	90.0%	88.2%
Avg. Units Sold	18.8	31.3	58.4	62.5	125.2

Of those selling major brands of flexible line trimmers, number of respondents handling the following brands:

Weed Eater	128	Toro	5
Black & Decker	45	K & S	5
Spin Trim (Garden Pro)	20	John Deere	3
HMC, Inc.	6	Other	20

Purchases	I	II	III	IV	V	VI	VII	VIII	IX	Total
					Region					
1. Percent of Lawn & Garden Purchases Made Through:										
Manufacturer	32.6%	15.4%	18.1%	14.1%	12.6%	20.3%	11.9%	5.6%	9.8%	16.1%
Wholesaler	50.2%	55.6%	51.4%	57.4%	59.4%	45.1%	64.4%	77.2%	65.9%	56.5%
Manufacturers Reps	11.8%	13.9%	16.6%	9.9%	12.8%	17.5%	13.1%	11.7%	13.6%	13.6%
Cooperative/ Franchise	5.4%	15.1%	13.9%	18.6%	15.2%	17.2%	10.6%	5.6%	10.7%	13.8%
2. Percent Belonging to Franchise or Cooperative	18.8%	28.6%	26.4%	36.5%	25.5%	33.3%	33.3%	22.2%	32.1%	28.5%
Name of Buying Group										
Cotter						16				
American Hardware Supply						14				
Sentry						5				
Agway						2				
Other						56				
3. Avg. Number of Wholesalers Purchased From	12.0	13.6	7.6	7.6	12.0	10.5	12.7	11.4	12.2	10.6

Purchases	Under $100,000	$100,000-$199,000	Dollar Volume $200,000-$399,000	$400,000-$799,999	$800,000 and Over
1. Percent of Lawn & Garden Purchases Made Through:					
Manufacturer	14.0%	17.4%	15.3%	20.7%	17.3%
Wholesaler	60.5%	65.3%	56.9%	40.4%	41.6%
Manufacturers Reps	13.0%	10.9%	17.7%	13.1%	22.3%
Cooperative/ Franchise	12.6%	6.4%	10.1%	25.8%	18.9%
2. Percent Belonging to Franchise or Cooperative	22.8%	17.4%	33.8%	43.6%	42.9%
Name of Buying Group					
Cotter				16	
American Hardware Supply				14	
Sentry				5	
Agway				2	
Other				56	
3. Avg. Number of Wholesalers Purchased From	6.4	12.6	15.8	15.1	9.4

394

| Capital Goods | Region | | | | | | | | | |
	I	II	III	IV	V	VI	VII	VIII	IX	Total
1. Percent Having:										
Computer Systems	3.1%	3.2%	5.7%	3.8%	5.5%	–	4.8%	–	3.6%	4.1%
Intercom Systems	28.1%	28.6%	26.4%	32.7%	29.1%	26.7%	19.0%	–	14.3%	26.2%
Computer Bank	–	–	5.7%	3.8%	–	–	–	11.1%	–	2.2%
Outside Computer Systems	3.1%	6.3%	8.0%	5.8%	1.8%	20.0%	–	–	10.7%	6.1%
Inventory Control With Cash Register	6.3%	12.7%	26.4%	15.4%	9.1%	26.7%	38.1%	22.2%	25.0%	18.5%
2. Percent Planning New Display and Store Fixtures in 1977	28.1%	33.3%	33.3%	28.8%	23.6%	33.3%	38.1%	33.3%	50.0%	32.3%
3. Avg. $ Invested in Store Fixtures & Displays	$48,313	$20,344	$25,468	$10,449	$17,780	$19,007	$14,824	$7,689	$17,031	$20,893

395

Capital Goods	Under $100,000	$100,000-$199,000	Dollar Volume $200,000-$399,000	$400,000-$799,999	$800,000 and Over
1. Percent Having:					
Computer Systems	3.3%	1.4%	1.5%	10.3%	14.3%
Intercom Systems	10.6%	20.3%	35.4%	53.8%	57.1%
Computer Bank	2.4%	1.4%	1.5%	2.6%	4.8%
Outside Computer Systems	3.3%	8.7%	4.6%	10.3%	14.3%
Inventory Control With Cash Register	26.0%	17.4%	15.4%	25.6%	—
2. Percent Planning New Display and Store Fixtures in 1977	27.5%	27.5%	44.6%	43.6%	42.9%
3. Avg. $ Invested in Store Fixtures & Displays	$13,631	$15,195	$15,822	$25,072	$99,244

Fastest Growth Over Last Five Years	Region									
	I	II	III	IV	V	VI	VII	VIII	IX	Total
1. Percentage Indicating Fastest Growth:										
Indoor Plants & Accessories	23.5%	22.9%	9.8%	17.9%	33.3%	10.0%	38.5%	40.0%	13.3%	20.1%
Nursery Stock	41.2%	8.6%	9.8%	17.9%	12.5%	30.0%	7.7%	—	13.3%	14.8%
Chemical	—	—	9.8%	5.1%	12.5%	—	7.7%	20.0%	20.0%	7.2%
Hose	—	2.9%	2.0%	2.6%	—	—	—	—	—	1.4%
Giftware	—	2.9%	2.0%	—	—	—	—	—	—	1.0%
Hand Tools	—	11.4%	3.9%	12.8%	8.3%	10.0%	—	—	13.3%	7.7%
Power Equipment	—	17.1%	29.4%	17.9%	16.7%	—	23.1%	20.0%	13.3%	18.2%
Repair Services	17.6%	14.3%	13.7%	7.7%	—	20.0%	—	—	13.3%	10.5%
Rental Services	5.9%	—	—	—	4.2%	—	—	—	6.7%	1.4%
Long-Handled Tools	—	2.9%	—	—	—	—	—	—	—	.5%
Landscaping Services	—	11.4%	9.8%	5.1%	4.2%	—	15.4%	—	6.7%	7.2%
Outdoor Furniture	5.9%	—	5.9%	—	—	10.0%	—	20.0%	—	2.4%
Other	5.9%	5.7%	3.9%	12.8%	8.3%	20.0%	7.7%	20.0%	—	7.7%

2. Percent Indicating *Second* Fastest Growth:

Indoor Plants &										
Accessories	13.3%	12.1%	4.2%	2.8%	4.2%	9.1%	7.7%	–	7.1%	6.5%
Nursery Stock	–	15.2%	25.0%	8.3%	16.7%	18.2%	23.1%	40.0%	14.3%	16.5%
Chemical	26.7%	24.2%	8.3%	16.7%	25.0%	27.3%	7.7%	40.0%	28.6%	19.0%
Hose	6.7%	–	4.2%	2.8%	4.2%	–	–	–	7.1%	3.0%
Giftware	–	–	–	2.8%	4.2%	–	–	–	7.1%	1.5%
Hand Tools	–	9.1%	12.5%	11.1%	8.3%	–	–	–	–	7.5%
Power Equipment	26.7%	18.2%	12.5%	27.8%	16.7%	9.1%	7.7%	–	35.7%	18.5%
Repair Service	6.7%	12.1%	20.8%	11.1%	12.5%	9.1%	23.1%	–	–	13.0%
Rental Services	–	3.0%	2.1%	2.8%	–	9.1%	–	–	–	2.0%
Long-Handled Tools	–	3.0%	–	–	–	–	7.7%	20.0%	–	1.5%
Landscaping	13.3%	3.0%	4.2%	8.3%	4.2%	18.2%	15.4%	–	–	6.5%
Outdoor Furniture	6.7%	–	–	2.8%	4.2%	–	–	–	–	1.5%
Other	6.7%	–	6.2%	2.8%	–	–	7.7%	–	–	3.0%

3. Percent of Sales to:

Consumers	84.4%	81.8%	83.2%	84.7%	80.4%	78.4%	86.7%	75.0%	82.1%	82.6%
Commercial	5.6%	10.9%	7.5%	7.4%	12.2%	10.8%	6.3%	16.6%	8.7%	9.0%
Institutional	2.6%	2.7%	2.5%	2.5%	2.2%	3.9%	2.7%	2.1%	2.6%	2.6%
Government	3.8%	1.4%	2.7%	2.9%	2.6%	2.8%	1.3%	2.9%	2.8%	2.5%
Schools	3.7%	3.2%	4.1%	2.5%	2.6%	4.1%	3.0%	3.4%	3.3%	3.3%

Fastest Growth Over Last Five Years	Under $100,000	$100,000-$199,000	Dollar Volume $200,000-$399,000	$400,000-$799,000	$800,000 and Over
1. Percentage Indicating Fastest Growth:					
Indoor Plants & Accessories	13.0%	24.3%	18.8%	36.4%	28.6%
Nursery Stock	16.9%	21.6%	18.8%	–	–
Chemical	9.1%	–	10.4%	4.5%	14.3%
Hose	2.6%	2.7%	2.1%	–	–
Giftware	–	2.7%	–	4.5%	–
Hand Tools	7.8%	2.7%	10.4%	18.2%	–
Power Equipment	13.0%	18.9%	16.7%	22.7%	28.6%
Repair Services	20.8%	2.7%	8.3%	–	–
Rental Services	2.6%	2.7%	–	–	–
Long-Handled Tools	–	–	6.3%	–	–
Landscaping	9.1%	10.8%	6.3%	–	–
Outdoor Furniture	–	2.7%	4.2%	4.5%	7.1%
Other	5.2%	10.8%	4.2%	9.1%	21.4%

2. Percent Indicating *Second* Fastest Growth:

Indoor Plants & Accessories				
Accessories	5.3%	11.1%	7.1%	5.0%	7.1%
Nursery Stock	17.1%	16.7%	11.9%	30.0%	14.3%
Chemicals	17.1%	19.4%	23.8%	15.0%	28.6%
Hose	5.3%	2.8%	–	–	7.1%
Giftware	1.3%	–	4.8%	–	–
Hand Tools	2.6%	5.6%	9.5%	20.0%	7.1%
Power Equipment	27.6%	11.1%	11.9%	25.0%	–
Repair Services	11.8%	13.9%	11.9%	5.0%	21.4%
Rental Services	2.6%	–	2.4%	5.0%	–
Long-Handled Tools	2.6%	–	2.4%	–	–
Landscaping	5.3%	13.9%	7.1%	5.0%	–
Outdoor Furniture	–	2.8%	–	–	7.1%
Other	1.3%	2.8%	7.1%	–	7.1%

3. Percent of Sales to:

Consumers	86.2%	79.8%	82.0%	78.9%	91.2%
Commercial	6.6%	11.5%	10.1%	9.9%	4.0%
Institutional	1.7%	2.8%	2.5%	4.5%	1.5%
Government	2.1%	2.2%	3.1%	3.4%	1.8%
Schools	3.4%	3.8%	2.3%	3.4%	1.4%

Grills	Region									
	I	II	III	IV	V	VI	VII	VIII	IX	Total
1. Percent Selling Outdoor Grills	12.5%	36.5%	26.4%	26.9%	21.8%	20.0%	9.5%	—	25.0%	24.3%

Of those selling major brands of grills, number of respondents handling the following brands:

Weber-Stephen Products	33
Charmglow	11
Structo (King-Seeley)	24
Other	9

Grills	Dollar Volume				
	Under $100,000	$100,000-$199,999	$200,000-$399,999	$400,000-$799,999	$800,000 and Over
1. Percent Selling Outdoor Grills	16.3%	18.8%	23.1%	41.0%	57.1%

Of those selling major brands of grills, number of respondents handling the following brands:

Weber-Stephen Products	33
Charmglow	11
Structo (King-Seeley)	24
Other	9

401

Pots	I	II	III	IV	V	VI	VII	VIII	IX	Total
					Region					
1. Percent Selling										
Plant Containers	46.9%	58.7%	42.5%	51.9%	70.9%	53.3%	66.7%	55.6%	50.0%	54.1%
Plastic:										
Selling	100.0%	86.5%	89.2%	96.3%	92.3%	87.5%	92.9%	100.0%	100.0%	92.3%
Imported	4.8%	5.6%	5.9%	9.2%	1.4%	–	1.4%	–	9.1%	5.2%
Domestic	95.2%	94.4%	94.1%	90.8%	98.6%	100.0%	98.6%	100.0%	90.9%	94.8%
Clay:										
Selling	86.7%	83.4%	83.4%	85.2%	82.1%	87.5%	85.7%	100.0%	78.6%	84.2%
Imported	49.7%	42.4%	27.0%	39.7%	46.3%	4.8%	6.0%	23.9%	50.7%	38.3%
Domestic	50.3%	57.6%	73.0%	60.3%	53.7%	95.2%	94.0%	76.1%	49.3%	61.7%
Ceramic:										
Selling	60.0%	73.0%	73.0%	66.7%	64.1%	62.5%	71.4%	60.0%	85.7%	69.4%
Imported	43.7%	12.2%	52.2%	28.0%	49.9%	–	35.2%	–	32.6%	39.9%
Domestic	56.3%	87.8%	47.8%	72.0%	50.1%	100.0%	64.8%	100.0%	67.4%	60.1%
Metal:										
Selling	20.0%	35.1%	40.5%	40.7%	46.2%	25.0%	42.9%	–	28.6%	36.7%
Imported	–	19.3%	45.5%	16.4%	1.5%	–	2.9%	–	–	16.9%
Domestic	100.0%	80.7%	54.5%	83.6%	98.5%	100.0%	97.1%	–	100.0%	83.1%
2. Avg. Number of										
Container Suppliers	6.4	4.9	6.0	6.8	3.9	4.7	7.6	3.4	3.8	5.4
Avg. Number Added										
in 1976	.8	1.5	1.2	2.1	.6	1.3	2.5	–	.5	1.3

Pots	Under $100,000	$100,000-$199,999	Dollar Volume $200,000-$399,999	$400,000-$799,999	$800,000 and Over
1. Percent Selling Plant Containers	41.5%	55.1%	67.7%	69.2%	71.4%
Plastic:					
Selling	94.1%	94.7%	86.4%	96.3%	100.0%
Imported	2.9%	8.2%	7.8%	4.2%	2.6%
Domestic	97.1%	91.8%	92.2%	95.8%	97.4%
Clay:					
Selling	72.5%	89.5%	95.5%	92.6%	86.7%
Imported	29.9%	43.2%	36.3%	39.1%	52.7%
Domestic	70.1%	56.8%	63.7%	60.9%	47.3%
Ceramic:					
Selling	58.8%	65.8%	79.5%	81.5%	93.3%
Imported	31.2%	36.5%	34.4%	54.8%	51.6%
Domestic	68.8%	63.5%	65.6%	45.2%	48.4%
Metal:					
Selling	27.5%	31.6%	34.1%	63.0%	20.0%
Imported	12.5%	11.4%	3.4%	22.3%	33.0%
Domestic	87.5%	88.6%	96.6%	77.7%	67.0%
2. Avg. Number of Container Suppliers	2.6	6.0	6.3	7.2	6.0
Avg. Number Added in 1976	.5	1.6	1.9	1.4	1.3

Indoor Plants	Under $100,000	$100,000-$199,999	Dollar Volume $200,000-$399,999	$400,000-$799,999	$800,000 and Over
1. Percent Selling:					
Indoor Plants	24.4%	40.6%	55.4%	48.7%	61.9%
Crafts	8.1%	11.6%	13.8%	12.8%	14.3%
Dish Gardens	10.6%	18.8%	23.1%	17.9%	28.6%
Potting Soils	42.3%	56.5%	61.5%	66.7%	71.4%
Indoor Plant Containers	35.0%	49.3%	58.5%	61.5%	66.7%
Plant Growth Lights	22.8%	34.8%	53.8%	56.4%	61.9%
Terrariums	21.1%	29.0%	41.5%	46.2%	42.9%

Indoor Plants	I	II	III	IV	Region V	VI	VII	VIII	IX	Total
1. Percent Selling:										
Indoor Plants	37.5%	34.9%	26.4%	38.5%	41.8%	53.3%	52.4%	33.3%	39.3%	36.7%
Crafts	9.4%	11.1%	8.0%	15.4%	18.2%	6.7%	4.8%	11.1%	–	10.5%
Dish Gardens	9.4%	14.3%	13.8%	19.2%	14.5%	13.3%	23.8%	11.1%	25.0%	15.7%
Potting Soils	50.0%	58.7%	41.4%	46.2%	63.6%	53.3%	66.7%	55.6%	50.0%	52.2%
Indoor Plant Containers	43.8%	50.8%	33.3%	50.0%	61.8%	40.0%	57.1%	44.4%	42.9%	46.7%
Plant Growth Lights	34.4%	41.3%	31.0%	38.5%	45.5%	20.0%	33.3%	33.3%	32.1%	36.2%
Terrariums	18.8%	33.3%	25.3%	28.8%	36.4%	26.7%	52.4%	11.1%	28.6%	29.8%

Appendix
I

Common
Garden
Problems[1]

[1]Courtesy of the University of Wisconsin—Extension, Madison, Wisconsin.

BENEFICIAL INSECTS

Avoid indiscriminant spraying. These insects destroy harmful insects. Diverse garden plantings aid in their establishment.

GALLS are caused by insect or mite feeding. Rarely cause serious injury. When necessary use:

CHEWING INSECTS

Capable of complete or partial defoliation of ornamentals.
Early observation and control is necessary.
Effective controls include:

SUCKING PESTS
Weaken plants by sucking juices.
When abundant use:

SOIL INSECTS
Symptoms appear in patches as browning with eventual death
of grass. If damage is extensive use one of these chemicals:

BORING INSECTS
Trees under stress are susceptible to
attack. Maintain good tree health.
Helpful insecticides include:

ENVIRONMENTAL DISEASES

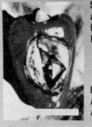

Sunscald is caused by exposure to the sun and hot, dry weather. Controls include balanced fertility and control of leaf diseases. Fungicides won't help.

Blossom End Rot is common in early fruit. Avoid heavy use of commercial fertilizers. Apply superphosphate and mulch.

Blossom End Rot is not controlled by fungicides.

APPLE SCAB

A wet weather disease causing leaf drop and deformed fruit. Some varieties are resistant. Rake up diseased leaves. Use one of these fungicides:

TOMATO BLIGHTS are a

complex of diseases attacking foliage and fruit. Controls include rotation, garden clean-up, and use of one of these fungicides as the fruit forms.

CEDAR-APPLE RUST

Fungus attacks susceptible varieties of apple and cedar. Select resistant varieties. Use one of these fungicides during May and June:

BLACK SPOT OF ROSE

Black spots, followed by severe defoliation. Provide good aeration and pick off diseased leaves.
Apply one of these fungicides routinely where the disease occurs:

FLOWER RUSTS

Colored spots on leaves with a powdery surface. Provide good aeration and sanitation. Use one of these chemicals when disease appears:

POWDERY MILDEW
White or gray covering on leaves and flowers. Apply one of these fungicides at first sign of disease:

LEAF SPOT AND MELTING OUT

Common in spring and early summer. Can severly thin the lawn.

Use resistant varieties, balanced fertility, and proper mowing height.

These chemicals can help:

Index